Murder in New York City

Murder in
New York City

ERIC H. MONKKONEN

UNIVERSITY OF CALIFORNIA PRESS
Berkeley   Los Angeles   London

University of California Press
Berkeley and Los Angeles, California

University of California Press, Ltd.
London, England

Library of Congress Cataloging-in-Publication Data

Monkkonen, Eric H., 1942–
    Murder in New York City / Eric H. Monkkonen.
        p.   cm.
    Includes bibliographical references and index.
    ISBN 0-520-22188-5 (cloth : alk. paper)
    1. Murder—New York (State)—New York—History.
    I. Title.
    HV6534.N87M65   2001
    364.15'23'097471—dc21   00-042614

Manufactured in the United States of America

10 09 08 07 06 05 04 03 02 01

10 9 8 7 6 5 4 3 2 1

The paper used in this publication meets the minimum
requirements of ANSI/NISO Z39.48-1992 (R 1997)
(Permanence of Paper). ∞

Contents

Tables and Figures

FIGURES

Acknowledgments

Major research grants from the National Science Foundation and the National Institute of Justice underwrote a significant amount of the work reported here. This funding enabled me to conduct a depth of research otherwise not feasible. Critical financial support also came from UCLA's Academic Senate, International Studies and Overseas Programs, and College Institute. Sustained organizational support of cross-disciplinary research requires a vision that I greatly appreciate. Needless to say, none of these organizations bears responsibility for my conclusions.

I wish to acknowledge the essential contributions of the many dedicated research assistants who have worked with me on this project. These include, in alphabetic order, Tyler Anbinder, Melissa Anderson, Paige Anderson, Andy Bodeau, Duyen Bui, Tom Chung, Tom Clark, Danny Contreras, Barry Dewalt, Gregg Doll, Mike Doyle, Cheryl Feiner, Cameron Fong, José Galvez, Matthew Gever, Brian Griest, Ed Hashima, Ryan Hemingway, Mary Herra, Laura Hollis, Julie Jarboe, Naoki Kamimura, Diane Kim, Catharine Lamb, Matthew Lee, Richard Lester, Anne Leung, Cynthia Lum, Susan Meyer, Rob Michaelson, Colby Moldow, Paavo Monkko-nen, Barnaby Montgomery Jr., Julie Myers, Tamara Myers, Marcus Nenn, Kristen Nickell, Sheila O'Hare, Sue Pak, Sanjiv Rao, Allison Rivera, Jane Roddy, Kristi Rolefson, David Schwartz, Kenneth So, Christine Statler, Lynda Thomas, Christa Welch, Robyn Wilkins, Carol Winter, and Jeffrey Wolfe. They have all experienced the strange frisson of snatching another murder victim from obscurity, just for a moment.

In addition, I wish to thank Randolph Roth, Graham Hodges, Phillip Walker, Richard Bessel, Daniel Scott Smith, Barbara Cantor, Paul Gilje, Bernie Heise, Stan Nadel, Jeffrey Kroessler, Richard H. Bezdek, and John Podracky (at the New York Police Museum). Every American should be grateful for the work of the New York City Archives, which with minimal funding has preserved a rich heritage for the future; in particular I am grateful to Kenneth Cobb, whose diligence and care for projects like this is remarkable. Phillip McGuire and Arthur Haimo at the New York Police Department took time to help me with contemporary data problems. For Liverpool, I wish to thank Joy Campbell, Paul Laxton, Roger Schofield, and David Farrington and the staff of the wonderful Radzinowicz Library at Cambridge University's Institute of Criminology. At the Integrated Public Use Micro Sample (IPUMS) at the University of Minnesota, Matt Sobek, Catherine Fitch, and Steven Ruggles all answered my questions and helped me download data. Several UCLA librarians, helping with everything from interlibrary loans to microform documents, have labored to make this project possible.

I am indebted to all of these institutions and individuals for their sup-port and assistance: simply put, I could not have done the research with-out their help.

Introduction

This book is like end-of-the-year stories about homicide in the media. These stories compare the just-ending year to the previous one. They rely on homicide counts as direct indexes to social life, asking two questions: Are things getting better or worse? And in either case, why? To acquire the homicide counts, journalists contact the police; to explain them, they often turn to politicians or "experts." This quintessential activity blends "news" with history and with underlying urges to predict the future and to assess personal safety. The resulting stories fit the bafflement, rage, and frustration at life's unfairness evoked by individual murders into a larger pattern that assuages, if it does not satisfy, our urge to understand. The same elements, in elaborated form, underlie this book as well.

The main difference is scope: I have looked back at two centuries, not 365 days. Such an extended retrospective requires different—and more

recalcitrant—sources than the end-of-the-year news story does. But a vital index to the underside of social life awaits the historian willing to pry
in forgotten places. Although the police can tell a journalist a city's homicide count for the current year, they do not place a high priority on long-
term recording. For a more thorough source one must turn to the coroner,
an ancient official whose duty it has been since the Middle Ages to determine and record how people died. When the coroner's inquests or tab-
ular summaries have been lost, other less consistent sources can supplement them. Whether in newspaper articles or through health department
summaries, long-forgotten murders can often be revisited. The results of
such reconstructions form the backbone of this study: two hundred years
of New York City homicides.

For the first three quarters of the nineteenth century, slightly fewer than
1,800 individual murders ground the statistics here. These murders also
provide elements of microdramas that lead to fatal violence. Nineteenth-
century coroners conducted inquests in barrooms, parlors, and the "dead
room" of New York Hospital. There they deposed witnesses, often including the offender, and took ante-mortem depositions from the dying
victim. These versions are as close as we can now hope to come to the actual events: confused, contradictory, opaque, and often unsatisfying,
these stories bring us as close as we can get to answering the "why?" question. I have reconstructed several such stories to illustrate kinds of crimes
and themes—yet most incidents hammer home multiple viewpoints,
multiple plausible accounts, and serve to make any reader wary of a simple explanation for homicides or homicide patterns.

For the years after 1875, vital statistics carry the statistical homicide
story forward. Adding violent death to the long lists of other causes of
death, medical doctors and public health officials changed details in their
recording formats quite often in the pioneering years of the mid nineteenth
century. Throughout, homicide definitions stayed relatively simple and
consistent in the context of newly discovered diseases. As the keeping and
reporting of vital statistics evolved, one can continue to find homicide usually located somewhere between "Senility" and "Ill-Defined Causes."

New York City merits close attention for several reasons. It is a city
whose long history, consistent government, and large size make it ideal

for a statistical portrait. Its boundaries changed only once, with the inclusion of the five boroughs in 1898; prior to that the city and county were Manhattan Island. The per capitized homicide rates did not change with this expansion.[1] From before the American Revolution, the coroner had responsibility for investigating all non-natural causes of death, including homicide. The antebellum sources include the coroner and the City Inspector, who also produced (less consistently) annual death reports. After the Civil War, the Department of Health gathered and reported death statistics, providing a consistent annual data source for the later nineteenth and twentieth centuries. In addition to its political consistency, the city has been big for a long time, so its urban character is never in doubt. Numbering sixty thousand people in 1800, New York City's population doubled in size by 1820, and by 1840 it had reached nearly a third of a million. For better or worse, New York has been *the* big city of the United States.

Chapter 1 surveys the long two-hundred-year sweep and the big events—wars, a severe depression, and a particularly vicious riot. In this chapter I clarify some of the "common wisdom" attending our conceptions of violence and broad social change and set the frame for the chapters dealing with the more direct aspects of murder.

Chapter 2 gets right down to gory details: how people did it, their weapons. The tools used in murders make a difference. Today's nasty bullets tear a person's insides apart and frustrate medical treatment, whereas in previous centuries slow and agonizing death from infection often resulted from knife and bullet wounds. Because this book is about the bad part—the killing, not the saving—I give medical treatments short shrift, just enough to try to estimate how medical innovation might have affected the statistics. In 1859 nearly 30 percent of the victims died within two hours of their assault, nearly 60 percent within twenty-four hours, and the rest painfully lingered for days, even weeks. We can guess that trauma care and anti-infection drugs might have saved one-third of the homicide victims in the nineteenth century. Would this have lowered overall rates? Would assailants have been correspondingly more vicious? Do the increasing availability and lethality of weapons counterbalance today's better medical care?

If murder weapons are the most basic part of killing, the next most basic may be gender. Most offenders and their victims are men. So obvious is this that the work of explaining why is in its infancy. Today, evolutionary psychologists look to the brain's biology. Chapter 3 provides information that may help to address this gigantic question, probing what people did and what they said as they did it, looking for what has changed and what has not, what still causes men—mostly—to attack one another.

Just as most violent offenders are men, most of them are between sixteen and fifty years old. Chapter 4 explores the changes in age and murder over the past two centuries. Some are unexpected. There have always been a few very young offenders, under age fourteen, perhaps relatively more in the nineteenth century than in the twentieth. But the large numbers of late-teenage and twenty-year-old offenders is new, a product—possibly temporary—of the late twentieth century.

The public murder of strangers, the form of violence that most unsettles civil society, was relatively rare in the nineteenth century, as it is today. Chapter 5 explores the circumstantial settings in which people murdered. Then, as now, some settings were predictably dangerous: men, darkness, and alcohol combined fairly regularly to fuel personal violence. But within these boundaries, certain triggering situations have disappeared: we seldom had murders over local elections in the twentieth century, for example. The Fourth of July and Christmas have become safer, though New Year's Eve may be as violent as ever. Chapter 5 brings out these fading settings of violence and discusses which still endure.

The victims and perpetrators of homicide vary in frequency among different ethnic and racial groups. Chapter 6 explores this variation over the two-century period. Prior to the late twentieth century, New York City's period of highest violence occurred in the mid nineteenth century, fueled by native-born whites and immigrants, the city's small African American population hardly making a dent in the bloody affairs of others. Racial components of homicide turn out to be somewhat unpredictable, with the high violence rates among Irish immigrants in the Civil War era fading by the late part of the century. Disproportionate African American victimization occurred most dramatically in the late 1930s and early 1940s, having been relatively low in the late nineteenth century and dropping almost every year in the second half of the twentieth century, including the worst years of the 1980s.

In chapter 7 I splice the experience of New York City with the discoveries of European medieval and early modernist scholars. Particularly in figure 7.1, the spliced data give us a better-quality picture of personal violence than ever before. Based on the work of dozens of historians and other social scientists, this final chapter should make clear how much we can learn from our past.

Throughout the chapters, at relevant moments I introduce the methodological and theoretical issues that inevitably arise in a study like this. The sources and provenance of the data I deal with briefly in the appendix. What is reported here is the best long-run series on homicide ever constructed—to date. These two centuries of New York City homicides form the basis of this study, but throughout the context is transatlantic and broadly American. This context undergirds the assertions and equivocations throughout the book. It forms the basis of my belief that our understanding can only grow when it is challenged with adequate information. This long span allows us to look back to a time when guns were rarer, when poverty was more widespread, and when racial discrimination was more intense, and to ask what differences these made.

The future of even more precise research than that presented here is exciting. Pushing our knowledge backward in time will take us into the future better able to understand ourselves, our society, and those who do not fit into it.

Chapter 1 The Long Sweep and Big Events

We rightly think of the United States as a stable country. Even so, the past two and a half centuries have witnessed several major cataclysms and social shifts that should have affected everyone's behavior, including behavior that turns into murder. New York has lived through a revolution and then enemy occupation, many riots, a draining of young men for a highly unpopular civil war, massive immigration from abroad and from the countryside, extraordinary growth, crowding and poverty, the disruption of two foreign wars, and a crushing national depression. The city also suffered several cholera epidemics in the nineteenth century and a lethal influenza epidemic in the twentieth (for which the population data used in this book have been adjusted). These events all make the city an ideal laboratory to test some of the major ideas that link social change to violence. Some of these ideas turn out to be little more than unexamined myths. This chapter challenges several. They include:

1.   Cities are cauldrons of murder, so why bother with all this work?

WRONG: For the twentieth century prior to 1958, New York City had *lower* homicide rates than the United States as a whole.

2.   The underlying social forces of mass society cause deviance. Big fosters bad.

WRONG: As New York City grew bigger, it often became safer. Late-twentieth-century violence increased as the city *lost* population.

3.   Crowding leads to deviance and violence, as proved by rat experiments.

WRONG: At times in the late nineteenth and early twentieth centuries, sections of New York City were *more crowded* than anywhere in the Western world—more crowded even than Bombay, said some—but the city was safer than it is today. People differ from rats in some ways.[1]

4.   Poverty explains murder.

WRONG: In some of New York City's most miserable periods, murder rates were at their *lowest*.

5.   A corrupt criminal justice system loosens morals and leads to violence.

WRONG: Morals may loosen, but at most identifiable times of immorality and corruption, homicide rates were *low*.

6.   We know what causes violence: young men coming home from war, trained to kill.

WRONG: Postwar times were some of the most *peaceful* ones we have seen.

7.   Riots unleash violence.

WRONG: Riots occur in times that are *already* violent.

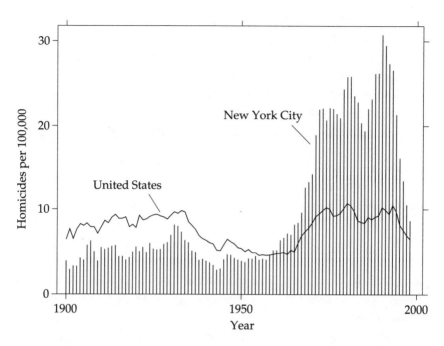

Figure 1.1.   U.S. and New York City homicide rates, 1900–1998. Source: see appendix.

1. Cities are cauldrons of murder.

Figure 1.1 shows twentieth-century homicide rates for the whole United States and for New York City. The biggest city in the United States looked benign compared to the nation as a whole—until 1958. Who would have guessed that in the years following, the city's homicide rate would zoom so high? Did New Yorkers even know that a kind of golden era was ending? No wonder that teenage gangs could be seen as romantic and cute, as in *West Side Story.* From the point of view of the remainder of the twentieth century, the idea that the biggest city could have a lower homicide rate than the country itself is unthinkable. Yet, in the year that *West Side Story*—a poetic, romantic vision of youth crime and gangs—became a Broadway hit, this was the case. By the late 1980s, the city of *West Side Story* contributed 10 percent to the total of all homicides for the country.[2]

The U.S. homicide rates plotted in figure 1.1 include both city and countryside. Prior to the 1920 census, half the population of the United States
lived in places with fewer than 2,500 inhabitants. Strangely, since Frederick Jackson Turner presented his seminal address "The Significance of
the Frontier in American History" at the Chicago World's Columbian Ex-
position in 1893, historians have been much more excited by the census
bureau's announcement (based on the 1890 census) of the closing of the
frontier than by the population's passing the 50-percent-urban mark. Sym-
bolically the frontier represented opportunity whereas the city, by the
twentieth century, represented trouble. That the frontier was the actual
site of violence seems irrelevant to popular conceptions—except that liberty and violence have often been linked in theory.

Although city size does bear some relation to violence, at least in the
second half of the twentieth century, we must observe that the growth of
cities does not inexorably lead to violence. Simply put, if urbanization
caused violence, then both sets of rates in figure 1.1 should have moved
upward together.

In the United States as a whole, the growth of the urban population as
plotted against crime looks like figure 1.2. The smooth lower line is the
proportion of the population living in cities, towns, and villages with more
than 2,500 inhabitants (the definition of *urban* used by the census bureau,
which is useful in its constancy but hardly reflects most people's sense of
the term). The jagged line is the annual homicide rate. (The homicide rate
is for the whole United States, not just cities, so it should not be compared
to the homicide rate in New York City.) There is a correlation between
homicide rate and urbanization, in that they loosely rise and level off together. But probably no one looking at this figure would conclude that
cities cause crime—the relationship is much too approximate.

Many other kinds of data corroborate the notion that city size alone does
not "cause"—or even have much relation to—violent crime. For example,
an appendix to one volume of the 1890 U.S. census lists all homicide arrests for 445 cities of more than 8,000 inhabitants, yet city size and the murder rate barely correlate ($r^2 = .01$). Similar information appears for 1903
on 175 cities of more than 25,000 inhabitants ($r^2 = .0025$), and in the FBI's

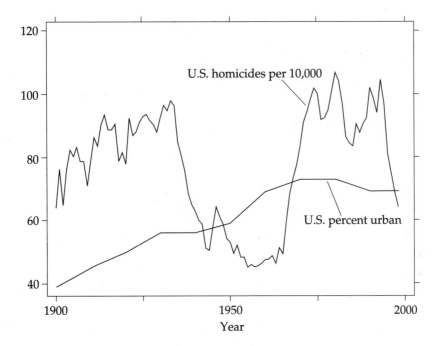

Figure 1.2. Percentage of U.S. population living in urban areas and U.S. murder rates (per 10,000), 1900–1998. Source: see appendix.

Uniform Crime Report for the late twentieth century on the 188 cities of more than 100,000 inhabitants in 1996 (r^2 = .07). In all of these slight positive relationships between city size and homicide rates there is little prima facie evidence to consider size itself as meaningful.[3] Although New York City usually has had the greatest number of murders in the United States, its actual rank in the per capita rates has always been well below most other big cities. As the city grew, its homicide rate varied considerably, with a slight positive relationship between size and murder rate appearing only in the twentieth century.[4] Perhaps if all things were held equal then larger city size might be shown to cause more violence, but given this unpromising start, such an effort seems unneeded.

If the commonplace idea that size equals violence is so wrong, where did it originate? The answer is not easy. In the preindustrial era, everyone knew that the countryside was dangerous and that cities were safer. Cities had walls and the gates were closed at night to keep highwaymen and brigands out, not in. In Europe, fortified houses were rural, not urban, architecture. They are charming now, but only because the countryside is so safe.

Why would popular impressions change in the urban industrial era, the nineteenth century? Data were available in the 1890 published census that would have allowed a straightforward graph plotting city size and murder arrest rates. Had someone plotted these data, they would have discouraged the notion that city size and crime were correlated: like the data from the early twentieth century plotted in figure 1.2, the 1890 census data showed no relationship between city size and crime rate. In his great work, *Suicide*, Emile Durkheim casually pointed to data showing that in 1887 suicide was an urban phenomenon, murder a rural one.[5]

As early as 1833, however, in the first American translation of Gustave de Beaumont and Alexis de Tocqueville's book on American penitentiaries, temporary New Yorker Francis Lieber claimed that cities produced more crime than rural regions. Supporting his point with logic (increased opportunity and decreased surveillance) rather than evidence, Lieber advanced arguments that were prescient if not immediately influential.[6]

If the idea that size equaled deviance came from theory, it did not come from the theory of the best American urban analyst at the turn of the century, Adna F. Weber. In his massive statistical study, *The Growth of Cities*, Weber questioned whether the city was more "wicked" than the countryside. Arguing that bars per capita measured morality, he found that in New York State, the smaller cities had more bars than the large ones. Dropping his tongue-in-cheek attitude, Weber argued that the city acted like a "spectroscope" or prism, transforming rural mediocrity into the "highest talent or the lowest criminal."[7]

In Europe at about the same time, an influential sociologist, Georg Simmel, was propounding the idea that large cities caused social breakdown. In a brilliant analysis that has permeated twentieth-century social thought, he argued that in large cities people lose connection with one another and social values lose out to rampant individualism, and that mental illness

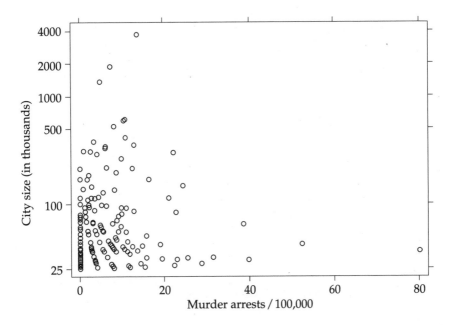

Figure 1.3.   City size (using log scale) and murder arrest rates, from the 1903 census. Source: U.S. Bureau of the Census, Statistics of Cities Having a Population of over 25,000, 1902 and 1903, bulletin 20 (Washington, D.C.: GPO, 1905), table 2.

and deviance, including crime, breed the "metropolitan personality." By the time of World War I American sociologists had taken up his ideas. It may be that this is where we get our sense that cities cause crime.

Yet when we look at the beginning of the twentieth century in the United States, using published census data from 1903, we find little to confirm the notion that the growth of cities causes increased crime. Figure 1.3, a simple plot of the populations of cities with more than 25,000 inhabitants against their 1903 murder rates, estimated from arrests, shows, if anything, an *inverse* relationship between city size and crime. If big cities caused crime, the point cloud should have run from the lower left to the upper right. Clearly, we cannot say that the idea of big cities causing crime came from this evidence plotted in a manner easily available in 1903. A more refined analysis of these same data shows that cities with more than

Table 1.1 City Size and Murder Arrest Rates for the Ten Largest U.S. Cities, 1903

City	Population	Murder arrests per 100,000
New York	3,716,139	13.9
Chicago	1,873,880	7.4
Philadelphia	1,367,716	5.0
St. Louis	612,279	10.8
Boston	594,618	10.4
Baltimore	531,313	8.1
Cleveland	414,950	10.8
Buffalo	381,403	3.4
San Francisco	355,919	12.9
Pittsburgh	345,043	6.1

SOURCE: U.S. Bureau of the Census, *Statistics of Cities Having a Population of over 25,000, 1902 and 1903*, bulletin 20 (Washington, D.C.: GPO, 1905), table 2.

a quarter million inhabitants did tend to have very slightly higher homicide arrest rates as their size increased whereas cities smaller than that had a very slightly negative relationship between size and homicide arrest rates.[8] In other words, among big cities considered by themselves, larger population meant slightly higher murder arrest rates; among cities smaller than a quarter million inhabitants, larger population meant lower murder arrest rates.

Finally, to sort out this puzzle, table 1.1 shows the ten largest U.S. cities in 1900 and their 1903 homicide arrest rates (per 100,000). Roger Lane has pointed out that New York City's arrest rates were out of line with those of other American cities, so one must keep in mind that these data are about arrests, not murders. If one looks only at the three largest cities and no further, there seems to be a relationship between size and arrest rates. It may have been as simple as this: the bad data on three cities confirmed a sophisticated European theory and, in the popular imagination, obviated any need to look further.[9]

The other possible source of the idea is that there are more *total* crimes in big cities, even when the crime rate is lower, because there are more people in big cities.[10] Perhaps if few thought, or—more appropriately— perceived and felt, in per capita terms, this was the source for the "big cities cause crime" formulation. Most social analysts knew better than to make such a mistake, but if this was popular perception, which then was reinforced by sociological theory, and then, after the mid twentieth century, even came to be true, these confluences may be the source of our misconceptions. By the mid twentieth century, the association of big cities with crime had changed to conform to the theory. Big cities did tend to have more crime per capita in the last third of the twentieth century. Given this circumstance, it was easy to project backward and think that the growth of cities had caused the crime surge.

In essence, the postwar world has reversed centuries-old trends. Violent crime began to increase. Big cities became the sources of problems, not solutions. It is important to remember that these developments are reversals. Our mechanisms for coping and understanding must be centered in this context rather than based on ignorant guesses.

2. Big fosters bad.

If the linkage between city size and murder is not a general law, what about another version of the same concept? As a city grows, social pressures increase, but it is the growth, not the absolute size, that causes the problem. In this sociological version of Boyle's law, the city is an urban compression chamber that substitutes population and crime for temperature and pressure. This is a dynamic concept, and thus New York City's history comes into play. Figure 1.4 displays the city's homicide rate and population over the past two centuries. This graph gives a nicely equivocal answer. Although the post-1960s violence burst came with a population decline, in some periods, such as the 1840s and 1850s, population and violence did march upward together. This shows the fragility of basing ideas on time series: because New York grew steadily until the last part of the twentieth century, virtually anything that increased would increase simultaneously with a population increase, whether or not there was any

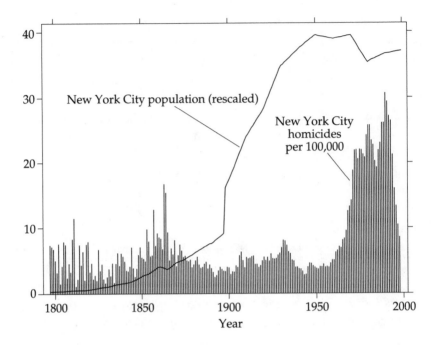

Figure 1.4.   New York City homicides per 100,000 inhabitants and population
(in 200,000s), 1797–1998. Source: see appendix.

causal relationship between the two. It is only the recent decline in population that belies the rigid correlation between population growth and violence and should make us doubt the pressure-cooker effect.[11]

3. Crowding leads to deviance and violence.

The portion of the graph in figure 1.4 for the decades just before 1900 also calls into question the linkage of population crowding and crime. The latter part of the nineteenth century and first decade of the twentieth were arguably the most crowded times in the city's history, as immigrants flooded in. (The 1898 population burst in figure 1.4 is caused by the city's expansion to include the outer boroughs.)[12] These were almost certainly the years of greatest impoverishment, the social welfare system struggling to deal with the millions of newcomers.

4. Poverty explains murder.

No doubt most murder victims were poor people, but poverty as a mass phenomenon did not automatically increase homicide rates. The Depression substantiates this: New York City homicides increased for the first two years until 1931 (see figure 1.4) and then fell throughout the rest of the Depression, paralleling homicide rates in the United States as a whole. On the one hand, we can say that sudden dearth did not provoke homicides. On the other hand, we cannot recapture deeper cultural influences of poverty. A two-decade depression is not the same as a substrate of continual poverty.[13]

A canny analyst here might ask if the Depression effect is not masked by the end of Prohibition two years later, in 1933. Legalization of alcohol should have slowed gangland murders. We cannot easily separate out homicides related to illegal alcohol sales, but we can look solely at women victims on the assumption that most organized-crime-related killings were of men. The numbers show that homicides began to fall before the end of Prohibition.[14] The number of male victims peaked in 1931 and then began to fall, whereas the number of female victims began to fall a year later, after 1932. Perhaps the additional fifteen men who died in 1931 represented those who were killed over illegal trade in alcohol. Otherwise, the counts show that all murders fell during the Depression and that this decline simply cannot be due to the end of Prohibition.

5. A corrupt criminal justice system leads to violence.

The vertical bars in figure 1.4 also bring into question the notion that corruption in the criminal justice system loosens morals and releases violence. The New York City police were beset with scandals during the post–Civil War era and into the early decades of the twentieth century, a period of low murder rates. The most famous investigation, the Lexow Committee, worked during the mid 1890s, years of the city's lowest rates. None of the corruption scandals included the suppression of homicide statistics, and there has never been a suggestion that the homicide counts were manipulated.[15] Police corruption involved vice and its illegal payoffs; murder was not inherently profit-making. In part, the homicide counts were separate from police business: the coroner determined which deaths were homicides and sent the data to the public health department. And until about 1910 the coroner prosecuted homicides. This is not to say that the counts were perfect, but simply to point out that they were never alleged to have been affected by corruption, and thus we can be confident that the period was the safest half century in the city's history.

6. Young men coming home from war cause violence.

Just as poverty and crowding are usually called upon to explain crime, so too is war, in particular the return of war veterans. It seems logical: young men, trained to use weapons, return to a society with their neighborhood ties disrupted after being gone for so long. It was a given in U.S. history that a period of violence and disorder caused by these men, north and south, followed the Civil War.[16] Perhaps this was true for the whole United States, but there are no national data to support the notion. It was not true for the nation's largest city.

Figure 1.5 shows the city's homicide rates with a vertical line in the year of cessation of every U.S. war. Only in the narrowest interpretation, after two of five wars (World Wars I and II), did homicides increase. More broadly, looking at a few years after each war, we see that only World War I was followed by an increase in homicides. Most significantly, none of the wars caused the burst in violence that has always been imagined.

The Civil War and the Vietnam War show some important similarities: during the conduct of each, there were either high or rising homicide rates. The only similarity between these wars was the widespread contemporary disagreement about the wars themselves, but to link this disagreement with violence seems implausible. The violence of war, we must conclude, occurs in the war itself and not in the homes of the soldiers.

What could have been the origin of the idea that war causes violence? Perhaps the presence of veterans among the convicted, perhaps the knowledge that often felons were allowed to enlist rather than go to prison,

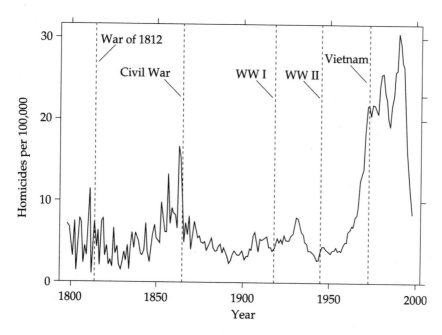

Figure 1.5.   Wars and murder, New York City. Source: see appendix.

or perhaps the presence of wounded men who had to beg to support themselves.

7. Riots unleash violence.

Unlike wars, there is a link of sorts between major riots and personal violence. The city's most violent riots occurred in 1806 (Christmas Day Riots), 1834 (Election Riots), 1849 (Astor Place), 1857 (Dead Rabbits Riot), 1863 (Draft Riots), 1870 (Orange Riot), 1935 and 1943 (Harlem Riots), and 1977 (Harlem Blackout Riot). Seven of the major riots occurred during times of high or rising violence rates and only three during eras of low or declining violence. In these three, special circumstances exacerbated the violence, whether ethnic conflict (the 1870 Orange Riots) or severe police repression (Harlem in 1935 and 1943). If it were possible to separate deaths due to rioters from deaths due to police or militias firing upon crowds, it is likely that the riots with crowd-originated violence would be even more closely associated with times of overall high personal violence.

This raises the question of just how different crowd violence is from individual personal violence. Because most riots have a rational explanation, it is assumed that the rioters who do violence are rationally motivated but take their political or protest actions to an unusual level of violence.[17] The notion that individuals yield up their personalities to angry mobs and that they become more violent than when alone is a commonplace. But is it not possible that violent individuals simply use the crowd as a mask, becoming more violent in riots?

If one wanted to predict riots, one could start by considering the general level of personal violence in a particular society. The possible paths to these results are multiple: violence creates more angry people carrying weapons for defense, violence becomes a more acceptable solution to problems, violent individuals gain power, public violence begets imitation. The general level of violence in a society does not trigger riots: they begin for reasons. But a more violent culture produces much greater violence during rioting than a less violent culture does.

HIGH VIOLENCE, LOW VIOLENCE: WHEN AND WHY

We can define periods of highs and lows in many ways. We can discuss what is high for New York City, or high for the whole United States, or high for a particular time period, or high compared to other similar places, say Liverpool or London. Figure 1.6 initiates this discussion with New York City's rates, each peak emphasized with a vertical line. Two related features of this picture can be visualized as a horizontal band of "normal" New York City homicide rates that covers the period 1800 to about 1960, and a triptychlike vertical sectioning of the graph into three eras or waves.

The normal range of homicide rates for the city has fluctuated between about three and six per hundred thousand for most of the nineteenth and twentieth centuries. Even alone, these rates represent dramatic variation,

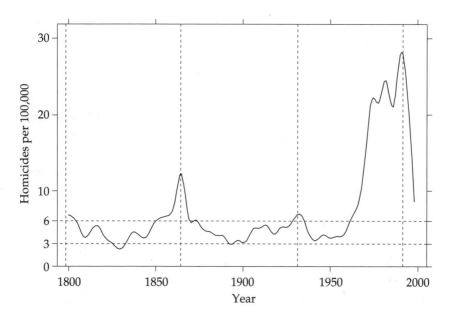

Figure 1.6.   New York City's violence waves. Source: see appendix.

a doubling from crest to trough. But a rogue tidal wave of violence in the last quarter of the twentieth century, which appears to be receding as abruptly as did the earlier smaller crests, has dwarfed these earlier swings. The regularity of these patterns confirms the unique magnitude of the late-twentieth-century violence boom.

Including both the normal range and the tidal wave, there have been three distinct periods of about sixty years each. The first two waves crested about 1864 and 1931, and the rogue wave crested in 1991. The troughs occurred in the 1820s–1830s, around 1890–1900, and in the late 1940s–early 1950s.[18] The periodicity of these waves, though regular, may not be meaningful because, as the dozens of individual cases discussed in this book make clear, each homicide has enough chance in it to make any grand wave-based theory suspect. The regular periodicity of the peaks raises two questions: Was there a peak around 1740? A trough in 1770? And will there be another peak in 2050? The data for the eighteenth century are simply too scattered to test this graphic implication.

These waves of violence suggest that there are distinct points at which violence changes course. The downturns are much more abrupt than the troughs, the times when low violence rates slowly and erratically turn upward again. When the limit to social tolerance is reached, for a whole range of reasons, violence abruptly diminishes. Then, when some lower level of violence has been achieved, the mechanisms for control and the value of peace get forgotten, and a slow rebirth of violence begins. Though it is vague in operational mechanisms—"violence is in the air"—the idea that eras encourage or repress violence across society is supported by evidence. White and black, male and female, very different kinds of homicide rates parallel one another through these waves of change. There is no reason that this should be—given gender differences and demographic and economic racial differences in murder—unless violence is in the air, a contagious virus.[19]

The three periods of sustained increases in violence are surprisingly similar in duration, about forty years each, though the increase from 1950 to 1990 looks longer because the slope is so much steeper. We can only speculate about why this has happened; the wisest thing is to stay with the empirical observation. Identifying historical cycles seems to be an unavoidable adjunct to looking at sweeps of one hundred years or more. Although the exercise is fascinating, it presents the problem that we like to believe that human events are driven by more human forces than the kind of cyclical forces driving climate, planetary orbits, and other nonhuman events.

What do we do with the cycles, once identified? In reintroducing his father's prescient analysis of American political cycles, Arthur Schlesinger Jr. never committed himself to a cycle theory of history, even as "legatee" of one of the most subtle of such analysts. As he concluded, the determinism implied in any cyclical theory "violates our deepest human instincts" such as freedom and responsibility.[20] The Schlesingers, father and son, handled this problem for political cycles by arguing that there are eras of optimism and reform, followed by conservatism and retreat.

One might extend such thinking to violence control, arguing that rising violence provokes a multitude of control efforts, many of which have long lags before their effects show up in the murder rates, and that the cumulative effect ultimately drives the rates down. When the murder rate ebbs, control efforts get relaxed, thus creating the multiple conditions causing the next upswing.

One can review the terrible period of increasing violence that began in the late 1950s as just such an era of slowly cumulating efforts—efforts that seemed not to work, at least initially. Everything from child nurturing (Head Start, for example) to increasing penal measures ("heads off," so to speak) may well have cumulated by 1991 to reverse what had seemed an irreversible tide. In past cycles, after three decades of decreasing violence, the violence reduction efforts fade from the policy agenda, laying the groundwork for the next upswing and a forced reinvention of prevention policies.

This gloomy scenario conforms with the position of many policy analysts in other fields, who describe "issue-attention cycles," as Anthony Downs identified them.[21] The primary insight that serious social issues fall into and out of the policy spotlight, irrespective of the actual social problems, supports the notion that violence cycles may not be natural at all, but influenced by policy vacillations. Confirmation of this would require measuring social effort: from the family to the schools to churches to popular culture to a myriad of virtually unmeasurable yet important activities.

Since the Civil War if not earlier, social observers have attributed violence at home to returning warriors. Turn this analysis of war and violence a different way and observe that periods of relatively low violence follow wars. Three, perhaps four, of the long periods of decline in violence follow wars—the Revolution (speculative, given lack of data), the War of 1812, the Civil War, and World War II. Another followed the most traumatic economic depression the country has experienced. The exception—as it is to everything—is the decline of the 1990s, unless one counts the Cold War. Perhaps we should, except that unlike the earlier wars, the Cold War did not have soldiers returning from the trauma of violence.

The one exception and explanatory problem comes from the war in Vietnam, which should have caused a decline in the 1970s. Perhaps it would have done so except that the rogue wave was already crashing ashore. This generalization—peace at home following war—holds if we lump the Vietnam and Cold Wars together, or if we rephrase it as "peacetime brings social peace." Both of these locutions analytically differ from that which links war to violence. For one thing, the notion that war begets violence is usually linked to the idea that military mobilization releases the beast within young men, and that this beast cannot be recaptured quickly. Analogizing to police officers unable to control their aggression after a dangerous pursuit, their adrenaline pumping, who attack the offender, the idea is that soldiers return to civilian life with their aggression and adrenaline pumping, ready to fight. This sounds believable until we consider it a little more precisely: soldiers are carefully trained to be aggressive in the right direction and to control their natural impulses, which typically include flight, dissociation, and withdrawal. A high proportion of soldiers do not experience battle. The "pumped" police officers are not pumped three months later. The soldiers return to civil life anxious to escape their military life. The post–Civil War phenomenon of soldiers flooding into prisons was simply an artifact of the widespread mobilization: it would have been hard to find any young male who had not had a war experience. The linkage of war and violence combines bad reasoning and little research.

In contrast, the linkage of peace and low violence is a more interesting proposition. What is special about peace? Not every peace lacks a standing army, so it is not actual military training. On the other hand, peace does mean prosperity in a very specific sense: young men follow occupational tracks, even if menial ones. And occupations help individuals develop a future orientation, increase the likelihood of family formation, and make late-night hours and drinking all but impossible.

Capturing Cold War tensions, *West Side Story* subtly tells us that gang warfare over turf is as old as conflict in the fifteenth century and as foolish as the carefully orchestrated turf violence in Europe during the Cold War. The musical's parallel between the fifteenth century and the 1950s has some historical accuracy: the upper classes in the early modern urban world had access to weapons and engaged in violence against rival groups. High society *was* violent then, and only the wealthy could afford weapons of quality. Access to weapons has drifted downward, as have the codes that govern the behavior of an armed class. Called the "civilizing process" by Norbert Elias, rules governing interpersonal violence began in late medieval courtly codes (hence the word *courtesy*).

The explicit conflict in the musical is over turf and ethnicity—Puerto Ricans versus "whites" who, we are reminded carefully, are themselves second-generation immigrants. The police, represented by Officer Krupke, are careerist and racially prejudiced; Officer Krupke is part of the problem in driving apart racial groups. There is no hope from intellectuals, either: a sociological analysis of juvenile delinquency as a "social disease" is mocked. The only saving virtue is young love, which obliterates racial barriers.

Two exchanges of the gang members with Doc, the owner of the candy store hangout, make these themes clear. He chides them for the escalating violence, "You kids'll make this world lousy," and they retort, "We didn't make it, Doc." Later he asks them, "Why do you kids live like there's a war on?" Here the underlying causes are shifted to the adult world and paralleled with the geopolitical fears of the Cold War era.

The early decades of the twenty-first century may have low homicide rates and bring social peace and boredom. The relaxation of the social effort to preserve peace will ultimately lead to rising violence. Then, on the upswing, there will be riots, new suspicion of big cities, and hand-wringing over the American character. The challenge for the next two decades is to maintain the social effort to preserve peace, to try to match other Western nations, and to consider every homicide deterred a major success.

Chapter 2 Lethal Weapons

In 1841, John C. Colt was on trial for murder. He was the brother of Samuel Colt, whom we now recognize as the most famous maker of repeating handguns—revolvers—and whose name is so charismatic that it now adorns a malt liquor can. The blunt irony should not escape us: did John use one of Samuel's soon-to-be-famous revolvers? Hardly. John hammered his victim to death. This thirty-year-old brother of the revolver's inventor taught bookkeeping on Chambers Street and Broadway, in the same office where he also murdered his creditor, Samuel Adams. After the murder John crated the body and tried to ship it to New Orleans. Before the ship left the harbor the odor became too strong, and Colt was quickly found out. To the end John Colt resisted the emergent technology for which his surname would soon stand. He died by his own hand just prior to his scheduled execution, using a dagger smuggled into his cell by Caroline Henshaw,

Samuel's pregnant, unacknowledged wife, whom John had secretly married (and thus made "legitimate") just hours before. Perhaps John lacked his brother's vision of the possibilities of the new revolver technology.

Certainly Samuel Colt tried to rectify this embarrassing public backwardness within his own family. His brother's highly publicized trial was lengthy for the time—ten days. Samuel took the occasion to demonstrate his new revolver to a packed courtroom. For some reason the defense wanted to prove that John had not used a Colt, and the trial included much forensic discussion of the kind of wounds a revolver could make. Although his demonstration had no hope of exonerating his brother, Samuel Colt managed to show the packed courtroom that his pistol, loaded with the firing caps but no powder, could shoot a bullet through only nine pages of a book. Even this demonstration did not go smoothly; on Colt's first attempt, the bullets fell out of the gun. Perhaps this explains why his brother had used a hammer to murder his hapless victim. The *Tribune* reporter noted laconically, "The Court suggested that hereafter the experiments should be performed out of the Court room."[1]

We associate murder with weapons, guns in particular. It is no news that most murders today are accomplished with pistols. Until their mass production, however, handguns were playthings of the rich. This explains early weapons' beauty, longevity, and attraction for collectors today. Prior to mass production of weapons, handguns were by definition custom-made and were items of conspicuous consumption; they were not utilitarian, as they were poor hunting tools, and at a close distance a dagger or sword was more reliable and therefore more deadly.

The contemporary handgun is a relatively recent product, the result of highly sophisticated engineering and mass production. The fundamentals of handguns got worked out over about a thirty-year period in the middle of the nineteenth century. First, handguns became mass-produced consumer items. American knives became mass-produced in the same era. While Eli Whitney gained fame for his interchangeable parts in military weapons, the same machine-age concepts helped to create the technology and marketing for nonmilitary weapons. Then, after the Civil War, ammunition became a mass-produced consumption product. The rapid-firing semiautomatic has come of age since World War II.[2]

The handgun's utility is as limited today as it was two hundred years ago. There is an inherent engineering tension in the design of pistols: the smaller and more concealable—in other words, the more pistol-like—the harder to aim and fire accurately. No technology has yet fixed this. Anyone who has fired a pistol and a rifle at a target is well aware of this distinction. It takes great skill to hit anything at a distance greater than a few feet with a pistol. The one advantage of a handgun over a more accurate long gun, whether shotgun or rifle, is its concealability. And concealability only matters to the assassin. For personal protection a shotgun is better, and its visible presence adds an element of deterrence. So the handgun provides protection only when it can be concealed and carried in spite of legal proscription.

Are we to believe, then, that the thousands of handguns sold starting in the mid nineteenth century were for would-be murderers? Or that so many men were fearful and in need of defensive weapons? This is the same era, after all, that saw the introduction of uniformed urban police in U.S. cities. The sales of handguns as purposeful tools of personal violence make sense only if we consider such weapons utilitarian. For rural people, rifles and shotguns made sense as tools; they could hunt and scare away predators and crop-destroying pests. But handguns are not very useful; rather, they are items of mass consumption for entertainment and pleasure.

After handguns became mass produced at midcentury, the market for such entertaining items expanded from a small and very wealthy proportion of the male populace to the ranks of well-off middle-class men. The expansion of the handgun market into the poor and working-class world is more difficult to date. One can guess that the price of consumer weapons such as handguns continued to fall throughout the post–Civil War era and into the twentieth century, although it is interesting to note that a good-quality automatic 9 mm pistol today retails for about $400, versus $12 for a Colt revolver in the 1850s. By the end of the nineteenth century, Sears was selling mail-order Colts for about $12, but it also offered its lowest-priced .22 "Defender" revolver for 68 cents plus 10 cents shipping. Sears offered an American Bull Dog for as little as $1.35, claiming that "these are not toys but good guns."[3] Measuring the prices of these guns against a workingman's daily pay of about $1 in the nineteenth century versus, say, $100 today, one can see the decline in the real cost of a high-quality handgun in the twentieth century and the advent of the very inexpensive handgun in the latter half of the nineteenth century. One can only note with awe that Sears stopped selling revolvers in 1930, a costly ethical choice made at the height of a homicide boom.[4] This would be equivalent to Wal-Mart dropping its handgun line today.

A different history has shaped bladed weapons. Like handguns, American mass-produced cutlery was also a mid-nineteenth-century phenomenon, but the key issues of availability and class status were very different for knives than for handguns. Sharp tools were essential to running all households until the rise of mass-marketed modern household devices, precut and prepackaged foods, and coal, gas, or electric heating. Kitchen ranges used wood or a combination of wood and coal; the use of petroleum-based fuels and gas was limited to better-off homes. Wood stoves, along with more exotic fuels, heated homes throughout the nineteenth and well into the twentieth century. Firewood and the sharp instruments to chop and shave it have disappeared from the household only in the second half of the twentieth century. Until then, axes had to be available in or near every wood supply. The sticks of wood themselves were lethal weapons, and were often used as such, and even the crudest instruments for splitting wood made kitchens into armories. The slow introduction of the gas range and central heating relieved households of these tools even as gas itself became the source of a surge in accidental deaths and suicides.[5]

There is less written on the history of knives than on that of guns, no doubt because knives are simpler, ubiquitous, and less exciting—no noise, no violent force.[6] We know of famous named knives, such as the very large Bowie knife and the lesser Barlow knife so much admired by Tom Sawyer. Folding pocketknives were available in quantity throughout the nineteenth century, although they were imported items until the late 1830s.[7] Because they were common tools, most knives got used up. So, what may have been the most common items in nineteenth-century kitchens are now the most rare collector's items. In a world of wood technology, pocketknives had great utility. Whittling was a major form of entertainment. Wooden pegs were all-purpose fasteners. When men shaved, they used potentially lethal straight razors. The "jackknife," an eighteenth-century American slang term, denoted an all-purpose and omnipresent tool. The knife has become less useful only in the twentieth century and, in particular, outside of the kitchen. For men, the jackknife has gone the way of the bowler hat.

Similarly, a man today using a dress cane is likely to draw attention to himself; therefore, the idea of concealing a weapon in one is ludicrous. Perhaps for this reason, sword canes merit little space in the histories of knives. Although some anecdotal histories of canes at least mention them, little systematic work has been done on the history of these weapons. Some sword canes are preserved in museum collections. Because of the nature of museum collections, these specimens are from relatively prominent locals. For instance, the Portland, Maine, historical society has a mid-nineteenth-century sword cane of a local newspaper publisher, who supposedly carried the weapon on his semi-vigilante night watch patrol. Other nineteenth-century sword cane holdings include one imported from Spain, one in the Ohio State Historical Society that had been owned by Joshua Buffington, and one in the Idaho State Historical Society that had been owned by Gus John Green.[8]

THE REVOLVER: THE CLASSIC AMERICAN WEAPON

Not only were early pistols cumbersome, they required considerable expertise in loading powder, bullets, and caps. Revolvers first had to have a cap for each charge inserted into the back end of each chamber. Second, powder had to be poured from a flask into each chamber, followed with a bullet for each. It was a slow process. Men who carried guns were well aware of the hazards of poor loading or loads that had become spoiled from damp, sweat, or jostling. When in 1855 New Yorker and future Democratic representative John Morrisey tried to shoot William Poole, a member of New York City's Know-Nothing party, he fired at least twice, his pistol failing both times. "It was kept loaded too long," witness Cornelius Campbell speculated.[9]

Smith & Wesson perfected a revolver using preassembled cartridges, which it began to mass market as soon as Colt's patent expired in 1857, but its technology limited the size to small .22 rim-fire cartridges.[10]

Completely assembled large-caliber metal cartridges did not become machine made and readily available until a few years after the Civil War. Colt pistols typically came with powder flasks, a container for the explosive caps, and tools for loading bullets. A shameless promoter, Colt probably intended his courtroom demonstration to show the safety of his revolver, for some of his competitors' smoky black-powder revolvers had explosive tendencies. Early ones could also flash over, firing off more than one charge. Of course, on this issue he took no chances, using a gun that was not charged with powder.[11]

At the time of his brother's trial, Colt was just months short of bankruptcy. He was desperate for any publicity for his innovative product. He did, in fact, go bankrupt about the time of his brother's jail cell death, yet his continued vigorous promotional efforts ultimately made his name and his weapon American icons. Gun collectors neglect this episode, perhaps because murderer John Colt represented the old, never really catching on to the new age of small repeating weapons.

Today such courtroom promotional shenanigans would surprise us, as would an advertisement from the Civil War era for the Remington pistol. A drawing of a pistol dominates the advertisement in the August 27, 1864, *New York Times*, more than twenty years after the Colt affair. It modestly proclaims that the Remington Army and Navy Revolver, a revolver "approved by the government," is "warranted superior to any other Pistol of the kind." The advertisement appeared above a picture advertisement for a scale. Below that came one for coffins, and below that, a small picture advertisement for the Elliot's Repeater, the "best revolver made, great power, small size, safe, durable, quickly loaded." Could this cartoonlike progression—gun, scales (of justice), coffins, and then another gun—have been the deliberate ordering of a witty printer?

New Yorkers must have been accustomed to the utility and reliability of revolvers by that time, as the advertisement relies for its impact on the notion of military might and expertise—after four years of civil war, a good testimony indeed. Today one does not usually encounter ads for the latest in handgun technology in newspapers, much less see promotional demonstrations in the courtroom. In particular, one would not see such ads during a virtual murder epidemic such as New York City was experiencing.

These advertisements and Samuel Colt's revolver demonstrations seem startling because we now know that most murders (about two-thirds) are committed with handguns. Our predecessors, rightly, did not connect the usage and availability of handguns with murders because at the time of the Civil War only about 30 percent of all murders were by gun. Colt's brother, in venting his fury on fellow businessman Samuel Adams, typified a murderer of the time, in his rage snatching the nearest reliable weapon at hand. Had he wanted to use one of his brother's new pistols, he would still have had to be cautious in its handling, first preparing a charge by loading firing caps, powder, and bullets. A careless firing could easily injure the shooter, so haste, anger, and vicious personal feelings were far more easily expressed with sticks, axes, knives, hammers, chairs, rocks, and boots.

Thus in 1841, John Colt, choosing a hammer for murder, represented the present while his brother Samuel represented the future. At the time this was not apparent except to a visionary, perhaps one like Samuel Colt, who had honed his promotional skills through laughing gas demonstrations at fairs. At the time of his brother's trial, he had manufactured fewer than three thousand of his revolvers. Within ten years, ten times as many Colts would be available, but still priced too high to be handy for a typical murder.[12] Even by the time of the Civil War, Colt pocket pistols were priced beyond the means of ordinary workers with scant discretionary funds, but well within the range of men who often spent that much on an elegant silk scarf. At midcentury, pocket pistols became the personal weapon of choice for gentlemen and the moderately well off.

For instance, when the ambitious young New Yorker (U.S.) Rep. Daniel Sickles—a prominent Tammany man—murdered his wife's lover, the U.S. district attorney Philip Barton Key, in Washington in 1859, he chose a pistol. Actually, he chose three, running clumsily out of his house and across a small square, where he shot down Key. Given the weight of even a single small pocket pistol, he must have moved in an ungazellelike manner. Ten years later, in 1869, when a deputy New York City assessor, Daniel

McFarland, murdered the popular *Tribune* reporter Albert Richardson, he too used a pistol. This murder is instructive. It was McFarland's second attempt on Richardson. In both he was accurate, usually not the case with handguns. In his first attempt, two years earlier, from a distance of one foot, only one of his three shots hit, and that not fatally. For this first assault he had purchased a "new four-barrel revolver," which he apparently also used in the second assault. This weapon was probably not a revolver, as stated in the newspaper, but the Remington Zig-Zag Derringer, which had four stationary .22 caliber barrels. McFarland's second, and this time fatally successful, assault was also at close range, three feet, so in both attempts his accuracy was no great achievement.[13]

One should note, in addition, that McFarland's choice represented less than impeccable taste: police captain Isaac S. Bourne was chatting with *Argus* reporter John Crawford Pollock, who was visiting Catholic churches for a Christmas story. Pollock showed Bourne his Derringer and Bourne invited him into his inner office. There he handed Pollock a Smith & Wesson Navy Revolver with a six-inch barrel, saying, "Now, Pollock, I'll show you a pistol that is a pistol." Unaware that it was loaded, Pollock promptly shot Bourne "quite dead."[14]

Other middle-class men often chose similar murder weapons. For example, when two brothers, Malcolm and James Campbell, "somewhat prominent members of the legal profession," murdered William Keteltas, son of lawyer Eugene, they chose guns. (The *Times* assured its readers that "there was a combined attempt to suppress the news of the affray.")[15]

Many murders demonstrate that guns were not completely restricted to the middle class, however. The young Scottish immigrant Walter Bell, "a notorious character" also known as "Scotty the Munger" (sometimes spelled "Muncher"), got involved in a shooting affray in a Mulberry Street porterhouse, in which eighteen shots were fired, several people injured, and Bell himself murdered. The *Times* article on the incident asserts that the shooters were "thieves and roughs" and that the murder weapon was a revolver. Bell's nickname was probably "Scotty the Monger," as in peddler, an apt moniker for someone involved with stolen goods. By contrast, a nickname did not determine the fate of murder victim Michael "Dick the Gun" Murray, for when he died nine days later, it was by mere "sheath-knife."[16]

All of these examples show that mass-produced pistols were middle-class males' culturally desired weapons of choice. These weapons enabled middle-class nineteenth-century men to mimic wealthy eighteenth-century men, who could display—and sometimes use—matched sets of exotic, imported dueling pieces. *New York Times* advertisements urged readers to buy the new mass-produced guns. They came with a surprising array of consumer-oriented gizmos, such as four barrels. In the exploding market for consumer items, handguns took their place as baubles for urban middle-class men. By contrast, women seldom used guns, whether or not they were mass manufactured. In the pre-1875 years only five of the ninety-two women who killed (about 5 percent) grabbed guns; for men the figure was about 21 percent.[17]

Although this point cannot be precisely demonstrated, table 2.1 makes it apparent enough that the handgun was the weapon of the better-off man, whether in a legal or an illegal profession. Looking at those killers whose nativity or racial identity was clearly known, and using ethnicity as a proxy for class status, we can see that gun use was highest among native-born whites and lowest among the poorer immigrants and African Americans. In the second half of the nineteenth century, mass production brought the price down a bit, and the handgun began to spread from more affluent males to middle-class men and to some better-off working-class and "sporting men." Comparing the two panels of the table shows that gun use doubled in the Civil War era, but in both periods native-born whites continued to lead all others in pistol usage.

Although estimating gun ownership is very difficult, there is some evidence that it was much lower in the eighteenth and early nineteenth centuries than has been imagined. Most historians of weapons have devoted considerable time and energy to discovering the manufacturing and mechanical characteristics of guns because they are interested in the objects, not the owners. Only one American historian, Michael A. Bellesiles, has tried to estimate the actual amount of gun ownership. He conducted his work to understand the context of the Second Amendment, in particular the weaponry of local eighteenth- and nineteenth-century militias. Ex-

Table 2.1 Groups Most Likely to Use Guns in New York City Murders, 19th Century

	(In Order of Likelihood)	
	Percentage of killers using guns (absolute number)	
Killer's race/ethnicity	*Before 1861*	*After 1860*
Native-born white	27 (10)	50 (21)
German	28 (9)	37 (19)
Irish	9 (9)	26 (26)
Black	3 (1)	26 (5)
Italian	0 (0)	21 (3)
Total, all ethnicities	14 (105)	27 (177)

SOURCE: see appendix.

amining probate records for quantitative evidence of gun ownership, he found that 15 percent of probated wills included guns in the mid eighteenth century, a figure that rose to 30 percent by the mid nineteenth century. He cites other statistics suggesting even lower levels of gun ownership and concludes that until at least the 1830s gun ownership was rare. Further, Bellesiles cites evidence from local militia commanders that existing guns were often nonfunctioning. Contrary to the idea that most Americans were armed, he finds a surprising lack of guns. His major point is that today we imagine a populace well armed and highly trained; the reality was quite different.[18]

Beyond Bellesiles's work with wills, it seems that there is little to be done if one wishes to measure the availability of guns, especially in a confined region such as a specific city. We can get counts by serial numbers to suggest how many of the better-documented weapons got produced, but this cannot serve as much of a measure of their prevalence, which should be a cumulative total of all guns manufactured minus those lost or broken— a pretty hopeless number to pin down, even today.

The functionality of nineteenth-century handguns as weapons is hard to assess. The mercury fulminate that ignited the black powder, as well as the powder residue itself, corroded the gun's inner surfaces. Intensive maintenance was essential if the weapon was to stay serviceable. Even today's highly engineered guns and modern powders require maintenance. Knives and axes work better if they are sharp, but they also work when dull. A jammed gun is useless except as a club.

Revolvers—handguns with multiple-firing power and some conceal-ment capabilities—were hardly the quick-firing things we see in movies. The weapons with fire power all weighed several pounds, and having one or two constantly next to a sweaty (and hence corrosive) body was both awkward and unpleasant.

In addition to the mechanical realities of concealable handguns, the range at which they were most effective was not all that different from that of a knife or a hammer. Accurately shooting a handgun at any dis-tance requires considerable skill, practice, and concentration. At the end of the twentieth century, the production of good-quality semiautomatic handguns meant that a motivated assailant got more chances to increase the probability of a hit simply because more bullets were fired. But as the killer Daniel McFarland's case should remind us, nineteenth-century gun assaults were most often successful murders at an intimate distance, at which a knife would have worked just as well. Anyone who thinks that firing handguns is as easy as playing a video game should visit a shoot-ing range for a dose of reality.

In contrast to handguns, knives and other sharp instruments were cer-tainly more prevalent in the nineteenth century than they are today, be-cause they served as essential multipurpose tools in a world of wood-using technology. People of Lizzie Borden's high social status do not have axes handy anymore.

Mary Booder killed her daughter Susan with a jackknife (worth "six cents") in 1821. According to her mother, little Susan had brought this on herself by injuring another child (we do not know who) with the same knife. Her mother testified that she "threw" the jackknife at Susan to pun-ish her. The knife penetrated Susan's lower abdomen. Susan told Dr. Valen-tine Mott that her mother had actually stabbed her and then pulled the knife out. "Haven't I got a very wicked mother?" Susan asked Dr. Mott before she died.[19]

Her mother also had another version accounting for her anger: she had been "teased" by Susan while cutting her corns. Whatever the actual cause for her anger, the point here is that a common jackknife, an all-purpose tool, was also the lethal weapon. One wonders: In a somewhat better-off household, would Mary Booder have had a proper fixed-blade kitchen knife?

THE RISE OF THE GUN

We know that gun murders at the end of the twentieth century were an American phenomenon. The contrast with Europe is especially stark. For example, in the 1990s in New York City nearly four in five murders were by gun, while in England this ratio was more than reversed, with less than one in ten murders by gun. It is difficult to discover precisely when this distinction arose. Thanks to economist John Marshall's *Mortality of the Metropolis*, published in 1832, we have considerable information about deaths in London. The clearest comparable information that can be extracted from Marshall's book suggests that while twenty people were shot between 1690 and 1739, thirty-six were stabbed and twenty-two died by the sword. Not all of the deaths by shooting were murders, but most of the stabbings probably were; the sword deaths probably were not a subset of the stabbings. If this is a correct interpretation, then there were at least three times as many sharp-instrument murders as shooting murders during the period. On the other hand, such a hint must be balanced against contradictory evidence: Thomas Birch showed 19 percent of eighteenth-century London murders to be by gun, which is very similar to the 18 percent of eighteenth-century New York City murders.[20]

For New York City, I have identified fifty-two murders prior to 1799. Of the twenty-two murders that had recorded weapons, four were by gun, five were by knife, and thirteen were by other means. This hints that in the seventeenth and eighteenth centuries knife murders were less common in the colonies than in London. One must avoid any absolute claims about guns and knives in the New World and the Old.

In New York City, eras of knives have alternated with eras of guns. For most of the nineteenth century until 1888, and one-third of the twentieth century, 1937–1967, knives dominated. Guns took over from 1862 to 1867, from 1889 to 1936, and from 1968 to the present. This tipping back and forth occurred in a context of gradually rising proportions of both weapons combined.

Figure 2.1 shows the proportions of murders using the two weapons. The predominantly lower line represents the percentage of all murders done with knives. Note the basic stability in knife usage until the 1930s, after which it increased until the late 1950s. Then knives declined and guns rose in step with the post-1960s rise in homicides.

Of greater import is the upper line in figure 2.1, tracing the proportion of murders using either guns or knives: here we see the constant increase of murders by these two kinds of concealed instruments. The statistical relationship suggested here is modest: the percentage of murders using guns correlates positively with rising homicide rates (r^2 = .18).

Two aspects of figure 2.1 deserve further examination: the change in proportions of weapons and the question of gender. Each illuminates the other, and differences in the weapons used by men and women killers emphasize that killers made choices, choices at least partly shaped by custom and culture.

Gun usage turned sharply upward in the mid 1850s, more so than is visible to the eye in figure 2.1. Before 1857, including the eighteenth century, of 520 murders where weapon is known only 12 percent were by gun: after 1857, of 715 murders, the proportion by gun doubled to 25 percent. At the same time, at least one newspaper editor commented on knife assaults, noting that assaults by the "hero of the knife" were frequent but that it was "singular" that "more lives are not sacrificed"—in other words, that so many were injured but did not die.[21]

Men, not women, engineered the turn to guns: only about 5 percent of murderesses used guns throughout the whole time period, a stable proportion. Women did not seek guns, even though they have often been called "equalizers," in the sense that strength may not determine the out-

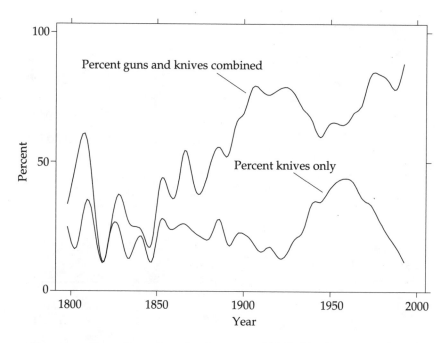

Figure 2.1.   Proportions of murders by guns and bladed weapons combined and by bladed weapons only, New York City, 1797–1994. Source: see appendix.

come of a fight. These gender differences suggest that weapons should be considered culturally chosen tools.

In the mid nineteenth century, guns became middle-class male consumer objects. After all, how many readers of the *New York Times* or *Harper's Weekly*—then, as now, written for the educated—needed a Remington's Army and Navy Revolver?[22] Yet picture ads for these and other weapons on the same pages that advertised fashionable shirts inveigled *Times* readers. Prior to the Civil War, Remington ads did not mention the military connections of revolvers. In the *Harper's Weekly* of August 1859, for example, the ad for "pocket and belt size" revolvers appeared directly above an ad for imported French Prince Imperial champagne (p. 512). By 1863, gun ads came with a reminder of the Civil War, but still retained their context as consumer goods (see figure 2.2).

The December 7, 1865, *Harper's* carried an ad (figure 2.3) for an Elliot's

Figure 2.2.   Advertisement from *Harper's Weekly: A Journal of Civilization,* Mar. 24, 1863, p. 208. Note that this gun advertisement is not for a particular brand but rather for a store with four locations—two in New York, one in Paris, and one in Birmingham, England—which also carried French and English "fancy goods." The ad placement, near other ads for in-line skates, gold pens, and shirts, makes clear that guns were consumer items. Courtesy Beinecke Rare Book and Manuscript Library, Yale University.

revolver above two ads for moustache "onguents" and "secret" enhancers, although the gender orientation of the intervening ad seeking agents for a fashion magazine is more difficult to determine: Were women magazine agents?

The February 4, 1865, *Harper's* (figure 2.4) carried on one page an ad

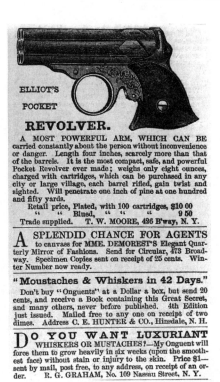

Figure 2.3. Advertisement from *Harper's Weekly,* Dec. 7, 1861, p. 783. This gun ad appeared adjacent to a story by Edward Bulwer-Lytton. It would have appealed to educated, urban, middle-class men. Presumably, they would not have noticed that this six-barreled "revolver" did not actually revolve. Reproduced by permission of The Huntington Library, San Marino, Calif.

for the National revolver below a watch ad and next to an ad for the *Atlantic Monthly*: the *Atlantic* carried Emerson and Mrs. Stowe, while the National was endorsed by police chiefs and one J. S. Vincent, editor of the *New Era*.[23] On the opposite side of the page, the Slocum's revolver illustrated ad appeared over ads for a securities dealer and Meerschaum pipes. Advertisement placements prove nothing, of course, but at least those placed in such New York City publications make clear that gun sellers were trying to appeal to an urban—even urbane—audience.

Nineteenth-century murder weapon usage contrasts starkly with con-

Figure 2.4.   Advertisement from *Harper's Weekly*, Feb. 4, 1865, p. 80. Note that the Cairo, Ill., police chief claims that at fifty paces the "pistol will kill at every shot." This "pocket" gun weighed slightly less than a pound. Courtesy Beinecke Rare Book and Manuscript Library, Yale University.

temporary practice, although muted gender differences still persist. Guns, as we all know, now account for a large proportion of all murders. Yet as recently as 1939, knives were used in as many New York City murders as were guns—33 percent each. By 1968, guns accounted for 65 percent of all murders throughout the United States (FBI data for this year do not allow a close examination of gender differences). The seeming inevitability of this transition to guns is belied by the fact that the city's transition was slower than that of the nation as a whole. In New York City, guns were still a minority of murder weapons in 1968—42 percent. This underutilization of guns did not make the city's murder rate lower, however: it had already begun to surge ahead of national rates.

New York City certainly caught up with the national trend toward the use of guns. By 1992, it exceeded the nation in gun murders: 81 percent versus 71 percent. Although reporting is not complete, the evidence for 1992 suggests that less than 50 percent of women used guns, both city-wide (40 percent) and nationally (47 percent). In other words, gun usage increased across the board, but women were still less likely than men to use guns. Thus, use of the gun as an "equalizer" is less significant than one might think.

There are many basic questions about weapons that we cannot answer with precision. How many were there? How many are there now? Did most people have them in their homes? On their persons? Surveys indicate that nearly half of all late-twentieth-century households had guns, and one-fourth had handguns.[24] Did nineteenth-century gun owners think of their guns as weapons for hurting other people, or did they think of them simply as tools for scaring away predators and for hunting? Were there unconscious cultural rules governing their use?

GENTLEMEN PREFER GUNS:
WEAPON CHOICE AND CLASS

The weapons people actually choose to hurt others may be the best indicator available of how they think about them: a heterogeneous mix of killing weapons implies that no particular tool is culturally highlighted as the instrument of killing. Most murderers, most of the time in the nineteenth century, did not use guns. Clear weapon choice has been recorded for 1,478 (out of 1,724) New York City murders prior to 1875: guns were used in only 19 percent, whereas knives or sharp instruments were used in 27 percent.[25] John Colt, literate and skilled with his hands, grabbed a hammer, not a knife or a gun. Given his status, would he have used a gun if he had not been acting on unchecked impulse? Would he have used a gun to kill a man who had wounded his honor, as opposed to one who asked to have a debt repaid?

At the very beginning of the nineteenth century, three murders by high-status men, one with a sword and the other two by gun, help explicate the linkage between status, weapon, and epoch. The best known, Aaron Burr's 1804 gun murder of Alexander Hamilton, did not take place in New York City, although the anger and arrangements preceding it did. A story familiar to many Americans, we tend to launder it by calling it a duel, and, we tell ourselves, duels are not murders. But in New York State duels were indeed murders, and arranging a duel was a felony. This is why the men moved their fight to New Jersey. Dueling could be prosecuted as a felony murder there too, and Burr was indicted for murder in New Jersey (and for fighting a duel in New York City) but was never prosecuted. Many thought that Burr had murder and not honor in mind, as evidenced by his practicing with his pistol beforehand.[26]

Hamilton fired first and missed Burr; he may have intended to do so, thus preserving his reputation—that is, showing that he was not a coward—without actually killing his opponent. Burr shot second and killed Hamilton. Rather than confront such a painful and ignominious interpretation of our early national history, we give the event a hint of glamour by calling it a duel. It is difficult to find an analogous situation today: a sitting vice president and a former Treasury secretary so hateful and so trapped by conventions of elite male behavior toward one another that the one agrees to a virtual suicide while the other commits a murder.[27] We would see such fragile egos, such cruel anger, as symptomatic of mental instability or at least moral defectiveness and cultural failure.

This incident is important in four ways. It shows, first, that high-ranking gentlemen engaged in what we now would call aberrant and unacceptable criminal behavior; second, that such gentlemen often chose firearms as their murder weapons; third, that murderers could escape prosecution; and fourth, that escape from prosecution did not mean social acceptance: Burr was rebuffed and even shunned for the remainder of his life, although some of this may have been because of his subsequent strange career and treason trial.

Another Hamilton, Alexander's twenty-year-old son, Philip, had been murdered by Capt. George I. Eacker in a gun duel in the same place only three years earlier. The conflict, though not as long-simmering as that between Burr and Hamilton, had brewed for nearly five months, from the day that Eacker had delivered a Fourth of July political speech to November 23, 1801, when he shot Hamilton.[28] Hamilton and at least one friend of his, a Price, apparently had mocked the speech, and after insults—which "began in levity"—and a public scuffle on November 20th, Eacker had challenged each of them to a duel. Eacker shot first with Price. Neither Eacker's nor Price's bullets made contact. After several tries, their seconds stopped them. Eacker evidently improved with practice. In his fight with Hamilton, his first shot was fatal. Young Hamilton apparently used his uncle's dueling pistol, modified for accuracy, the same one used by his father. The pistol fired huge bullets, nearly a half inch in diameter, and had a "hair trigger" option for increased accuracy.[29] The murder occurred outside of the city, in New Jersey, but both Hamiltons died in the city; *The New-York Evening Post* of November 24, 1801, referred to young Hamilton being carried back on a ferry.

Eacker may have been prosecuted, but evidence of this is hard to find. Eacker was no stranger to conflict, having paid a recognizance (virtually a fine) for an unnamed sum for an unnamed offense in 1798 to the Court of General Sessions. Typically such recognizances served as bonds for good behavior. Eacker himself died only three years after murdering Philip Hamilton. Of course, neither man was as distinguished as the elder Hamilton or Burr, both were young, and the affair carries the hint of a "sporting man" element to it.[30] Some of the insults were exchanged in a theater box. Such boxes were often the sites for contact between fast young men and prostitutes, and between different classes. The exchange continued into the lobby and then into a tavern. Political identity fueled these duels: both Eacker and Burr were connected to Tammany Hall politics, as was Rep. Daniel Sickles, nearly sixty years later.

A third high-status murder demonstrates that pistols had not yet become the only weapon of choice among well-off New York City murderers. In 1819 Robert M. Goodwin murdered James Stoughton.[31] He attacked Stoughton, the twenty-year-old son of the Spanish consul, with a "sword cane" (worth "one dollar") on Broadway. The anger had been simmering between the two men for several months, and Goodwin had traveled from Baltimore to commit his crime. In the indictment and trial the murder weapon was variously described as a dagger and a sword cane. The blade of the weapon, ten inches long and one inch wide, was technically too short to be called a sword, and its width was greater than that usually associated with a sword cane, which requires a narrow blade to be concealed within the cane.

The weapon was probably not a manufactured item but one of the many variations of locally made knives in circulation in early-nineteenth-century America.[32] Goodwin, the killer, caroused with several military officers at his hotel before the murder. He traded his bladeless cane for the murder weapon with one of the officers the night before the killing, and it was noted several times in the trial that the cane was only loosely held around the blade with a thong. The sword or dagger cane in many ways more easily met the fashion needs of a gentleman than did a pistol, for a cane could always be fashionable but the pistols of the day were cumbersome, to say the least.

Because Goodwin planned a surprise attack on a crowded sidewalk, he may have selected his weapon for stealth and accuracy. Although a gentleman could certainly step out well-armed with pistols, he would have had to spend some time loading the cartridges before the expedition, and could never be quite sure that they would fire cleanly and powerfully. Early-nineteenth-century handguns required deliberacy. The examples of these higher-status men typify their kind, able to afford guns, able to use them, and likely to have one nearby. The information is too fuzzy to draw the positive conclusion that guns were weapons of the upper or middle class, like swords in the Middle Ages, but the implication is strong.

By the fourth decade of the nineteenth century, the sword cane was no longer restricted to gentlemen, perhaps because gentlemen had turned to guns and their sword canes had trickled down to the inexpensive used market. Peter Kain (Irish, age thirty-six) used a sword cane in a New York

City murder in 1841, stabbing Catherine Riley through a door. Early on Sunday morning, September 3, 1854, John Bushnell ordered his barkeeper, Charles, to attack a rowdy customer, John Moran. Charles went to with vigor, stabbing Moran with a sword cane, then finishing the job with decanters.

Yet the sword cane must have kept its aura of elegance. When Dr. Henry Otto Clauss, a thirty-two-year-old German, murdered Charles Carson in 1865, he used a sword cane. Carson, proprietor of the Carson Shades, a bar that had musical entertainment as well as gambling, had tried to settle a gambling dispute between Clauss and a bagatelle player named Busby.[33]

"The hero of the knife" by midcentury was clearly a lower-class man. When the *Tribune* editorialized on "The Knife," on Christmas Day, 1858, it noted that "the majority of these stabbing affrays take place in low groggeries, and are tragical terminations of petty quarrels or altercations about some trivial matter."

CLASS AND CONCEALED DEADLY WEAPONS

A Metropolitan Police Board report by its president, Thomas Aston, reprinted in the January 5, 1865, *New York Times* made clear that the problem was not guns, but rather "concealed deadly weapons." The report stated that "since the commencement of the civil war, the practice of carrying concealed deadly weapons by the violent and vicious classes of the city, has become common." The report continued to argue that a "slight provocation" turned into a deadly encounter because of this practice. Note that Aston's statement can be understood to mean that the middle and upper classes had carried such weapons but posed little danger, and that the problem was the spread to the "violent and vicious classes."

The report makes clear that both knives and guns were the weapons for killing, and that the problem was not the kind of weapon but its concealment. Concealment has two implications: first and most obvious, an unconcealed weapon announces the subject's potential for violence, and presumably this warning enables others to be cautious. Concealment has a second and possibly more lethal implication: the constant and easy availability of deadly force turns impulse into action. This second implication is certainly as important as the first. Aston commented that lesser "affrays . . . are likely to result in murders or homicides, where deadly weapons are present."

Aston's comments came as the proportion of killings by both knives and guns tripled. But at the same time, the total homicide rates began to fall. The way people murdered had begun its long transition to guns and knives, but for the next century there would be less killing.

MURDERS WITHOUT GUNS AND KNIVES

If guns and sharp-edged weapons account for somewhat less than half of all nineteenth-century New York City murders, what did assailants use? Certainly contemporaries feared such exotic and undetectable weapons as poison. But only a tiny proportion of murders can be attributed to poison. It was greater then (about 2 percent) than now (less than 0.1 percent), but one wonders why poison is even discussed, given its near absence.

Murder by poison has become a favorite device of mystery writers. Is this because it is more complex and therefore more interesting? Because it implies intimacy and planning? Or because most food preparation and even drug administration is by women? Simply put, very few murders have been done with poison. Of the more than 1,700 cases of murder prior to 1875, only 37 (2 percent) were by poison. Of these, slightly more (54 percent) were by men, but since more than 90 percent of all murders were by men, this does confirm that proportionally women used poison more than did men. And slightly more than half of all killings by women were done with poison. The question arises: How many deaths by poison escaped the coroner's notice? Nineteenth-century forensic medicine was poor, to say the least, but so was knowledge about sophisticated poisons. Common poisons were readily available, in particular rat poison. Finally one is left with speculation: How many deaths from undiagnosed stomach ailments were actually poisonings? Conversely, how many alleged poisoners were innocent?

In the contemporary era of better forensic pathology, the evidence suggests that poisoning is rare. Of the 446,256 murders in the United States between 1968 and 1992, only 314, less than 0.1 percent, were by poison. In New York City alone, poisonings constituted an even tinier proportion, 0.03 percent—twelve in all. Women comprised about one-third of the poisoners for the whole United States. Have the killings by poison diminished? Or were there more unfair accusations in the nineteenth century? The evidence simply will not let us decide.

Most murderers used whatever was handy, including hands, feet, sticks, rocks, chairs, and combinations of them all. In a murder with Biblical overtones, two German peddlers, ages twenty and twenty-six, murdered an old man, Jacob Bertrand, the father of someone with whom they had initially fought on Christmas Day three months earlier. On March 24, 1859, they resumed the fight, first stoning the son. When old Jacob came out to help him, they fractured his skull.

Finally, consider this whodunit, a true low-tech murder: On August 30, 1821, J. Hopson, coroner, found a true bill for manslaughter against Sarah Dennison for knocking Francis, "her husband[,] overboard, whereby he was drowned." Depositions were taken from Bridget Plato, John Devoe, and Sarah Dennison. Both women were illiterate and signed with a mark. All agreed that Francis had gone overboard from the Mink, a sloop "lying at the Walnut Street birth and had drowned," but they disagreed on details.[34]

Sarah elaborated on how she and Francis came to be on board. Francis and she had married about three years earlier, he a French seaman and she a widow. (She added, in a Dickensian touch, that her former husband, James Wilson, the father of both of her children, had died in the War of 1812 on the privateer Governor Tompkins.) Sarah and Francis had been staying at Alice (?) Benson's on the corner of Cherry and Walnut for about five weeks.

They had spent the evening wandering about and "at length went aboard a sloop at Walnut Street wharf where she saw Bridget Plato lying in the arms of a man when the said Bridget Plato took from the mouth of the said Francis a segar that he was smoking." She "would not stand that from her or from any other whore like her," Sarah told Bridget.

According to Sarah, Bridget replied "that she had slept with her [Sarah's] husband and would again—and did not care a dam for this examinant [Sarah] or for any bloody bitch of cow like examinant, and then the said Bridget rolled up her sleeves and challenged examinant to fight. When this examinant's husband [Francis] interfered and struck this deponent [Bridget] with his open hand in the face, which blow knocked examinant['s] hat overboard—when he the said Francis gave examinant [Sarah] his hat to hold, while he would get hers which was in the river—when the said Francis went down by the side of the sloop and then into the water—this was the last examinant saw of him and does not know whether he was drowned or not. . . . The hat here present is the hat her husband wore and which he gave her."

Bridget and John's version, on the other hand, had Sarah pushing Francis, no gallant leaping into the water to fetch her hat. Bridget said that Francis "unbottoned [sic] his pantaloons and was easing himself over the side of the sloop when the said Sarah his wife gave him a blow in the breast which knocked the said Francis into the river—which caused the said Francis to be drowned—The hat of the said Francis fell on the deck as he fell overboard."

Devoe said that he had called to Francis "to give him his hand" and that Francis swam a short distance, then sank.

"Let him go," Sarah cried.

"My Dear Francis come here," Sarah then said, having changed her mind.

Devoe called for the night watch, to whom Sarah confessed that she had pushed Francis.

Sarah was indicted for manslaughter on September 1, 1821. The indictment added the information that she had hit Francis on the left breast with her right hand. On September 11 a jury acquitted Sarah.

Was this a murder? Or was Francis gallantly recovering his new wife's hat? Assuming that it was a murder, the weapon was no more than a well-timed push, and whether the victim had landed in water, on stairs, or on the ground below a window mattered little. Given his probable alcoholic befuddlement and the lack of swimming skills typical of the era, such a push was the only weapon needed.

THE TOOLS OF MURDER

Whether nineteenth-century murderers used guns, knives, or other less sophisticated devices, most murders occurred at intimate distances. Mc-Farland shot Richardson at a distance of three feet or less. Short swords, pocket knives, and sticks worked best in close physical contact. Weaponry, haste, and the context of a physical struggle all caused murders to be affairs of close, messy, physical contact. The technology of killing varied in its effectiveness, with sharp instruments probably being the most fatal, pushes and kicks or perhaps guns the least.

Forensic anthropologist Phillip Walker has examined thousands of skulls from different cultures and different eras for blunt-force trauma. He has discovered that prior to the late nineteenth century and the rise of professional boxing, few traumas were to the face, but by the early twentieth century, such traumas predominated. He concludes that the popularity and visibility of boxing caused a change in the way people fought, and they began to focus on the face. The significance of his finding is that here a popular cultural practice has influenced what we now take to be a "natural" form of physical conflict.[35]

The fists of "prize fighters" were feared and respected weapons by the mid Civil War era. For example, when Tammany boss and future mayor Richard Croker defended himself at a murder trial in 1874 he claimed that he never carried a gun. The unspoken point: he was well known for his bare-knuckled fighting ability. On October 29, 1864, the *New York Times* reported the depredations of a gang of "prize-fighters"—"the worst class of bruisers, blacklegs and thieves"—on the New York and Erie Railway.

This leads, finally, to a question the answer to which tells us as much about the late twentieth century as it does about weapon choices of earlier eras. What are the common ways of categorizing weapons? Our primary distinction between guns and knives, or between semiautomatic pistols, "Saturday Night Specials," and shotguns, say, demonstrates that average people conceptualize the range of murder weapons the same way most murderers do. To at least a limited extent, the murderers' culture is our culture, and we can speak the same language.

There is a trend more significant than the contrasts between guns and

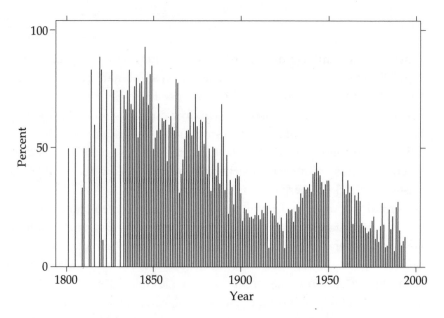

Figure 2.5. Percentage of murders not by gun or bladed weapon, New York City, 1800–1994. Source: see appendix.

knives: that between these two instruments of death and the messy category of "other." "Other" includes sticks and kicks, blows and pushes, rocks and ropes. The obverse of figure 2.1 is a bumpy overall decline in murders by sticks, rocks, and kicks. Murder weapons have changed dramatically from those at hand to those more purposive. The change overall has been a long decline in the use of miscellaneous weapons—or a rise in the use of knives and guns. This change has not been steady, but has moved in two large looping curves, the first from the early nineteenth century to the first decades of the twentieth, and the more recent from the Depression until very recently.

These two loops have had very different consequences. The first essentially drove the homicide rate. That is, when miscellaneous weapons increased, so did the homicide rate; when they decreased, so did the homicide rate. The second loop has had exactly the opposite relationship: knives and more particularly guns drive the homicide rate, no matter which way

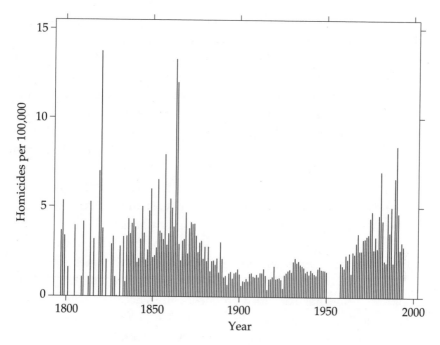

Figure 2.6. Number of non–gun / knife homicides per 100,000 residents, New York City, 1800–1994. Source: see appendix.

it goes. The transition between the two relationships came sharply in 1932 (see figure 2.5). It was a change hardly visible at the time because the concern is always with the number of homicides and with the weapons that seem responsible for them.[36]

What does this change in murder technology mean? Is it a sign of our mechanized century? Even impulsive anger gets realized through tools? Geoffrey Canada traces changes in weapons technology at the level of young people and street fighting, showing how access to weapons and the handgun culture made youth conflict more lethal in the 1980s.[37] His argument is careful and he makes no exaggerated claims about controlling violence by controlling handguns. Rather, he shows how the changing culture of carrying and using handguns has made contentious relationships and confrontations far more lethal than before. An implication: simply making guns less available would reduce some violence.

Canada makes no easy arguments that other weapons would not be sub-stituted for guns and knives, a speculation intriguing but impossible to confirm. One can examine the rates per hundred thousand population of non–gun/knife homicides (see figure 2.6). Even without guns and knives, the homicide burst of the 1970s and 1980s would still be there, but the lev-els would be more similar to those of the mid nineteenth century. If it were to last as long as previous bursts, something like thirty-five years, then its course would now be over. Note that this graph puts an end to the notion that strict gun control alone would make the United States more like other Western countries, for the twentieth-century rates of non–knife/gun homi-cides in New York City are still well above those in London. (All of En-gland still has fewer murders per year than New York City has.)

Neither guns nor knives alone can account for the high homicide rates of late-twentieth-century New York City or the United States. The num-ber of murders by other means keeps the rates high, even though these kinds of murders have declined proportionally since the nineteenth cen-tury. But today, handguns and knives, lethal, easily accessible, and con-cealable, are an enormous component of the homicide problem. Since the Depression, murders by guns and knives have pushed the rates around. This suggests that for control policy, a focus on such weapons makes sense, even though they should not be mistaken for the cause or the whole problem.

Even this most violent and often impulsive crime, murder, has been and still is conditioned through cultural, technological, and mass-consumption standards and fads. When and how people hit is not "natural" but pat-terned, and these patterns change. Some, unfortunately, are more likely to be lethal than others.[38] Almost all are forms of violent force—whether delivered by boot or hammer, bullet or ax. Almost none are by the favorite means of novelists and nineteenth-century newspapers: poison.

Chapter 3 Gender and Murder

One might wonder why I begin a chapter on gender with a murder involving only men, men participating in an exclusively male cultural activity. In the discussion of violence issues, all too often the label "gender" means that the topic will be women, either as victims or as perpetrators. It is almost as if the overwhelmingly male activity of personal violence is not gendered behavior. Yet it is, and as such it is a puzzle that too often strains explanation and calls for reliance upon cliché.

The November 20, 1858, *New York Tribune* reported that David Fox, the captain of the Fox Musketeers, a "political target company" (armed supporters of political parties), had taken his group of Democrats up to Harlem on Thanksgiving Day. He was anxious to avoid hostile onlookers. He especially did not want the captain of a rival group of Democrats such as the Brady Guards hanging about. Yet Daniel Stackpole, the captain of the Guards, managed to follow and foolishly insisted on watching the Musketeers' afternoon of shooting and drinking. After dinner the Musketeers dropped their shooting for drinking and quarreling, and only then did they turn on Stackpole.

"You hit me!" Charley Moore said to Stackpole.

"No, I did not strike you; keep away; don't lay your hands on me," Stackpole replied.

Then three Musketeers, Moore, A. D. Thompson, and Captain Fox, chased Stackpole with swords.

"On!" someone (perhaps Fox?) ordered.

"Stop you s[on] of a b[itch]. . . . Stick the s[on] of a b[itch]!" someone cried. Then one of the three men stabbed Stackpole in the perineum, using either a bayonet or a dress sword, as he desperately tried to scramble up a bank.

"Sheath your sword," an onlooker yelled to one of the three "pioneers."

"I guess he has got enough," the pioneer responded.

Stackpole died of internal bleeding in about fifteen minutes, leaving behind a "widowed mother and five helpless sisters to mourn his loss."[1]

The Stackpole murder is almost impossible to imagine with genders reversed, with women instead of men. Murder, particularly political murder, is principally a man's business. Just how much more male than female is murder? Table 3.1 lays out comparable urban figures. Note how similar the figures are for the proportion of male offenders (third column), particularly when child victims are excluded. Over the past two centuries the proportion of New York City offenders who are male has stayed remarkably stable; Liverpool and London have had a slightly higher proportion of women offenders than New York City has had. Victims, on the other hand, were proportionally more male in the late twentieth century than in the nineteenth century. As interesting as this apparent decrease in female victims is, it should not obscure the basics: over a two-century period most murderers and their victims have been and now are men.

How do we account for male violence? Testosterone via natural selection? Behavioral evolution? Pan-species maleness? Culture? Historical contingency? Psychology? Politics? Conversely, what makes women so much less likely to kill than men? Mothering? Oppression? Inherent good-

A TARGET EXCURSION IN BROADWAY.

Figure 3.1. "A Target Excursion in Broadway," satirical cartoon, *Harper's Weekly,*
Oct. 23, 1858. Only six days after the Fox Musketeers murdered Brady Guard leader
Daniel Stackpole, *Harper's Weekly* published this cartoon accompanied by a satirical article in pidgin French. The gist of the satire—how silly and childish these
companies are—demonstrates the insouciance of New York's elites in the face of
political violence. Note the two gang members walking arm in arm, bullying the
aged woman out of the way, in the lower left foreground. Courtesy Beinecke Rare
Book and Manuscript Library, Yale University.

ness? Serotonin? We sometimes forget that murderers are mean and want
to hurt: they take advantage of those weaker or less violent. Does this exclude women because they are nurturing? Since killers tend to pick on
weaker (hence, smaller) people, why aren't there far more women victims?[2]

These puzzles and the answers to them no doubt are interrelated. But
at this point in our understanding of gender differences, researchers have
not yet been able to produce a single convincing and coherent explanation. Rather, the questions and implied answers can be grouped into two
broadly plausible accounts, neither of which can be refuted even though
each excludes the other. In some ways these two broad groups conform

Table 3.1   Gender Proportions of Victims and Offenders

Place	Time	Percentage of offenders male	Percentage of victims male
New York City	1968–1994	90	66
New York City (excluding child murders)	1968–1994	93	86
New York City (excluding child murders)	1797–1875	93	76
London (excluding child murders)	1719–1856	85	64
Liverpool (excluding child murders)	1852–1865	89	63

SOURCE: see appendix.
NOTE: London data are based on a fairly small number of cases (54), so they may be biased.

to the older arguments about human culture and to the camps that emphasize either nature or nurture.

One recently developed approach comes from evolutionary psychology and is best summarized in the work of Martin Daly and Margo Wilson.[3] They argue that the psychological mechanisms have evolved to differentiate between genders so as to maximize genetic survival both of a particular genetic lineage and of larger groups. The dyadic family contains one aggressor who can fight and defend and who is not essential to nurturing. Likewise, larger human groups select for childbearing and nurturing by one gender, and select for aggression and defensive protection by the other. This scenario, thus, accounts for the presence of much more testosterone in men and serotonin in women through natural selection. The emphasis here is on level, for the chemicals have similar if not the same behavioral effects in both genders. This scenario also accounts for differences in whom each gender attacks: women more typically attacking spouses or anyone who threatens the family unit, men also attacking spouses but more typically strangers and other men.

The evolutionary psychology perspective—which I have presented here far too simply and starkly—has generated considerable experimental support. This theory also predicts the time-independent uniformity in the gender proportions of offenders shown in table 3.1 for New York City. (Of course, in an evolutionary prediction two centuries is the blink of an

eye.) In her readable summary of the scientific research on the brain biology of men and women, Deborah Blum brings together current under-
standings of testosterone, serotonin, and other chemicals. The presence
and behavioral consequences of these chemicals differ between the sexes,
and a further complexity arises from the fact that the chemicals are caused
by behavior, as well as vice versa. The research cannot resolve the question of natural selection reinforcing chemical differences that promote behavior versus behavior promoting the chemical differences. As Blum says
in her chapter on the "Big T" (testosterone), there is a "chicken-or-egg
dilemma of linking testosterone to violence."[4]

    Yet this theory is unable to account easily for cultural and historical vari-
ation in levels of violence even as gender differences persist. Sociologists
and historians would automatically look to external, contextual, nonpsy-
chological reasons. But evolutionary psychologists would criticize the so-
ciohistorical view as incomplete, unable either to account for the nearly
universal male predominance across space and time or to explain the physiological gender differences. Some evolutionary psychological research
deals with the problem of variation. In *Culture of Honor*, for instance,
Richard Nisbett and Dov Cohen show how different cultural patterning
can repress or encourage aggression, and demonstrate that these cultural
differences in turn can have differing psychochemical effects.[5] They press
the issue, arguing that herding-based cultures foster male aggression because grazing ranges are less easily bounded than cultivated fields, and
that in the United States, the South was settled by herding cultures. This
argument makes most historians and sociologists balk, to put it mildly.

    The second group of explanations of gender differences—sociohistor-
ical explanations—locates the causes in the nearly global oppression of
women. Power—the argument goes, following Marx—is too universally
valued for any group, whether a social class or a nation or a gender, to
cede it willingly. Women have been historically and culturally forced into
subservience by male violence or the threat of violence, and women's only
viable strategy for survival has been to avoid conflict and to suppress violent impulses. The gender differences in levels of violence, then, are historically contingent, not inherent or essential. Some evolutionary psychological research supports this interpretation. Nisbett and Cohen report

that testosterone in men can rise after conflict; that is, testosterone is both caused and causal. The sociocultural approach would criticize the evolutionary psychology arguments as "essentialist"—that is, tautological (women kill less because their nature is to kill less)—and therefore as nonexplanatory.

Of these two broad theoretical approaches, the first has a stronger if more controversial body of literature directly addressing the question of gender and violence, whereas the second has much more literature, but of a more diverse, diffuse, and particularistic nature. Because of differing disciplinary locations—the first group in psychology and biology, the second in sociology and history—there is less dialogue between proponents of the two views than one might expect. And because neither has created a theoretical argument with a clear place for critical tests allowing refutation of the theory, intelligent confrontation—much less resolution—is unlikely.

A detailed look at New York City's two-centuries-long historical record provides some support for each theory, completely contradicting neither. The historical record can incorporate several different sets of explanations. It requires an open acceptance that virtually every explanation can account for a piece of the puzzle, but that to see the puzzle whole, one must avoid the expectation of a single "factor" or a big bang. Evolutionary psychology helps, and so does historical contextualism. So does accident, including cultural fashions that have consequences disproportionate to the causes. (The idea of a cultural fashion captures the notion that some activities, transient cultural habits, may not have deeply meaningful causal roots.) Usually fashions do not have significant social consequences, but it is easy to imagine others that do—cigarette smoking, for example. The carrying of various lethal weapons can have an element of fashion; the difference between the lethal weapon fad and a clothing or shoe fashion is in the consequences. The former can promote an escalation in carrying weapons, and an epidemic in fatalities may be the result. Youth counselor Geoffrey Canada hints at this in his book *Fist, Stick, Knife, Gun,* as he shows the deadly consequences of young people's weapon fads in the late 1980s and early 1990s.[6] David Kennedy, who works in violence prevention in Boston, suspects that the youth preference for Glock pistols comes from their status as police weapons.[7] The concept that relatively minor causes can trigger epidemics is familiar enough in scientific theories, but from a policy point of view it is very challenging, for the means to change a fad are not easy to discern. The very triviality and capriciousness of such triggers make monitoring and control more elusive than for bigger causes.

BIG TRENDS

Figure 3.2 displays the proportion of New York City murder victims who were women. The solid curve smooths the actual percentages (the small dots). The rare times that the percentages spike over 40 percent are almost always when the numbers are small, so that the difference of one or two victims could have changed the proportions dramatically. Over the pictured two hundred years, women averaged 17.9 percent of all victims, indicated by the horizontal line.

One can interpret the graph as confirming that murder is mainly a men's affair, even for the victims, and one can even note the relative consistency of the proportions. But is the "relative" consistency enough to support an evolutionary psychology approach, or does it challenge the theory? If the gender differences in homicide were accounted for by evolutionary aspects of human psychology, then these differences should be broadly consistent over time. The important feature of evolutionary psychology is that it explains a stable proportion, not a historically changing one. On the other hand, because no gender theory makes precise, testable predictions, none can be rejected.

We are left noting the visual impression of a slight, ragged decline in the proportion of victims who are women, an impression that fits the broader picture hinted at in table 3.1. This is confirmed by a negative correlation of this proportion (with time), declining about a half percent every decade.[8] One could even read this slender trend as indicating that the women's movement from the mid nineteenth century onward has had a measurable impact on women's safety, their likelihood of being murdered—compared to men—declining from at least the middle of the nineteenth century. One must be cautious about this interpretation, how-

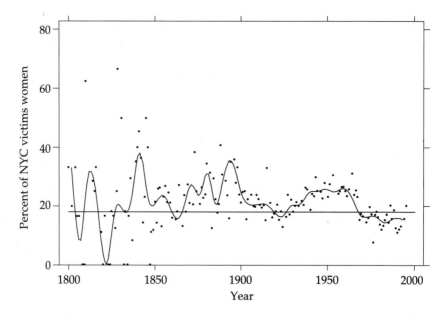

Figure 3.2.   Percentage of victims who were women, New York City, 1800–1995. Source: see appendix. Note: The nineteenth-century gap years come from averaging to get larger numbers; the 1950s gap years come from recording lapses in the public health and police records.

ever, because, like men, women experienced a dramatic increase in murder from the early 1960s until the late 1990s.

Although it is easy to notice that the decrease in the proportion of women victims seems to correlate with increases in overall homicides (especially in the post-1950s era), a more refined approach is in order. Figure 3.3 offers such a refinement. It displays the rates of women victims per one hundred thousand women (the vertical bars) and contrasts this value with that for men (the jagged continuous line). The actual values are not as important as the shape of the lines, which also indicate a data gap in the 1950s and some early years when there were no women victims. This reveals a step increase in the murder rate in the 1950s, when women, like men, were murdered in ever-increasing numbers. The two series correlate highly, r = .79, confirming the visual impression.

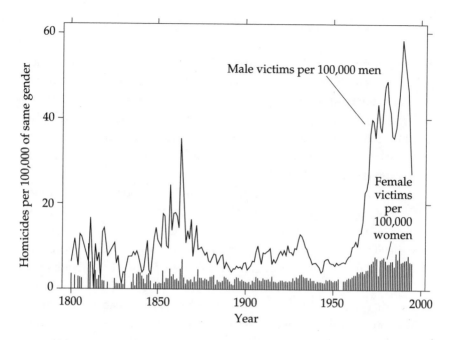

Figure 3.3. Women and men murder victims per 100,000 women and men living in New York City, 1800–1995. Source: see appendix.

To probe further, we can ask if it was not high violence itself, rather than the historical era, that correlates with increased proportions of women who are murder victims. It turns out that when the homicide rates were "low"—say, below 10 per 100,000—the distribution of the proportion of women victims is random. High homicide years, on the other hand, shift toward male victims. Figure 3.3 makes clear that women are dragged along in high homicide years, but the proportion of women victims decreases when homicides soar: essentially, the sudden bursts are for men.[9]

This distinction demonstrates that the murder of women is less sensitive to overall violence, or, conversely, that men make up a more sizable disproportion of victims in extreme homicide years. Violent times pull women into the maelstrom, but on an elastic tie, so that their rate does not soar to the violent heights of men.

Some time periods had low murder rates for women: the 1820s, 1830s, and a few years in the 1840s; 1883–1903; 1918; and 1944–1945. Taken chronologically, the earliest block of low homicide years came during a period of high population growth and internal migration, the second during a period of high East European Jewish immigration, and the twentieth-century low came at the end of World Wars I and II. Each era had discrete and unpredictable historical circumstances.

Some blocks of years were particularly high homicide years for women: 1855–1866, 1906–1915, 1929–1935, and the recent post-1960s. The first block of high homicides came during an era of violent riots, mostly understood as male affairs. During riotous years, women were murdered more often than usual: these were not directly riot-related, as direct riot deaths have been excluded from the data plotted and analyzed in this book. The second block occurred during a period of high East European and Italian immigration—but simultaneously overall low homicides. The third came in the early Depression years and the fourth during the recent abatement from record overall highs. Some of these periods—the two in the early twentieth century—seem high principally because the overall homicide rate was so low, which suggests that on occasion the killing of women and the killing of men are influenced differently. The high rates of murder of women that accompany some violent years do not necessarily contradict this: the mid-nineteenth-century violence, like the post-1960s violence, was the product of a time violent in other ways.

A whole generation of late-twentieth-century American college students and their professors—social scientists and historians—grew up learning about the rational, politically oriented, and calculating mob.[10] We have all learned how to "understand" group violence and to avoid our predecessors' foolish condemnation of the mindless crowd. Typically, then, when we think of riots and civil disorder, we forget that these events include an enormous amount of plain murder. The year 1857 began a period of violent riots in New York City—some between rival ethnic gangs, the Bowery Boys (Protestant, native-born, and nativist) and the Dead Rabbits (Irish Catholic)—a period that culminated in the Draft Riots of 1863, which claimed more than a hundred victims.[11] All of the riots had racial overtones, whether Yankee versus Irish (who were seen as a different race) or Irish versus African American. The racism filtered through economic conflict and gender. Typically mobs spared women, murdering men. No doubt the male riot deaths came in large part from the greater preponderance of men at risk, on the streets, whether participating or just watching.[12] Yet we cannot help but wonder if rioters went after men just as genocidal soldiers often do. To repeat, the reported homicide data throughout this book exclude riot deaths, so gender distortions from riots do not figure in the visual data. During eras of riot, however, there were more murders of all kinds, including murders of women; for example, an era of unprecedented personal violence began in the mid 1960s in parallel with urban riots.

The nineteenth-century sources clearly show that spouses, lovers, or other intimate family members murdered two-thirds of the women victims as opposed to only 5 percent of the male victims. Almost by definition, then, times with high levels of women victims were times with high levels of family tensions. "Family tension" is such an all-encompassing phrase that it does not really account for much. It can include increased drinking because of increased real income for very poor immigrants, more leisure time, new role expectations for each gender in the context of host societies, and failure to fulfill traditional gendered expectations in new societies—any and all of these translate into "family tensions."

A murder reported in the November 9, 1874, New York Tribune fuses all of these abstractions and demonstrates how any single explanation is impossible to isolate. Joseph Rosenstein, age thirty-five, pushed his wife, Mary, age thirty-two, off the roof of their five-story tenement building while their eight-year-old son, Matthew, watched. On payday Joseph had come home from his job as a porter at a coffee and spice "establishment" in Coenties Slip. His pay must have made him feel powerful. He may have begun drinking on his way home from work. Once home, he began fighting with Mary about the quality of the supper she had prepared. He angrily announced that he would leave "to get something to eat, and meet friends with whom he could enjoy himself." Mary, wanting him not to squander his week's wages, whisked little Matthew out and locked Joseph in the apartment. She and Matthew went to the roof of the building to take in the laundry. Joseph bolted from her trap, climbing out to the fire escape and then to the roof, where he attacked Mary and finally pushed her off. She died instantly. He then went back down the fire escape to the street, headed for a barber shop, and had a shave. Matthew described what had happened to the police. Joseph ultimately returned home, and the police arrested him.[13]

What "tensions" were here? Challenges to patriarchy? Mary locked Joseph in. Independence of children? Little Matthew told police what his father had done. Money enough to drink and carouse? Joseph had the alternative of spending the evening in taverns instead of either working or eating at home. A new living environment? Mary hung the laundry on the roof of their building, nearly one hundred feet high. Waged labor? Joseph had his week's pay, Mary had none.[14] No doubt Joseph's testosterone levels were high, but just as surely the cultural context permitted his aggression and channeled it into personal violence.

Over the past two centuries, the worst three years for New York City women were 1864 for the nineteenth century, and 1986 and 1988. The first of these, 1864, with thirty-one women victims, came after the Draft Riots; should one conclude that war itself caused the high rate of murder of women, then one would have to ignore the extraordinarily low rates for the last two years of World War II. Perhaps the Civil War, as a local war, was different. The test case would be the Revolution, about which it is almost impossible to reconstruct a clear record of personal violence. One oddity: eight of the thirty-one 1864 victims were murdered by other women, at least four from within the family. Ordinarily, we would have expected only two or three women victims of women offenders in that larger group. The victims' gender failed to immunize them from whatever evil was afoot.

None of the newspaper reports about the murders of these women suggested what that evil might have been in 1864. In January, Sarah Dillon threw an intoxicated sixty-year-old Margaret Roundtree down the stairs, killing her. In the same month, Catherine Henry, who was "very old," quarreled with her daughter-in-law, Bridget, who then beat her to death. In June, Mary Miller went to Fishkill Landing for a summer of "quiet and repose" to relieve her spells of insanity; instead she killed her two children. Dora Clinton, a twenty-year-old Irish woman, killed three-year-old Mary Gerrity, whom she had adopted from a poor widow six months earlier. "Mama Clinton threw the slop-pail at me, and cut me on the chin," Mary told witness Ann Dowell before dying.[15] Mr. Clinton testified that he had seen his wife "slap" the child, but not abuse her. On the other hand, Dr. George B. Bouton found sixteen different bruises on the child's head alone.[16]

In the mid 1980s—considered the crack cocaine epidemic's worst times—there were 320 women victims in 1986 and 354 in 1988, about 25 percent more victims than was to be expected. There are few clues. The average ages were similar; the FBI coding of the circumstances of the killings is too sparse to tell us much; and the proportion of the attacks by men is consistent with less violent years.

AGE

An evolutionary psychologist would say that at the onset of male puberty, the rules governing reproductive strategies take command and competition becomes lethal. Evidence to support this notion should come from the killer and victim gender distributions: after puberty males should be the victims of other males. For recent twentieth-century New York City the distribution does indeed conform to evolutionary psychology's prediction: only 52 percent of the young or old victims were male. For the United States as a whole the current picture is just as dramatic: young and old victims split almost evenly by gender.[17] Compared to females, males become more at risk to be murdered somewhere between ten and thirteen years old. Prior to that age each sex is killed at the same rate. Why should we take as expected the violence toward or by boys once they are no longer completely dependent on others? Is it that males increase their public socializing or, as Deborah Blum would argue, decrease their willing subservience? Or do they increase their aggression? Does it have something to do with the family formation and reproduction strategies that attend the onset of puberty? Is there something flawed about our thinking that what distinguishes men only operates on certain age groups? Is this biological? Cultural?

Although nineteenth-century New York City data on very young and very old victim/killer pairs are scanty (about two-thirds of all pairs are incomplete), they do not support the evolutionary psychology thesis, in contrast to data on the current situation. Of the forty young (under age fifteen but not infant) victims of men in nineteenth-century New York City, 78 percent were also male; of the twenty-two victims over age fifty-nine, 82 percent were male; and of all 1,348 pairs where offender and victim sex are known, 75 percent were male. These proportions are similar enough across age groups to cast some doubt: Does evolutionary psychology work only for recent times and less well in New York City? Did fewer youth murders get reported or did data-gathering errors compound the small numbers? Or did the nineteenth-century pattern reveal other secondary gender rules and roles? Perhaps mothers kept their daughters away from men. Or might we detect an influence of evolutionary psychology, but one that does not always predominate?[18]

FEMININITY/MASCULINITY AND VICTIMS

Official attitudes toward infanticide—predominantly an offense by very poor, unmarried women—have varied considerably.[19] From slim evidence it appears that in seventeenth-century New York officials prosecuted infanticide. By the late eighteenth and early nineteenth centuries New York officials obviously looked the other way. They did so for two reasons: a growing sympathy with the plight of poor pregnant women, and a realization that the causes of infant death were difficult to discern. Infanticide was a crime that the sympathetic police of the nineteenth century tried not to discover: laconic listings of "dead babies found" often appear in annual police reports. Because many infants died of causes unknown, the medical decisions were often less than certain. When a desperately poor mother said that her newborn died from her rolling on it in her sleep— "overlayment"—who could, or wanted to, place blame?

Occasionally we get a glimpse of these interpretive conflicts:

Supposed infanticide.—Coroner Gamble held an inquest at Trinity
Place Police Station yesterday, on the body of a female infant, which,
while alive, had fallen or been thrown into the sink of premises No. 63
Greenwich Street. Mary Ward, the mother of the deceased, arrived
recently from Wisconsin and being without money or friends took
lodging in the above tenement house. She stoutly denied having
thrown the infant into the sink and says it fell there by accident, but
the majority of the Jurors did not believe her statement. Dr. Wooster
Beach made a postmortem examination of the body and ascertained
that deceased was born alive. The Jury rendered a verdict of death
from "suffocation by being thrown in the sink of the house No. 63
Greenwich street, on the 15th day of August, 1859, by her mother Mary
Ward." The accused, who is in very feeble condition, was conveyed
to Bellevue Hospital for medical treatment, and will remain there a
prisoner until she is able to be taken in charge by the police. (*New York
Tribune*, Aug. 18, 1859)

Already in the article we see "Mary Ward's" desperate personal situation,
the rather slender evidence on which to prosecute the case, and a potential defense line. "Mary Ward"—one of at least thirty-four women with
that name in the city—could have expected her problems to disappear into
the urban mass. No wonder the case disappeared.

Only at the end of the twentieth century did medical examiners begin
to develop infant and child death protocols to discover with accuracy and
regularity whether the accidents that took children's lives were actually
intentional. This new quality in child and infant death reporting shows
that the death rates of children has a specific age distribution: infants die
four times more often than one- or two-year-olds, nine- to eleven-year-
olds are the least at risk, and the rates for fifteen-year-olds begin to soar.
In the nineteenth-century data on New York City, for the sake of consistency I have excluded the identified infanticides and included only
definite child murders. The irregular reporting and questionable accuracy
of infanticides would make inclusion highly uneven. Including infanticides over time is an exercise in measuring changing medical practices
and adult perceptions.

If "Mary Ward's" probable infanticide illustrated a "woman's" crime,
then in the same year John McCue and Samuel Reeves acted out a "man's"

crime. John Armstrong witnessed the sequence of events (reported in the
New York Tribune on November 19, 1859), suggesting that this was all
played out in the streets and at least one saloon in front of several other
men. All involved knew each other. The drama required it. John McCue,
age twenty, Irish, saw Samuel ("Forty") Reeves pass a "grocery store" at
Grand and Crosby and ran out, trying to throw a brick at him but missing. An hour later he found Reeves sitting and drinking with several others at James Cunningham's saloon.

"Forty, I can lick you," McCue challenged Reeves.

Reeves followed McCue outside and hit him in the face. McCue then
pulled a knife and "made several plunges" at Reeves, penetrating his
lungs and slashing his face. Reeves staggered and died. McCue ran. Armstrong and others chased McCue down and caught him at 444 Broadway,
probably near his home, where his wife and sister-in-law tried to rescue
him.[20]

These two young men contested for dominance in a very social, public setting. In front of several others, probably all Irish and all known to
one another, one boasted of his prowess, the other rose to the challenge
and died. The stakes—local reputation—required that the event be enacted in public, before an audience of peers. The newspaper notes that
McCue was a "Five Points rowdy and a thief," and implies that his claim
of self-defense out of fear was lame. Probably not: to maintain power and
respect in front of his peers, McCue was simply continuing the male
power challenges by going after Reeves. Reeves played the willing victim, leaving the saloon to fight. Street reputation required some sort of
cooperation in the fight: had Reeves run, he would have suffered a dam-
aging, even dangerous, status loss. The echoes of the Hamilton-Burr duel
reverberate.

Men and women often demand and reinforce gender roles. Just as men
insist on what women are or should be, women make role demands on
men. In October 1810, James Johnson murdered Lewis Robinson (both
African American) at a dance that Johnson and his wife were holding in
their cellar oyster bar.[21] This establishment, a cellar room entered from the
street by going down under some stairs, was furnished with trunks to sit
on and a table with oysters and liquor. Apparently a candle or a lantern

provided the lighting. And there was dancing. It was the kind of establishment that gave meaning to the word *dive*.

Johnson, known to be mean when drunk, was "capering" about rather than working while Mrs. Johnson collected the entry fees and served the food and drink. She and Robinson argued about the cost of the dance, one shilling, and had settled that issue. He paid her only nine pence. Then she accused Robinson of stepping on her toes.

"*Are you a man* [emphasis added], and will you tread on my toes?" she angrily asked Robinson. Apparently her husband did not leap to her defense, so she turned on him, using the same logic.

"*Are you a man* [emphasis added], Johnson, and suffer me to be insulted in my own house?" she was heard to "cry out."

At Johnson's trial, the defense played up this provocation, saying that Mrs. Johnson's "pungent expression . . . would be powerfully felt even by those in whom higher education might control the workings of natural passion, but among men of the lower class, the pride and point of honor lies in their courage and strength; and whether his wife had been trod upon, or pretended to be so insulted, . . . such a cry, in such a moment, must have greatly aggravated his passion."[22] The court did not consider whether Johnson's capering had anything to do with his subsequent knife attack on Robinson, but Mrs. Johnson certainly egged her husband on. (The court, however, could not decide if he actually heard her, so busy was he dancing and fighting.)

Mrs. Johnson evoked two manly traits: from Robinson, physical deference toward the delicate feelings of a woman (the toe-treading), and from her husband, violence toward other men in defending a mate. The defense lawyer, one Mr. Hopkins, pointed out to the jury that such gender feelings were "natural passion" but that class and education modified such passion, making it less strong, but still present, in the educated classes. Education, then, obscured but did not obliterate to the educated men of the court just how deeply such slights could be felt. (Presumably, the higher classes felt grander passions, which would be equally difficult for the lower classes to understand.) The court, either unswayed by the argument or, more likely, unswayed by its application to an African American, convicted Johnson, who was subsequently executed.

RELATIONSHIPS

Most nineteenth-century murders took place in same-sex environments. In these homosocial worlds, social bonding and gemütlichkeit could spill over into violence. In 1854 Jerome B. King, a twenty-one-year-old coach painter from Pennsylvania, killed his friend Peter Garrison Post, a stone-mason. They "had both occupied the same bed for some time," the *New York Times* reported, their fight originating after King had spent a week on a drinking spree. They fought and made up over a period of twenty-four hours. The last fight turned fatal when Post slapped King, then threw him to the floor of a grocery.

"Damn your big soul," King "exclaimed."

He grabbed a butcher knife and ran out to the sidewalk, where he stabbed Post. At the inquest, King stated that he had had no "ill feeling" toward Post until Post slapped him.[23] Other than the comment that the two were bedmates, we learn little about the nature of the relationship between these men. Were they blue collar workers sharing lodgings in a city with a tight housing market, something like Queequeg and Ishmael's port lodging in *Moby Dick*? Their pattern of fighting and making up suggests a more affectionate relationship, as does King's apparent remorse at Post's death. Or did King's reference to Post's size, his "big soul," indicate that defeat in front of the other men drinking in the grocery was a shameful status loss that only further violence could restore?

If the precise point of most male power struggles cannot be clearly reconstructed, the power contests in pre-election-night politics differ: these were struggles over asset control. The male electoral politics of New York City incorporated a barroom society that stretched from the gilding of Tammany Hall to a tavern network directly tied to elections. Late-nineteenth-century Tammany boss—and future mayor—Richard Croker used his influence to keep two incidents from being investigated by the police, and was himself a participant in a third. At the time of this 1874 barroom election fight, Croker was a coroner (an elected position). In the brawl, John McKenna was murdered by gunshot. Though Croker was indicted, the indictment was dismissed. Alfred Lewis, his biographer, reiterates the defense claim that Croker "never owned nor carried" a pistol. Croker's defense was not a claim of pacifism, but rather of his aggressive and violent reputation, of his highly reputed bare-knuckle boxing ability.[24] He was too tough to need a gun.

The murders in this microcosm involved small male groups angrily confronting each other, often as voting gangs or toughs intimidating voters (or other voting gangs). These violent confrontations protected the nineteenth-century equivalent of cocaine—access to the jobs and graft political power offered. The men involved protected this male asset via the electoral process and sometimes the voting booth, using calculated and highly public violence. When in 1869 city council candidate Florence Scannell tried to stop a voting gang from assembling in the bar of Tammany operative Thomas Donahue, Donahue took careful aim and shot him in the back of the neck. Scannell lingered, paralyzed, for seven months before dying. Florence's brother, John, a political worker for Richard Croker, in turn stalked and finally murdered Donahue nearly two years later.[25] These men made bluntly clear that they owned this political world; the violence was contained within it. There was absolutely no room for the unwanted, and that certainly included women.

Most murders between men were over less lucrative prizes. Actually, there were few lucrative prizes open to men whose only potential was for violence: most vice was unregulated. The large number of brothels and easily opened drinking establishments, including the curiously misnamed "groceries," meant that the kind of violence used to control the drug trade in the late twentieth century was unneeded.[26] The typical male killing in mid-nineteenth-century New York City is a comic book exemplar of assertive male dominance. Dominance could be enacted in a range of manners from physical superiority, as with Reeves and McCue, to wealth or simple generosity. One man's refusing another's offer to be "treated" to a drink, for instance, could be interpreted as a slight and thus could lead to murder. A hint of disdain could ignite a power struggle. Thus the act of turning down a gift could become the insult precipitating violent aggression.

Men could also lay claim to the manliness of others: behind this lay a peculiar concept of ownership, a conception of one's manliness as being possessable by another, but being expressed in an odd way. Women could never start a fight with words like "I am your woman." The word *man* carried freight enough to kill. Consider this lethal script from 1854:

"Do you want to fight? If you want to fight, *I am your man* [emphasis added]," Hugh Hagan challenged an unnamed man, possibly Dennis Carrick.

"Go about your business," another man responded.

"Hold on, I will give you fighting enough," Dennis Carrick chimed in.

The latter apparently did join the fighting, killing Hagan with a cart rung.[27]

Hagan insisted to his eventual killer that he was *his* man, offering his manliness as an aggressive act. When we think of violent interactions, we usually think of taking, but here, in a sense, the violence began with a giving. The concept of manliness as a possession blurs into the notion of the prey belonging to the predator, even prior to the kill. It extends to the twentieth century, when a deer hunter referred to getting "his" deer. Commenting in 1931 on a late-nineteenth-century interview, muckraking journalist Lincoln Steffans discussed his friendship with New York mayor Richard Croker: he admitted that Croker, whom he liked, "had killed *his* [emphasis added] man."[28]

Often, men simply acknowledging one another disrespectfully could lead to death.[29] Earlier in the year 1811, the woodcutter Joseph Killey had made fun of Samuel Stivers and had called him a thief. On Sunday, December 3, when Killey was cutting wood in the middle of Harrison Street, Samuel Stivers walked past, drunk, and Killey smiled (or perhaps sneered) and laughed at him. Stivers stepped off the sidewalk into the street and shook his fist at Killey.

"Damn you, are you the man? If you are the man, walk out in the street with me. Damn you I'll knock the [saw] dust off you," Stivers snarled.

"Go away. I want nothing to do with you," Killey responded.

"I am in the street, and I will stay as long as I please," Stivers continued.

"Go away, or I'll make you go away," Killey threatened, trying for one last time to avert a fight.

They then fell to fighting with wooden sticks. Killey hit Stivers a fatal blow on the head and returned to his sawing. Stivers died the next day.[30]

"You are the man," or "I am the man," were phrases signaling a challenge to fight. Again, the challenge has as much to do with the act of identifying who was who as it did with the manliness in question. One could say that the manliness inhered in the right to assert manliness.

When not killing one another in bars or in the street, men often turned on their spouses. Of the nineteenth-century murders where the killer's sex is known, at least 193 killers (14 percent) were men murdering their spouses; conversely, 20 women murderers (18 percent) turned on their men, a small and statistically insignificant difference.[31]

The criminologist Marvin Wolfgang once startled his readers by declaring that the "bedroom has the dubious honor of being the most dangerous room in the home" and the second most frequent site of murder overall, more frequent, for instance, than bars.[32] Of course, that so many killings involve family members and intimates and occur in homes does not make homes particularly dangerous. At a minimum, one spends a third of one's time, and probably most social interactions occur, in the home. When one considers the time "at risk," then the home is what most people feel it to be: a safe and secure place.

One might expect a different quality to nineteenth-century murders, especially prior to the 1840s. Family historians have demonstrated that the nature of marriage relationships changed over the course of the nineteenth century, family sizes declining and the companionate marriage rising. One supposes that this qualitative difference might decrease the prevalence of spousal murders, although it might be argued, on the contrary, that the spread of companionate marriage from the newly forming middle class to the more traditional artisan and working classes would create a class or ethnic difference in such murders.

How do the spousal murders of the early nineteenth century look? Table 3.2 shows the ethnicity of victims or, when that is not known, the ethnicity of killers (if known). Of 393 intergender murders, 216 were clearly identified as spousal, and of these, 134 have ethnicity stipulated. The only ethnic/race group that stands out is the Irish, who had more spousal victims than expected when compared to all murder victims. If one considers that the proportion of Irish in the population averaged over the period was about 30 percent, this predominance is even stronger. There is a possibility that newspapers overreported Irish ethnicity, though there is

Table 3.2 Ethnicity of Spouse Victims, New York City, 19th Century

Ethnicity of victim	Frequency	Percentage of total spouse murders
Native-born white	15	14
Native-born black	9	7
French	4	3
British	5	4
Irish	79	59
German	17	13
Italian	2	2
Varied European	3	3
Total	134	100

SOURCE: see appendix.

no indication that this occurred. My interpretation has been conservative to avoid this possibility, but even if all unspecified spousal murders were considered to involve native-born couples, the Irish accounted for 33 percent of the spousal murders.

An attempted spousal murder that went awry exemplifies the typical features of such conflict. Patrick Stackpole, a stevedore, arrived home late and drunk on October 19, 1858. He became "enraged" at "something saucy" his wife said and, trying to hit her with a stick, hit and killed their three-month-old infant instead.[33]

The theme of spousal ownership rights and the control they are supposed to confer still is a part of spousal abuse and wife murders.[34] In 1838, after Edward Coleman coolly slit the throat of his wife, Ann, in midday on Broadway, he asserted to bystanders that he had a "*right* [emphasis added] to do it." They had had a brief, rocky marriage and she had left him prior to the murder. The defense argument that he was "under the control of a monomania" failed to sway the jury, and Coleman was convicted, sentenced, and executed. Was his severe punishment carried out because of race? He and his wife were African American. Of nine African

American spouse murders, three went to trial, but only Coleman was executed, so it is doubtful that race alone motivated the jury. Statistically, there was no relationship between the race of the spouse offender and the conviction rate.[35] Perhaps the jury could not discount his cruelty because it was in front of witnesses? Clearly, his notion of a "right" to slit his wife's throat, though not unique, was not persuasive in this instance.

WEAPONS AND GENDER

If we think of murder weapons as enacting a combination of cultural preference and easy access/availability, the gender changes in weaponry tell us more about the things people have than about gender itself. In the nineteenth century, women rarely poisoned, but they were three times more likely to use poison than to use guns. A woman was much more apt to choose sticks and kicks than poison, a gun, or a knife. Men, on the other hand, were the least likely to use poison. Only about 5 percent of women killers used guns, contrasted with 20 percent of men killers. In the late twentieth century, the proportion of women killers who shot increased by ten times to about 56 percent. In the nineteenth century there were fewer handguns and they were male accessories; today there are many more handguns and although they are still male consumption accessories, women are far more likely to have guns in their homes than poison, wooden sticks, or axes. The kinds of tools both genders use have changed as well: the kitchen, the workshop, everyday life in general have all become more mechanized. Few people need to split wood for fuel anymore. As new technologies appear, their gender access diffuses. Access can determine gender just as gender sometimes determines access.

Poison makes this most clear. No one has easy access to poison today. Rats may even be less common. Poison seldom appears in the kitchen, sometimes among gardening chemicals, and almost never among household supplies. Its use as a weapon has subsequently declined to a tiny tenth of a percent. Yet, because women still do more food preparation than men, they are three times as likely to use poison. Probably as food preparation tasks become more evenly divided, so too will poisoning.

Historian Elliot Gorn has argued that in the mid nineteenth century conventional masculinity required manly men to fight with their bare hands. Lewis Baker's 1855 gun murder of William "Butcher Bill" Poole, the nativist political tough, was "an anomaly, a violation of the street culture's unwritten assumption that a reputation for toughness must be won bare handed." Certainly Poole could use his hands aggressively. Testimony in Baker's trial identified Poole as "brutal," not deserving the title of a "pugilist" but a "fighting man." One witness explained, "a pugilist is an artist, and the fighter is a blackguard."[36]

When it came to the fine points of male violence, Poole got eliminated for his manly if not completely upright style, which dictated his weapon choice. Winning mattered. For the large group of political combatants participating in this murder, including future member of Congress John Morrisey, guns had become manly accessories. The weapons involved in a series of brawls shifted from fists and fingers for eye-gouging (Poole's specialty) to knives and handguns. In the ultimate battle in which Baker murdered Poole, several of the combatants had guns, ranging from either five- or six-cylinder revolvers to the "ordinary" Colt revolver that Baker used on Poole. These manly men were none too skillful with their guns: one combatant, James Turner, carefully laid his gun (an eight-inch Colt Naval Revolver) across his arm for better aim and shot himself. Unskilled though these men may have been, they were quite familiar with handguns, speculating at the trial about why Morrisey's gun (a five-barreled Allen revolver) did not fire, and observing that it may have been improperly loaded.[37]

The puzzles of gender differences and violence mix historical contingency and cultural patterning with a fundamental disproportion that will continue to challenge theorists. In order to avoid circular reasoning, or no reasoning at all, we should maintain an intellectual awareness that this issue, like other human puzzles, keeps its very humanity in its irresolution. The only failure in our efforts to understand comes if we yield to oversimplification.

The long record sets out clear areas of persistence: the high proportion of murderers and their victims who are men. There is some increase in the proportion of victims who are men. Gender violence rates parallel one another, with the exception of a few periods in which women were more likely than usual to be murdered. On occasion, over New York City's past two hundred years, the highest women's homicide rates have been higher than the lowest men's rates at other times: variation over time is greater than the gender differentials at any one time. For example, in 1825, Unity Gallagher, Elizabeth Adams, Bridget Carrol, Rosana Lade, and Mary Ann Cunningham assured a women's homicide rate greater than the rates for men and women combined in the 1950s. The puzzle is this: the ratio of male to female offenders stays the same, but the overall rates vary enormously.

Chapter 4 Age and Murder

What would a video have recorded when Adam Smith, age ten, pushed seven-year-old Daniel Mashafer through a hole in the Gouverneur Street dock and into the East River in 1856?[1] In an era when drowning occurred with depressing regularity, surely the older boy knew the lethal danger of the river, equivalent to traffic flowing down a busy freeway today. But did he know that Daniel would die? Or what death meant? Would the video have shown a calculated murder? Or childish roughhousing, skylarking as it was then called? Or the pushes and shoves of a neighborhood bully, picking on younger children?

Most killers are in the prime of their lives. So are their victims. This was true in the Middle Ages; it is still true. The basic determinant of victim and killer ages has first to do with opportunity—access to people, to weapons, to free time, to unruly situations. In general, children and old people have less access to these four essentials. Size also makes a big difference, so small children—and especially infants—are very vulnerable. Size is the equivalent of strength; thus the old, when weak, are vulnerable also.

The tighter the situational rules—that is, the minute-by-minute structures of life—the less likely it is that people can murder or be murdered. Social "scripts," rules of etiquette, steer most people away from unpredictable exchanges.[2] Killers, in particular, are people with unstructured liberty. Killers and victims tend to be people outside of socially controlled and circumscribed situations. In practice this means that children, very old people, and people living very structured lives do not kill.

There are, of course, exceptions. Inmates in institutions, whose lives are supposed to be monitored closely, occasionally kill one another. American TV watchers probably think that violent murders regularly punctuate prison life. Prisoners sometimes do kill other prisoners, sixty-seven in the United States in 1994. Given that prisoners tend to be more violent than nonprisoners, prison violence should not surprise us; what should is how much safer men are when they are in prison, for their demographic equals outside prison died at more than four times the rate that prisoners did.[3] This simply reiterates the general point: tight rules and clearly structured situations minimize the likelihood of killing.

So why have we worried about very young killers recently?

First, despite all the reasons that there should not be very young killers, there are. Accounts of several well-publicized cases have given us such graphic details that they have alerted a sheltered world to inexplicable evil. One chilling video recorded by a Liverpool shopping mall's surveillance cameras, for example, showed two ten-year-old English boys leading a toddler off to his death in February 1993.[4] The banality and seeming innocence of the image can leave no one complacent.

Second, although the numbers are not precise (we do not know the ages of those who do not get caught), it appears that there are recent increases in youth homicides. For New York City, the percentage of killers who are younger than age eighteen quickly rose from about 9 percent in 1976 to a peak of nearly 16 percent in 1993. Using more precise data, research for the state of California confirms an increasing rate of young killers.[5] Note that the last two years of increase came at a time of declining overall homicide rates. If these youths continue their practice into adulthood, then the near future could be very grim. A fifteen-year-old murderer will be out of prison by the time he is twenty-two, with a long and potentially lethal future before him—and us.

But the nineteenth-century experience suggests that we should make these predictions very cautiously: about 9.7 percent of the killers in early New York City were younger than eighteen. If we set our definition of youth a bit lower, the historical comparison changes: 5 percent of the murderers in nineteenth-century New York City were younger than sixteen, contrasted with only 3 percent of those in late-twentieth-century New York City. Annualized, these recent data showed a nasty trend in the early 1990s, rising from only 2 percent in 1976 to 6 percent in 1993. By 1994 the proportion dropped back down a bit to 4.4 percent, and in 1995 things improved even more to 2.7 percent. Would complete information change these percentages? Curiously, the offender age information is complete in about 30 percent of the contemporary cases, not much different than the record from the early nineteenth century, when only about a fourth of the New York City cases gave precise ages. Age reporting standards were less critical in the nineteenth century: I could not quantify notations such as "lad" or "old man." Might greater accuracy have changed the results?[6]

Given that unknown ages of killers increase the possibility of error, the age comparison of nineteenth-century to twentieth-century New York City must remain suggestive, not definitive. What it suggests is of interest, however. There were more very youthful offenders in early-nineteenth-century New York City than in the recent United States. Not until somewhere between the ages of sixteen and seventeen do the contemporary murderers outnumber their nineteenth-century counterparts.

Consider that of the nineteenth-century murders by very youthful (younger than age seventeen) murderers, only three of the twenty-four were with guns: children did not have access to high-quality weapons. This means that twenty-one murders were done with knives, stones, kicking, and beating. Two of the gun murders occurred in 1873, well after the advent of preassembled ammunition.

If further research and better data continue to confirm the high proportion of youthful murderers in the nineteenth century, we should not be surprised or turn to moral evolution for the explanation. Rather, we should chalk these up to the higher proportion of youths in the population and to the prevalence of youths not under intense supervision, whether in school or at home. In addition, young boys participated in a culture that valued and encouraged physically aggressive masculinity. Apprenticeships, the traditional way of training the young, were supposed to be carefully monitored, time-intensive, and heavily controlled. The master was supposed to incorporate the apprentice into the master's family life, shrinking the apprentice's free time. But that system broke down in the nineteenth century, with apprenticeships no longer leading to secure and highly paid craft occupations.[7] Newspapers seldom called the young workers apprentices, but instead identified their occupations as though they were adults. Apprentices themselves, when launched on the town with money to spend and no age limits on drinking, were the source of much public disturbance.

While both boys were working at their leather strap–making benches at 277 Tenth Ave., twelve-year-old Thomas Miller stabbed to death William McElroy, also twelve, with his shoemaker's awl in March 1859. A month later Judge Davies in the Court of Oyer and Terminer sentenced Miller to the House of Refuge until the age of twenty-one. He would have been released, at the latest, in 1868. (Could he have been the same Thomas Miller who lived in the twentieth ward in 1870?) McElroy, the court heard, had teased an annoyable Miller, "seizing his wax ends, removing his tools, and constituting himself an excessive and unremitting grievance." McElroy should have been cautious, for Miller had on an earlier occasion "stabbed a boy, though not dangerously; and, if phrenology be true, the occipital regions of his skull are somewhat of a dangerous character," noted the *New York Times*.[8]

This case raised the specter of "criminal capacity," a problem in the late twentieth century. By customary law, very young children, those under age seven, were not culpable for committing crimes, and those between seven and fourteen had to be shown, in court, to be culpable before they could be charged.[9] The *New York Times* editorialized on the day after the trial that justice had been "slandered," for the prosecution had failed to even try to show that Miller understood what he was doing.

Despite the *Times*'s editorial about age and the law, the few relevant statistics suggest either that age fourteen was not an actual breaking point—rather sixteen was—or that cultural and criminal practice made sixteen a threshold age. Table 4.1 shows the percentages of young people (of the totals) executed in the whole United States, identified as killers in New York City, or identified as killers in the twentieth-century United States. The proportion of executed killers and nineteenth-century New York City killers jumps between ages fifteen and sixteen; for all offenders in the nineteenth and twentieth centuries the jump is one year earlier.

An older boy's "teasing" at the work site similarly enraged sixteen-year-old James McMahon. McMahon, who had been fired from regular wagon driving at a soda-water manufactory because of his "careless habits," had taken to working for the other employees, cleaning their horses and doing odd jobs. As a demeaning joke, eighteen-year-old William Scanlon paid him only $1.50 on Saturday, withholding 50 cents. Poor McMahon returned on Sunday, only to be told by Scanlon, "I'll never give you that fifty cents." Then Scanlon "thrashed" McMahon and told him never to come back. McMahon ran to a nearby grocery, stole a bacon knife, and returned to the workshop. Others tried to grab him, but he escaped and stabbed Scanlon. Scanlon fell, "saying, 'My God; I am stabbed; send for a priest.'" He died within minutes. McMahon ran, saying to a pursuer, "If you don't stop following me, I'll fix you the same way as I fixed the other fellow."

Here age, power, gender, public humiliation, and money all contributed to propelling McMahon to act. One senses his desperation and the lack of any other workplace assistance. With no friendly workmates, any hope of help was gone.

The late-twentieth-century phenomenon of callous, very young murderers stands apart from the nineteenth century, even though the nineteenth century had high numbers of young murderers. The story of fifteen-year-old Willie Bosket, compellingly researched and told by Fox Butterfield, exemplifies the extreme case of the nation's late-twentieth-century murder spree. Bosket, on different occasions, shot and killed two

Table 4.1 Very Young Offenders

	Percentage of all killers in each age group		
Age	All U.S. executions	NYC killers, 1800–1874	U.S. killers, 1976–1994
12	0.04	1.0	0.13
13	0.04	0.3	0.30
14	0.13	0.78	0.69
15	0.09	1.31	1.41
16	0.57	2.35	2.37
17	1.49	2.61	3.33

SOURCE: see appendix.

men, both strangers to him, in separate robbery incidents on New York City subways in the late 1970s. Bosket, it must be noted, lived in impoverished circumstances with a dysfunctional family. He was not starving, however, and his many robberies seem to have been motivated by power seeking and excitement. He killed his first victim when he was alone, with robbery as his partial intent. The murder netted him thirty-five dollars and a feeling of power. Two days after this murder, a family court judge—unaware of his act—refused to jail Bosket on a previous robbery charge, overruling the prosecutor's assertion that he was likely to kill if free. About three weeks later Bosket was with a friend for the second killing. The friend acted as a lookout while Bosket murdered a man who refused to hand over his welfare card and two dollars. Both victims were Latino, but their race seems to have been irrelevant. More important, they were alone (in one case asleep) and vulnerable. Bosket betrayed his youthful incompetence by choosing poor victims, making his violence unsuccessfully instrumental. He is now serving a life sentence.

A case paralleling that of Willie Bosket may have occurred in late September 1853. Fewer details than for the Bosket case were available concerning the apparent murder of a young German immigrant (so identified from his dress), name unknown. Police arrested William Matting, known

as a "hard character" in the neighborhood. A seventeen-year-old, irregu-
larly employed butcher, Matting had been sleeping in a butcher shop next
to a cooperage. The night of the murder, someone burglarized the cooperage. Matting claimed both innocence and ignorance. He was, he said, out
walking that night when he came across the murdered man, and as he
went to find the police he also came across a cooper's adze. He took the
adze with him the next day on a sloop, captained by his uncle, bound to
Albany.[10] Was he a Willie Bosket, preying on the weak, opportunistically
taking what he could, where he could?

Another case resembled that of Willie Bosket. The "steady and indus-
trious boy" James (Jimmy) Rogers attacked and killed John Swanson in
the bloody year 1857. The case attracted much attention and resulted in
Rogers's execution. On Saturday, October 17, 1857, three boys including
Jimmy were walking arm in arm, drunk, down Twenty-first Street about
10 P.M. when they saw Swanson and his wife, complete strangers. Jimmy
deliberately hit Mrs. Swanson with his elbow, and when Swanson turned
toward them, Jimmy stabbed and killed him. Jimmy was between seventeen and nineteen years old and lived with his mother, Bridget Rogers,
who averred that he was as "quiet and peaceable as any boy could be."
The boys had begun their evening about 6 P.M., intending to watch a fire-
men's parade, which they never found. Later in the evening they had tried
to attack another boy who refused to give Jimmy an apple. Then they ha-
rassed Mary Brannigan and her husband, who knew one of the boys. They
tried to rob the Brannigans, hit her, and threatened them both with either
a knife or gun. The Swansons, then, were victims of a fairly random attack by very hostile young men out on the town.

Yet the case also differs from Bosket's in several conspicuous aspects.
First, Rogers was not alone, but with friends; they were a small band of
"shoulder hitters" or "corner loafers," who more typically attacked other
gangs or used their violence for political ends. Second, Rogers's assault
was close to a random attack, with the only latent motive perhaps being
class: Swanson was a "respectable" man. Third, the assault was risky.
Bosket, at least as a young prisoner, took pride in his recklessness, but actually his victims were vulnerable, defenseless, or unarmed. Rogers challenged an adult (if unarmed) male. Fourth, Bosket did not seem capable

of remorse, whereas Rogers, awaiting execution, claimed that he had been so drunk that he remembered nothing of the murder. Though not exactly wracked with guilt, neither was he cocksure. A reporter wrote of him: "he seems stunned—stupefied."[11]

Another young murderer awaited trial in the Tombs where Rogers was housed, Maurice or Morris O'Connell. A "hard looking youth," even in prison O'Connell kept up "a wicked, rowdy, Dead Rabbit expression of countenance," noted the *New York Times*. O'Connell, who was somewhere between fifteen years old (his claim) and seventeen (his mother's and the media's), had committed a crime that sounds eerily like some from the late twentieth century. He and three friends raped and murdered fifty-five-year-old Theresa Spiztlein, a Swiss immigrant, on November 6, 1857. She had been in the United States less than two years; her husband and child had drowned on the passage from Switzerland. She slept on the floor in a back cellar of Christian Martin's beer saloon at 32 Greenwich Street for six cents a night, and worked at a nearby apothecary shop. Martin, quite an entrepreneur, testified that he was a tailor as well as a barkeeper, and that he kept prostitutes in his cellar as well as rented out sleeping space.

On the night of the murder Spitzlein left work about eight, going directly to Martin's saloon. Half an hour later the four boys broke in and tried to rape Mrs. Martin. Spitzlein intervened, telling them to keep quiet. (We do not know if she said this in German or in English.) O'Connell and another boy pulled Spitzlein into the bedroom and threw her on the bed, where they strangled and then raped her. According to the *Times*, "Before they ended their fiendish assaults their victim was dead."

O'Connell, a native-born New Yorker, lived at 64 Greenwich Street and worked as a "car driver." He blamed the rape and murder on two of his friends, "Sailor Dan" ("a mere boy," noted the *Times*) and James Toole, the latter a sixteen-year-old native-born bartender. Ultimately he was identified as the last to rape Spitzlein and leave her for dead. After the attack the boys went across the street to a dance house. O'Connell was arrested, escaped, and then was caught. The attack had several significant elements: there was a latent racial undertone, the attackers either second-generation Irish (as two claimed) or Irish, the victims either German or Swiss ("Dutch"-speaking). The attackers were associated with the Dead Rabbits, an Irish Catholic gang, at least by adjective. (Because of their cute name, we have trouble today imagining just how ferocious the Dead Rabbits were.) The attackers seem to have been employed. Like Bosket, these attackers bragged about their exploits until the police came after them. And most obvious, like Bosket, they were completely callous and uncaring about this murder of their neighbor.[12]

House painter James Smith's murder of James Davis a few years earlier, on Sunday, October 13, 1853, gives a sense of the more "wholesome" social circumstances of a youthful murder. Seventeen-year-old Smith, originally from New Haven, testified that he was drunk and had begun to quarrel with Davis—his "good friend" until that moment—when he stabbed him. As the assistant coroner took Smith to the city prison, he broke away and escaped. "Watch! Murder! Stop thief!" a deputy cried futilely. Smith must have been quite a sight as he zipped off in his "light blue frock-coat, red figured brown vest, dark cassimere pants, and . . . a blue cap."[13]

Many young murderers were not street children with time on their hands, suggesting that often conditions of child labor could promote child violence, as in the case of twelve-year-old Thomas Miller, the shoemaker, discussed earlier. Today we think that orderly occupations and structured situations prevent unpredictable and potentially violent conflicts, and perhaps the nineteenth century would have had even more youth violence had boys not worked from an early age. But the winter murder of Michael Driscoll by Cornelius Cuddy, or Curdy, should give us pause. Driscoll, an eighteen-year-old newsboy, sold both the *Herald* and the *Express*. He and Samuel Murray came into the coffee cellar at 7 Spruce Street, where Cuddy, a "small boy about 15 years of age," worked. It was about 10 P.M. on a Wednesday night, January 10, 1849. Driscoll, drunk, ordered pies (or cakes) and coffee for himself and Murray. Cuddy may have said something to anger Driscoll.

Driscoll challenged Cuddy when he was served. "Who are you giving sauce to?" Driscoll demanded. He warned Cuddy that he would die that night. Driscoll and Murray both threw plates at Cuddy, and hit him in the face twice.

"You son of a b[itch], what did you strike me for?" Cuddy screamed.

Cuddy ran behind the bar, reached into the till, and pulled out a "large dirk-knife which he plunged into the breast of his assailant." The wound, more than six inches deep, killed Driscoll, who died in the cellar within a few minutes and was laid out on a table there.

The police took Cuddy, "weeping with grief and alarm," to the station house. The coroner's jury, meeting a day and a half later, concluded that he had acted in self-defense and let Cuddy go. A year later he still lived at home, now working as a tailor.[14]

All of these boys behaved like their elders: impulsively, unable to control their own rage, displaying physical challenges likely at any moment to turn lethal. That they worked until late at night becomes irrelevant. This victim almost certainly precipitated his own death, but on the other hand poor Cuddy did not seem to have considered escape as an alternative. Where was the coffee cellar proprietor, Richard Marshall? Would Cuddy have been fired if he had run? Maybe gainfully employed teenagers living on their own in an unstructured, or badly structured, world cannot be expected to deal with erratic uncertainty and violent threats.

In this case and so many others, one wonders about the concept of the neighborhood bully. Would this term have described the otherwise unnamed lad, "Punchey"? In November 1855, Punchey kicked nine-year-old William Wood, who was turning somersaults in Mulberry Street. Wood, though injured, "made the best of his way home," where he went to bed and then died. The coroner's jury apparently did not indict Punchey.[15]

Adults not only tolerate bullying, they can actively cultivate child violence; in the late twentieth century the focus was usually on the media's role rather than on direct, personal encouragement. There is at least one clear instance in mid-nineteenth-century (1855) New York City where we can see a neighborhood catalyst. The issue was also clearly one of manliness as enacted through fighting, boys being explicitly stimulated to fight. Bernard M'Hugh, who lived in the same house as Michael Butler, probably as a boarder, came home drunk. In front of the house, M'Hugh encouraged a group of neighborhood boys to scramble for the twenty-five cents he threw to them. This not being enough fun, he then offered a sixpence to any boy who would "whip" another. Hugh Dyer and Michael Butler, both about twelve years old, began to fight. Butler's mother

stopped the fight and then went back in the house. The boys began fighting again, and when Dyer had Butler down, he took his collar and
"jammed the back of his head against the pavement." Five days later Butler developed a headache and died shortly thereafter in the hospital.

Not all victims of youth violence were other young people. In a culture
foisting a violent understanding of manhood on boys who often worked
and had money to spend, boys could be expected to try out their reputa-
tions in a wider and older world. Sixteen-year-old Robert Hill, an Irish-
born plumber who lived at 38 Greenwich Street, stabbed thirty-year-old
William Hurley (also Irish) in a bar at 9 Rector Street.

"I never stabbed no man in my life," Hill told the coroner's jury. That
jury may not have believed him, but later the grand jury dismissed the case,
no doubt because the evidence given to the coroner's jury was contradictory and incomplete.

The problems on Saturday night, September 6, 1873, began in a confusing commotion involving an unspecified argument "about politics" between "Irish" Mahan and Phillip Conklin in a liquor store at 109 Greenwich Street. This fracas, in which they may have been involved, caused
Hurley and his friends John Shaunnessey and Martin Donohue to move
around the corner to the Rector Street bar.

Things were no quieter on Rector Street, for the threesome immediately
got into a scuffle with three other men, Daniel O'Keefe, John Petty, and
Clancy; Hill may have made a fourth with them, but the record is unclear.
They were on their fourth round of drinks in that bar, O'Keefe having
treated first, Clancy second, and Petty third. Petty claimed that Hurley's
friend Shaunnessey grabbed O'Keefe and began fighting, so he left.
Shaunnessey's friend Martin Donohue corroborated this.

Hurley may have left at this point, but leaving the bar could mean three
things: just leaving, leaving to have a fight, or leaving to avoid attack.

Martin Donohue testified that he was very drunk. "I messed my own
trousers and went out. When I got to the door I saw deceased [Hurley]
lying in the middle of the street and about four kicking at him," Donohue
remembered. He did not know who was kicking Hurley because he only
had a "glimpse" of them, and, of course, he was drunk. Hurley may already have been dead at this point.

"[Did you get] out of the scrape in Rector Street?" Hill asked Petty when he met him the next evening. He asked Petty how the man was getting along. Petty, perhaps not knowing that Hurley was dead or exactly what Hill meant, said, "Well."

"I'm glad of that," Hill responded.

Petty asked him why.

"The man got a hold of me by the smock and I stabbed him," Hill answered.

Petty may not have been as naive as he seemed, for it is likely that he was one of the men kicking the prostrate Hurley. If Donohue's blurry recollection can be trusted, it suggests that the Hurley party came into the Rector Street bar, started a fight, and as they dribbled out, one—Hurley—was attacked. How Hill fit into these drinking and fighting clusters is unclear, but he must have been affiliated with the Petty, O'Keefe, and Clancy group.

Though it is impossible to interpret this bar-to-bar brawl with absolute certitude, it could well be that teenaged Robert Hill, participating in an evening of roaming, drinking, and fighting, displayed his inexperience by using a knife when the acceptable weapons were feet and fists. This could explain Donohue's bafflement the next day, for he remembered seeing blood on Hurley's face, blood that resulted from a slit throat and not the kicking.[16]

Robert Hill's excessive violence may have reflected his immaturity. On the other hand, was eleven-year-old Henry Docket equally immature when he chose an empty building for target practice? Docket shot and killed forty-year-old John Fitzgerald, a private watchman, standing outside the building. He said it was an accident: he had been practicing using the pistol. Docket was arrested, though it is not clear if the action went further than that.[17]

Sometimes the very young victims clearly precipitated their own deaths. Alcohol, a fuel to violence, must have spurred a wounded teenage male ego and propelled sixteen-year-old, New York City–born Peter McCann to heave mugs at bartender James Ozab in 1871. For drinking and fighting men, treating, like beating, established reputation. And feckless young McCann seems to have established a reputation of not being able to pay, at least in Ozab's bar. He and Ozab had had a fight about McCann's refusal to pay three weeks earlier, so Ozab must have been concerned when McCann and two friends, all drunk, came in at ten o'clock on a Monday night.

The witnesses all told somewhat different stories to the coroner's jury.

Mary McCann, Peter's mother, testified that Peter went out a little before ten to look for his brother. By the time he entered Ozab's at ten, he was drunk. This implies that he left home already drunk. His mother helpfully informed the coroner's jury that McCann was a "good boy."

Timothy McCarthy said that he and James Lyons were walking along when McCann asked them to go to Ozab's for some beer. McCarthy told McCann that they had had enough, and McCann responded that they should go into Ozab's for "one glass of beer and then go home." Stephen Whalen was in the bar with Patrick Maher, whom he had just treated, when McCann, McCarthy, and Lyons came in and asked for beer. Ozab asked who would pay for it. McCann responded that he would, and then Ozab refused to serve them.

"You better go home," McCarthy told McCann when Ozab refused to serve them. Instead McCann had some "high words" with Ozab. McCann twice tried to grab a glass of beer, Ozab shoved him back, and then McCann threw an empty glass at Ozab.

McCarthy may have thrown more, though he denied to the jury that he had thrown an empty beer barrel at Ozab. None of the young men denied trying to hit Mrs. Ozab or Susan O'Connor with a chair. Both of the women had tried either to calm them down or to throw them out.

Ozab ordered McCann to quit, and pulled out his pistol to back up his command. He then told McCann he would shoot him. Ozab fired once, some more glasses were thrown, and McCann grabbed a butcher knife (according to O'Connor).

"Blaze away," McCann shouted. Ozab did, firing his second and perhaps third shots. The second shot went through Whalen's coat and vest. One witness mentioned that at one point in this wild melee, after the first shot, McCann was on the floor near the door. Whalen said that even with the first shot McCann had left the bar and was just outside, in the doorway. When Dr. Joseph Cushman performed an autopsy, he only noticed one bullet, to McCann's forehead, suggesting that all of the shots were fired before McCann fell, or that he uttered his challenge to "blaze away" after already being shot.

The police came to the bar and took both Ozab and McCann in, Mc-Cann dying shortly thereafter.

The coroner's jury, after listening to testimony from the bar's patrons, found that Ozab had fired in self-defense.[18] We might well agree, but the point here is that a teenager had been acting like a young adult of his world, participating in an escalating violent interchange that revolved around the sensitive issue of paying for drinks. "Real" men treated in order to establish their social position. In this McCann had ventured and failed.

What is special about the nineteenth-century youth homicides? Three things stand out. First, many teenagers, like McCann, were not very youthful: they had occupational identities, went barhopping for fun, and in essence had moved into the bottom part of the working class. The only thing missing was that they still lived at home and had despairing mothers instead of wives. Second, youthful play could get violent, and at least in the case of Hugh Dyer, adult supervision could make it worse. And third, impulsive and aggressive behavior, even in work situations, made twelve-year-olds with awls seem like the precursors of those who committed late-twentieth-century job floor massacres.

If youth murders reflect both the adult culture and youthful immaturity, what should elder murders be like? Why, in general, don't more old people commit murder? For men, could it be physiological? A decline in testosterone? For women, could it be fading competition for mates, fewer children to protect, fewer children to care for?

And why do we think it "natural" that old people kill so little? Whenever we think of some habit as "natural" we should be on the alert: labeling something thus is often our way of avoiding examining it.

Virtually the only obvious reason old people have for not killing is their age. That is, the decline in killing accompanies a decline in vigor. What else about age would stop killing? Here the answer gets at the philosophical essence of murder: control of another person. The murderer, whatever the circumstance, is trying to gain control of another individual, whether to stop some behavior, to change emotions, or to permanently assure compliance. Whatever the reason, murder is strangely future oriented. (Never mind that it is, in general, ineffective. I make no claim that murderers are effective thinkers.) Could it be that the decline of murder in older people reflects a decline in their future orientation? Does age actually bring with it a sense of mortality? A kind of wisdom? Or was the lawyer Mr. Anthon correct when he observed of killer John Sinclair in 1810 that the "passions of seventy-seven are not naturally strong."[19]

Only 2 percent of New York City's nineteenth-century killers were older than age sixty (ten of the 382 with known ages). This is almost identical to the city's proportion of killers who are older than age sixty in the late twentieth century. But because the senior population today is proportionally more than ten times larger than it was in the nineteenth century, the age-specific homicide rate by seniors was much greater in the nineteenth century than it is today. Have old people become wiser over the past century?

When seventy-seven-year-old John Sinclair, German, murdered his landlord, David Hill, in April 1810, he became the oldest murderer in early-nineteenth-century New York City. The trial transcript leaves it unclear as to whether Sinclair was a pitiable, poverty-stricken old man, worried about being evicted, or merely a vindictive lodger in an abusive relationship. Sinclair had been one of British general Burgoyne's Hessians, perhaps one whom the Americans captured when he was foraging for food (August 16, 1777); he would have been forty-four at the time. Strangely, his final fight with his landlord began after he had been foraging for food. He had just returned to their shared home carrying a sack of potatoes when Hill "flew at him and pulled him down."[20] After brooding about this for two days, at 8 A.M. on a Sunday morning Sinclair stabbed Hill to death while Hill sat by the fire, either reading a book or drinking. (Witness Hetty Talmadge contradicted the reading testimony, saying that there was only one book in the house and it was hers.)

Sinclair emerged from his bedroom and stabbed Hill once, with a "square, blunt pointed clasp-knife."

"Oh dear, I am a dead man," Hill said, looking "wonderful pale."

"Oh, I am a dead man; old John has stabbed me and run away," he repeated.

Hill died three days later in a hospital, on April 10, 1810.[21]

The household was a bit peculiar: Sinclair boarded with Hill and his wife, Elizabeth, and had Mrs. Talmadge staying in his room. Mrs. Hill said that Mrs. Talmadge stayed with them because she was sick. The whole crew had just moved to new quarters three days earlier.

Hill was gentle and mild according to his wife, though Hetty Talmadge elaborated that he could be "high spirited when raised, but mild take him one way with another—mild when he was not imposed upon." On a roll, she added, "Hill was a mild man by times, but when he was in liquor very rash."[22] The attack about the potato sack must have been one of those rash events.

The jury found Sinclair guilty, and he was sentenced to die in January 1811. There is no evidence that this sentence was carried out.

Nearly half a century later, on May 30, 1853, seventy-four-year-old Thomas Kine, Irish, murdered his sixty-year-old wife, Catherine. "I struck her lightly with the flat side of the ax," he told the coroner's jury. After killing her he was taken to the Blackwell's Island Lunatic Asylum, where he still heard her voice. A jury found him insane.

Two months later, sixty-six-year-old John Price stabbed Samuel Freeman to death. Price's wife, Rachel, was somehow involved but did not have to testify against her husband. Freeman and Price were both black; their relationship and the circumstances of the murder are obscure. The murder occurred in the Price household at the rear of 27 Leonard Street. Whatever the circumstances, Price seemed to the reporter and to the participants in the trial a very "old man, of large stature, but much debilitated." There was trouble assembling a jury, apparently because of his age and debility, which made the possibility of a death sentence seem wrong. Many potential jurors were dismissed on the "ground of 'conscientious scruples'" against the death sentence in this case. When finally assembled, the jury acquitted Price for lack of evidence "without leaving the box."

Fourteen years later, in 1869, sixty-four-year-old John Hilbert killed his common-law wife, Eliza Cahallan, age thirty-six, Irish. Hilbert, either German or French—definitely foreign-born—was a scavenger and had an eleven-year-old son, Joseph. His previous wife had died in June 1867 under suspicious circumstances; that is, she was found dead outside the shanty door, and there was no inquiry into the cause of her death. In the case of Eliza, police followed up a rumor about a death on Scavenger Hill (a shantytown between Sixty-fifth and Sixty-sixth Streets and Eighth and Ninth Avenues). They found Eliza beaten to death inside the shanty. The *New York Times* had a Dickensian description of the scene, calling it the "antipode" of Murray Hill. Built on rocks, the area is "the abode of so many of those squatters who follow the avocation of night scavenger, that it has gained its distinctive name, and is, moreover, noted for its squalor, its brutality and its shiftlessness. Human life can go no lower than the point it has reached in this abode of the horrible."[23]

Though the newspaper listed Hilbert as German, and though the area had mainly German and Irish inhabitants, the 1870 census enumerated him as French. Given the area's bad reputation, it is surprising that enumerators came near Hilbert. Clearly his neighbors resented and mistrusted the police. None would say that they had heard any noise. Young Joseph Hilbert had told Margaret Meh of Eliza's death at 5 A.M., and then had gone to Christina Schack's at six o'clock with the same news. His father came to Christina's and sat down a bit later. As opposed to Sinclair's apparent rebellion, Hilbert seems to have been a habitual spouse abuser who had killed at least two victims. One year later, in 1870, Hilbert and young Joseph still lived in their house, valued by the census enumerator at $100, with no new spouse listed.

The Civil War sharply affected the age of killers, whether by removing potentially violent youths, by removing potential victims, or by other means that are still unclear. The percentage of murders committed by those younger than age eighteen dropped dramatically: 13 percent before the war, the proportion dropped to 3 percent during the war, rising to 9 percent afterward.[24] The average age of killers also reflected the war's impact: prior to the war, the mean was twenty-eight years old. It rose by four years to thirty-two during the war, remaining there afterward. It is possible that the age shift is only an artifact—maybe the young were less likely to be arrested, or maybe age reporting became even more haphazard during the Civil War, editors losing interest in local problems in the face of national ones.

The increased average age of wartime murderers makes demographic "sense": young men leave to fight. What does not make sense is that wartime murder rates soared to frightening heights in New York City when they should have dropped, the more volatile age groups having left for the Civil War. One could guess that the most violent, the most criminal, did not actually go to war. Thus though the at-risk age group diminished in size, the most dangerous individuals of all ages stayed behind, creating a more lethal mix. Recent research that demonstrates that a high proportion of middle-class men went off to fight in the Civil War reinforces the notion that those who stayed home may have been more crime oriented. Certainly the nineteenth-century idea of class supports this idea. The Draft Riots of 1863, for example, were understood by the city's middle class as an outburst by its "dangerous class." The "dangerous class" constituted at best a rumbling "volcano under the city" (the title of a book published after the Draft Riots), and as a class it could hardly be expected to contribute to the war effort.[25]

"Jimmy" White, age thirty-five, exemplified one of the older wartime killers. White shot John Cussick dead on November 10, 1863. White was Irish-born; Cussick, age twenty-three, was native-born. It is difficult to discern how the Civil War figured in this killing, except by its absence. A crowd of men was drinking at Joseph King's fourth ward porterhouse about 5 A.M., when another group of five came in and started "bantering" (here used in the original sense of ridiculing). One Thomas Brown, age thirty-four, Irish-born, announced that he was a "strong Morgan Jones [fourth district councilman, 1859–1864] man."

At this Cussick "laughed, and said he was a strong Billy Welch [Walsh] man [second district alderman, 1862–1863]."[26]

"Never mind politics—we will drink," ruled one of the group. They had another drink.

"Go away boy; you are a foolish boy. I think you have run away with the idea you can whip me," Brown ordered Cussick.

"I am sure I can whip you," Cussick replied.

Barkeeper William Furlong got them to let up. Cussick began singing. Brown in turn began "brandishing" his pistol. "We are all fighting men here. . . . Let us give it to them," he exclaimed.

At this point White joined in the fighting. First, he shot himself in his pants with his Derringer. Then he shot Cussick with his Colt revolver.

"Take that, you son of a b[itch]," he said.

"Jimmy you have shot me!" Cussick said as he died.

White left the bar with Brown, giving him his Derringer. "Take that. It is not worth the powder. I have shot myself with it," he complained.[27]

This affray, which is hardly unusual with its elements of drink, temporal separation from the workaday world, masculine posing and childish blaming (White blames his gun for his self-inflicted wound), and politics, differs from similar incidents five years earlier only in involving more guns. Otherwise it seems like a normal brawl, completely isolated from the Civil War. Thomas Brown's self-identification as a "fighting man" suggests that his fighting world did not include an actual war—his fights were all contained in the city's "dangerous class."

Did other wars similarly raise the average age of killers? Possibly, but the data have not yet been gathered to answer this question. Whatever the answer, other wars—except, perhaps, the Revolution—differed from the Civil War in that the rates of homicide went down, not up, during wartime. For the time period 1976–1994, when data on the average age of killers do exist, there were no wars and little dramatic fluctuation except for the increase in youth homicide.

We can use one indirect, and possibly deeply erroneous, estimate of killers' ages over a long time span by examining the age at death of all those executed for murder. These are contained in a remarkable data set gathered by Watt Espy, who set out to document every execution in the United States since the early seventeenth century.[28] In this collection of nearly fifteen thousand cases, Espy recorded the ages of about 50 percent of the 11,564 executed murderers. Because so few murders went to trial, and even fewer resulted in executions, it is very difficult to claim that the ages of these people represent the ages of actual offenders as opposed to those who were seen as most deserving to die. These data on executions, for the whole United States, show clearly the decline in prosecutions during the war years—so few as to make averaging ages difficult. For the five years of the Civil War, there were only sixteen civil executions. The preceding five-year period saw fifty-one, the following one saw seventy-nine. (Curiously, executions for *all* crimes went up during the Civil War. The same thing happened during World War I, murder executions dropping dramatically, then rising afterward. World War II differed: the executions dropped, as before, but then stayed at new, low levels.)

The average age of those executed for murder rose abruptly for the whole United States during the Civil War decade. In the previous decade the mean age was 29.25; during the 1860s it jumped a whole year, and then fell back during the 1870s. It is risky to say on this basis alone that the age of the typical murderer was also increasing. Rather, there was an inadvertent policy change during the war years. That there is a two-centuries-old reluctance to execute the young is suggested by contrasting the mean ages of the seventeen executed murderers with the mean age of the 366 who were not executed: for New York City, these are age thirty-four versus age thirty. Surely neither judges nor juries held different policies for sentencing during wartime, but just as surely they turned away from harsh sentences for all offenders during war, even when actual homicide rates soared. Did war make violence more tolerable? Or did violence make war more tolerable? In any case, the Civil War stands as a unique period in crime history.

The novelty of young and old murderers seems to be a historical constant. This may be why they, like serial killers, attract the attention of the media and forensic psychologists rather than that of historians or sociologists. Because of their rarity, they do not constitute a social problem. Instead, we tend to view them as symptomatic of social, cultural, political, familial, and individual failure.

"Normal" murderers, whose ages run from the late teens to the mid-fifties, are normal in that they are both independent and also culpable; not only that, but they constitute almost all murderers. A positive benefit of youth and old age, then, is that the compulsion and enabling circumstances to hurt others are so dramatically diminished as to make murder by young or old killers a rarity in any era.

Thus far in this chapter, nineteenth- and twentieth-century murderers have been compared to each other. Things get more complex, even puzzling, when we consider the demographic situations in which they lived. Overall, the nineteenth-century world was much younger than the late-twentieth-century world: families had many more children and the adult life span was shorter. In any case, a younger world should have produced more total homicides because research on recent homicide patterns shows a very high rate of offending among the young.[29] That, for example, seems to have been the case on the gold-mining frontier of the American West.[30] Figure 4.1 gives a snapshot of the age distribution of all males in mid-nineteenth-century New York City (solid line) compared with the age distribution of all males in the city in 1990 (bars). The image shows clearly that the over-thirty population of the 1990 city is relatively large compared to the dwindling group traced by the smooth line for 1850.

Immigration complicated this demographic picture in New York City, as immigrants tended to be young adults with few or no children.[31] Native-born white American males had a mean age of about sixteen, Irish and Germans twenty-eight, and African Americans about twenty-five. The immigrant groups create the very visible and sharp hump in figure 4.1, which shows in the age distribution of the city's male population in 1850. For native-born people, with so many young men, this distribution should have been especially productive of violence. Yet we know that the homicide rates, although high, were not *that* high. What does this suggest?

One way to adjust for these different age mixes is to look at age rates, for example, to look at the number of native-born sixteen-year-old killers per 10,000 native-born sixteen-year-olds.[32] Unfortunately, the somewhat casual age recording procedures of the nineteenth century frustrate this procedure: many young offenders were noted as being "lads" or "boys"— not precise enough labels to allow us to construct age rates for every race and ethnic group. On the other hand, enough killers' ages were recorded to make possible a focus on men only in the whole group; anything finer requires much more complete information.

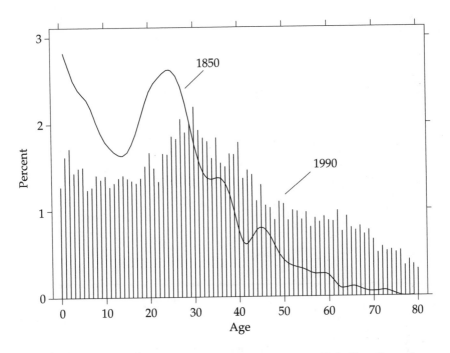

Figure 4.1. Age distribution of the male population, New York City, 1850 and 1990. Source: see appendix.

Figure 4.2 shows the age rates for male killers in New York City in the nineteenth and late twentieth centuries. This figure shows a startling difference between nineteenth- and twentieth-century New York City murderers, a difference many have sensed. Homicide offenders used to be relatively smoothly spread through the population older than age ten; today there is an enormous bulge primarily in the ages between fifteen and thirty. (The figure also shows something slight but surprising at the youthful end of the scale: a higher proportion of very young killers in nineteenth-century New York City, even when expressed as age rates.)

High rates of recent homicide do not come from just anywhere, but from a specific age group. In essence, earlier homicides were produced from a broad spectrum of ages; that broad spectrum is still present, but now another group of killers is superimposed on it. There is some evidence that

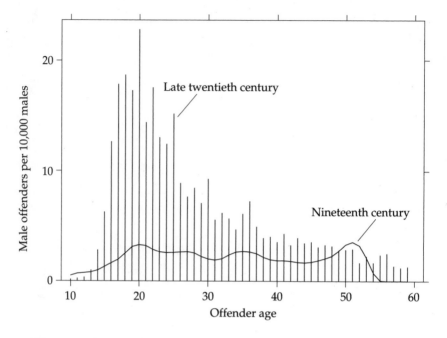

Figure 4.2. Age rates (per 10,000) for male offenders, New York City, 19th and 20th centuries. Source: see appendix.

New York City's nineteenth-century pattern was a norm: data from Philadelphia in the late 1940s and France in the late nineteenth century look very similar in distribution to those of nineteenth-century New York.

If the current age rates of homicide had occurred in the past, when there were proportionally so many more young people, the overall levels of homicide would have been very high. It is fortunate that the late-twentieth-century homicide epidemic among young men occurred in a time when there were relatively few of them.

There are several reasonable places to look for long-term explanations of what may be a trend toward a second, demographically separate group of young homicide offenders. These include physiological and sociocultural changes in aging; changes in the family structure, particularly in its social control functions; and age-related changes in the cost, lethality, and cultural desirability of weapons.

The place to begin explaining the long-term shift in homicides is probably with nutrition and age at puberty. Although exact details are hard to get, we know in principle that better nutrition has played a part in reducing the age at which children reach puberty, which in turn means that male testosterone levels are higher earlier. Testosterone levels relate to violence, though in which direction and exactly when is clearly open to sociocultural mediation; for example, testosterone rises in males after seeing or being victimized by violence as well as before. Thus, testosterone alone cannot be used as a straightforward biochemical explanation of violence.[33] In addition, testosterone levels increase with nutritional quality. Nutritional quality has increased throughout the late nineteenth and twentieth centuries. There are some solid research hints in the literature on height, nutrition, and the age at leaving home that link improved nutrition with younger physical maturity as measured by growth speed.[34] A precise measure of how much and among which groups nutrition has increased would allow us to quantify, but we can say that to an unknown degree diets have improved for all classes of society and that these dietary improvements have increased testosterone levels (as well as energy available).

Even the most careful age rate adjustments may miss another long shift in the meaning of age for young men. There are several suggestive bits of evidence that although demographic distributions have decreased the proportion of young men in the population, social and economic changes have shifted residential circumstances in another direction. For instance, the age at which children leave home has drifted steadily downward in the twentieth century from a median age of twenty-eight in the mid nineteenth century to twenty-one in 1980. For most of the nineteenth and early twentieth centuries, slightly more than 5 percent of New York City's population was composed of men aged fifteen to fifty-four living alone. The proportion fell dramatically for the years 1920–1970 to around 3 percent. In 1980 and 1990 it shot back up to about 6 percent.[35]

Thus even though the U.S. population continues to age, the proportion of young people leaving home has increased and the mean age of home leaving has moved downward. One estimate suggests that the proportion of the population in the home of origin has fallen from two-thirds to only one-fifth of the population. Another estimate, that for the proportion of the population between the median ages of home leaving and first marriage, gives simultaneous increases, though much less extreme. Young men away from their parents' supervision must have increased dramatically.

A second way of measuring changing at-risk populations is to examine the percentage of the city's population that was male, older than fourteen and younger than fifty-five, and who lived alone. This population proportion represents both potential offenders and potential victims. It decreased from just under 6 percent in the mid nineteenth century to a leveling at 2 percent from 1910 to 1960. It then doubled between 1960 and 1990.[36] These estimates resolve a major puzzle: the median age of the U.S. population has been getting increasingly older since the early nineteenth century, with a deviation introduced by the baby boom, but violent crime has not followed such a steady trajectory. By focusing instead on the male population outside of the traditional family control, we see a different trend, with the at-risk population decreasing until the turn of the twentieth century, remaining low until 1960, and then increasing.

Historians from John Schneider to David Courtwright have written on the effects of the "bachelor subculture."[37] This "bachelor subculture" has structured the free time of young men. As conceptualized by historians, this subculture often contributed to an increase in violence. Sometimes the violence and confrontational masculinity was as lethal as today. Both Clare McKanna's and Roger McGrath's studies of western towns hint at high age-specific homicide rates, for example.[38] In any case, what the data suggest is that there was a diminishing population at risk to participate in the bachelor subculture until the abrupt shift at the end of the twentieth century.

These long-term explanations offer only imprecise possibilities. Measuring what kind and size of family best controls its members, for example, may be impossible. Might not the cultural habits of young men ebb and flow for multiple reasons? Only when the demographic setting is ripe would a dangerous trend—a nasty and aggressive mode of "bantering" or the fad of a highly lethal new weapon, for example—matter.

Chapter 5 Circumstances: When Do People Murder?

When a "rowdy white gang" of Brooklynites stabbed Charles H. Rodgers in 1866, they had made clear that their target was an African American. At first glance, the attack appears to have been a racial hate crime. Given the racial hatred exhibited during the Draft Riots three years earlier and the often angry Democratic politics of urban New York, this would not have been surprising. But the narrative of this event is not so transparent. Had Rodgers provoked the attack? Was race an additional contingency?

According to the account of the incident in the August 29, 1866, *New York Times*, Rodgers sat (or stood) in front of a house on Battle-row on a bright, moonlit Saturday evening in August. A group of six white men passed, "skylarking among themselves." Rodgers seems to have been with three of his African American friends, Hezekiah Chester, Richard Gear, and another unnamed person.

As the group of whites came "down the road, swaggering back and forward," one of them, Charles Kelly, either stumbled or was hit by something.

"Show me the black s[on] of a b[itch] who struck me and I will cut his damned guts out, or shoot him," he demanded.

"There's the black s[on] of a b[itch]; let's give it to him," someone else in the group, probably Joseph Kelly, said.[1]

"We have put it on the black s[on] of a b[itch] good," Charles Kelly bragged after stabbing Rodgers.

Emma Carpenter, standing in front of her doorway twenty feet away, saw the fight. Immediately after stabbing Rodgers, Kelly turned to her and asked again, "Where the black s[on] of a b[itch] was who had hit him," suggesting either that the precipitating incident was a pretext or that Kelly had decided Rodgers had been the wrong target.

Robert Peterson, also African American, who lived near the fight scene, had just started to go outside when a boy ran in.

"For God's sake, don't go out—there is a bad set of people [meaning the white gang] out there," he begged.

Peterson went out anyway and Kelly acted as though he wanted to continue fighting, challenging Peterson. Peterson thought that Kelly had a knife in his hand. He told Kelly that he did not want to fight, noting later that Kelly's friends "appeared anxious to get Kelly away." The white men stayed across the street until the police came and arrested Kelly. By this time, he had no knife.[2]

This homicide's setting—including what we can infer about it—contains all of the elements discussed so far in this book, including groups of drunken young men and a concealed weapon. Add to this mixture race, cultural scripts, and a virtual stage on which to act out the issues and the result is lethal. Exactly which scenario happened mattered to the participants, but does not matter for illustrative purposes here. Perhaps Charles Kelly, noted as the tallest man in the rollicking group, simply stumbled and felt humiliated in front of his audience, a combination of male drinking companions and mixed sex, racially different onlookers. His stumble pulled the rug from under his social standing. The power conferred by his stature, race, and gender took a tumble. He defensively transferred

public attention to an onlooker, Charles Rodgers, who simply by observing Kelly had participated in his fall. By dominating Rodgers, Kelly could
regain his status as tallest, whitest, and most male. If, on the other hand,
Rodgers had actually hit Kelly, the same scenario was essential for Kelly
to regain the moment.

The African American onlookers and victim were part of a neighborhood—all friends and relatives—but Kelly did not need to know this.
Charles Kelly was with friends and a probable relative, or even brother,
Joseph Kelly, but these friends and relative could just as well have been
drinking companions recently acquired. Kelly behaved like a small child
blaming something else for his own mistake. The audience, and Kelly's
stumble in front of it, were the key circumstantial elements enabling a violent action. If he had stumbled on a tree root in the woods, would he have
stabbed the tree? Probably not, though he might have kicked it. Kelly's
concealed weapon helped guarantee that his action would be dangerous,
and the elements of race and gender in the circumstances made the action more meaningful. Why did Kelly hang around after the murder, if
not to bask in his restored status?

In our contemporary parlance, this homicide was "expressive" as opposed to "instrumental."[3] That is, Kelly did not get anything material out
of his action; the murder was not a consequence of a robbery attempt, for
example. The word *expressive* misconstrues Kelly's action, however. In a
display of masculine dominance, Kelly's action could help his reputation,
save him from a similar attack in the future, and ensure that on the street
he would get respect, or at least generate fear. The expressive/instru-
mental continuum helps sort out the multiplicity of homicide situations
at the end of the twentieth century, but is not adequate to the nineteenth
century. As Roger Lane once noted, a robbery murder then was so unusual
that when one occurred in New York City in 1895, it made the Philadelphia news.[4] The circumstances of about half of the New York City homicides in this study were not clear enough for me to accurately categorize
them, but it is clear that those few that could in any way be construed as
robberies composed only 2 to 4 percent of all homicides.

For post-1976 New York City the FBI data have not recorded the circumstances of most murders, but we can turn to a more complete data set

on Chicago to draw some inferences. There, 17 percent of the homicides were instrumental, a figure that is smaller than one might have guessed but between four and eight times the comparable nineteenth-century figure.[5] Although most homicides are still not for clear monetary gain, gain provides a motive for far more homicides today than in the past.

Previous chapters of this book have illustrated a variety of settings in which issues of gender, in particular, have been played out, often as issues of manliness. In the varied settings explored in this chapter such cultural scripts will be clear, but here I want to illuminate the actual stages— social and physical—on which these real life minidramas played. In the first example, Charles Rodgers occupied a visible boundary position— between private home and public street. He and his friends, and presumably their households if not the whole street, were African American. Brooklyn and New York City had a small African American population— less than ten thousand in Manhattan and five thousand in Brooklyn. For African Americans, each must have felt like a village.

On the other hand, the group of attackers, white men, two probably relatives, were a carousing group out in the big city. They lived in a world of strangers, where visual attributes, including race, had to give social cues. They were as touchy as explosives as they "skylarked" down the street. Wiser neighbors hid inside, avoiding their dangerous, alcohol-blurred notice. Almost anything could detonate these rowdy men, who became white in this racial context. The street was their public stage: dimly lit in the late evening, it provided a setting where strangers could invade neighborhoods, where manly confrontations could be enacted, and where the audience could seem random to the stranger but familiar and comfortable to the local. Kelly would have been dangerous anywhere that night; having a public stage heightened his attack's melodrama, as did the presence of his group of friends and the racial boundaries within which the attack occurred. What the public street gave him was a ready-made scene in which he became the protagonist.

Other street murders partook far less of this public stage. These homicidal encounters flowed through public and private space, in essence making the private public and the public private, drifting from home to barroom and back. Where the final blows were struck had little to do with scene. For example, the sprawling conflict in which John Masterson, a twenty-one-year-old Hoosier, killed twenty-four-year-old Max Beck, a German immigrant, in the spring of 1851, finally concluded when Beck died in the New York Hospital (Bellevue) two days after Masterson struck the last blow, shoving skull fragments into poor Beck's brain.[6]

This angry drama contained elements of youthful foolishness, male drinking, romance, ethnic conflict, and, in some confused way, a hat. Perhaps it was the cement of romantic relationships, real or imagined, that gave it the energy to cross in and out of the public-private divide. By contrast, surely Kelly's attack on and murder of Rodgers would have fizzled had it been enacted on a stage much more complex than a street.

Patrick Martin's testimony at the coroner's inquest throws some partial light on Beck's murder. Martin and three others—David Dunn, Calvin Hoyt, and Samuel Wallace—were with Beck on April twenty-first, when they stopped in front of Mary Ann Dubois's house. Beck shouted, "Mary, come to the corner with me and we will have a drink."

Masterson, who must have been in the house, responded, "Suck my asse."

Beck replied, "If you'll come down here, I'll kick it for you."

Masterson came down and Patrick Martin headed for the corner bar, apparently thinking that they would all have a drink after this friendly chat. Only when Martin finally noticed that none were in the bar drinking with him did he return.

Other witnesses appearing before the coroner's jury filled in the scenario. Mary Ann's father, Smith Dubois, testifying first, claimed that he was sleeping soundly about eleven o'clock when a noise outside awakened him and he heard someone say, "Come out of that or [undecipherable and blotted] you out." Dubois "jumped" out of bed, looked out the window, and saw six or seven men "upon" another whom they were "striking and kicking." He heard the victim of this fight—John Masterson, it turned out—say, "This is not fair play. . . . Give me fair play and I can whip the whole of you."

Smith's daughter, Mary Ann, called to him while Masterson was being attacked, and at that moment Masterson escaped and ran into the Dubois house and up to "his room" (his sister lived a block and a half away, though he did not live with her). On the stairs he and Mary Ann both asked Smith Dubois where the ax was. Smith refused to tell them.

(At this point the coroner's clerk confused Masterson and Beck, and although Dubois signed his name to the testimony, it was in none too steady a hand, suggesting that he could not have read the document.) Smith would not let Masterson go, telling him, "You are safe inside."

Masterson replied, "No, it won't do for me to stay here. I can go out the rear way, run across the lots, and so get home."

Mary Ann said, "No, don't go. They are at the door watching for you."

Masterson waited a while and then left by the back door.

"They have seen him," Mary Ann said to her father. "I see them start and run toward the corner [Fifty-fourth Street and Tenth Avenue]."

Masterson returned to the Dubois house once more, armed with a stick, saying, "We have met again and had another battle."

Martin, returning solo from the bar, saw the fight between Masterson and Beck end with Masterson running into the house (where, no doubt, he beseeched Dubois for the ax). The group, including Martin and Beck, then headed for the corner bar, where Beck realized that his hat was missing. Martin and David Dunn went back for the cap, no doubt hoping to keep Masterson and Beck apart. But they misjudged the tenacity of the two, for as they headed back to the corner bar with the hat, they saw Beck and Calvin Hoyt running down Tenth Avenue. Then they heard John Masterson, who had exited the back of the Dubois house and apparently found some support: "There goes the son of a bitch who has got my cap!" Had Beck taken Masterson's cap by mistake? Or did their hats look similar? How had the hat become the issue?

Martin, seeing eight or more men chasing someone down the road, left the scene, wisely deciding to spend the night at his brother's on Tenth Avenue. (Martin signed his deposition with a + mark.)

Samuel Wallace, part of the Beck group, also testified, telling a story similar to Martin's. David Dunn's version, while corroborating the earlier ones, added some significant detail. The group did in fact go to the Dubois house, and Beck kicked the door before he and Masterson had words. When Masterson came out, they clinched and hit, falling off the stoop. Dunn's subsequent narrative agrees with the others.

Calvin Hoyt added that he actually did see a man with a club strike Beck, and the man's voice sounded like Masterson's—an Indiana accent perhaps? (It was the middle of the night in the pre-electricity era.) Hoyt reported that as Masterson struck with the club he said, "There is the son of a bitch who has got my cap on."

That same April night, police officer William Post, of the fourteenth ward police, at his captain's request, went with two Germans to find Beck and bring him back to the station. Officer Post first found his hat, lying in the road. This in turn led him to Beck, lying on the stoop, covered in blood. Post lifted Beck, who "remarked, 'Be careful my [written over with *his*] arm is broken.'" As they walked to the station house, Post asked Beck what had happened. Beck said that he "knew little about the cause" but that he would let Post "know in the morning as it hurt him to talk." That morning Beck arrived at the hospital unable to walk or talk.

The relationships here can be amplified a bit with some census information. Most of the participants lived in the nineteenth ward. Dubois may have been the same Smith Dubois, age forty-one, who was a farmer in Franklin County, Indiana, the year before. Masterson, remember, was also a Hoosier, and the census enumerator wrote his occupation as a contractor. Masterson lived in a house with nine other Hoosiers, two of whom might have been his uncle and aunt.

Beck, on the other hand, was a stage driver, and the year before he had been boarding in a house with six other stage drivers of varying ethnicity. At least one of his friends on that Sunday night was also a stage driver, David Dunn, age twenty and a native New Yorker.

These details raise a question: How did Mary Ann, the farmer's daughter, know Max Beck, the immigrant stage driver? If the Duboises really were migrants to the city, the mixed ethnic culture and night life must have seemed threatening to them. One wonders if John Masterson had pulled together his Hoosier roommates to launch the fatal attack on the carousing stage drivers.

Sometimes murders occurring in public space and even following what might be called public rules were in actuality the acting out of gendered power claims and local intra-ethnic conflicts between acquaintances. These could even take on some aspects of dueling. Throughout this book I deliberately downplay duels as a separate category of murder for several reasons. First, there were very few duels in New York City, in part because New York combatants typically went to New Jersey to carry out their lethal acts. Second, the rhetoric of duels hid and still hides their basic action: two men fight and try to kill each other. The upper-class monopoly on the duel in early modern Europe and the American aping of such conduct allow contemporary Americans to look back on duels as though they were something other than fights leading to what I—and nineteenth-century law and most nineteenth-century Americans—consider the proper context for understanding the duel: murder. Understanding the duel as ritualized murder leads to awkward conclusions, such as that Andrew Jackson was a murderer. Does it redeem his action that his victim, Charles Dickinson, tried to murder him, too? If so, then the same logic should apply to street gang members today. My strategy for thinking about duels is, therefore, to avoid glorifying them and to contextualize them with other murders.[7]

Most historians of American dueling work on the South, and most show the rigid class dimensions of dueling, with weapon-based duels reserved for elites and close physical combat duels occurring among poor men. Sometimes the language and ritual of the duel was incorporated by immigrants and the working classes, part of the American democratization of everything. When William Dinan attacked James McCarty on September 8, 1851, the apparent barroom brawl had the gloss of a duel. McCarty, Irish, age thirty-seven, got into an argument with Dinan, a forty-three-year-old tailor, also Irish, in James McGlaughlin's oyster house after a benefit concert at Castle Garden for the Catholic Half Orphan Asylum.[8] Though not wealthy men, they were not poor either, as the benefit had cost fifty cents admission. When their quarreling escalated, McGlaughlin made them leave and the two fought in the street. Dinan and some friends clubbed first McCarty and then James McCort when he tried to stop the beating. McCarty died from his injuries four months later, in January. Dinan was arrested and posted bail to the coroner, but it is unclear if the case ever went to trial.

The depositions to the coroner show that this fight had elements of the ritualized argument that would have led to a duel among gentlemen. The oyster bar confrontation began in the context of men who all knew each other, either directly or indirectly. McCarty was with James and Patrick McCort (probably brothers and probably Irish, but neither is in the 1850 U.S. census manuscript), and all three were acquainted with McGlaughlin, the oyster house keeper. Dinan and his four companions were all strangers to McGlaughlin, but not to McCarty and the McCorts. Sketches of the rising level of exchanges leading to McCarty's fatal beating and of a later nearly successful attempt by Dinan to force Thomas Sayles into a fight show the trappings of the duel: one man insulting another or implying that he is a liar followed by a demand for "satisfaction," the use of go-betweens, and in the first case a bloody conclusion, in the second, running away and the intervention of a coroner's jury.

> McCarty asked Dennin [sic] if he was the man who beat Charles O'Neil. Dinan replied that he was not, and asked McCarty if he saw him. McCarty replied no, but that his wife saw him.
> Upon which Dennin [sic] asked McCarty if he wanted *satisfaction* [emphasis added].
> McCarty replied no.
> I [James McCort] then understood Dinnan [sic] to say *you must have satisfaction* [emphasis added].

McGlaughlin, seeing that they were getting "irritated," told them that he would not have fighting, and Dinan left, soon followed by McCarty and the McCorts. McGlaughlin added at the inquest that Dinan was a "quarrelsome man."

McCarty died from his injuries on January 25, 1852, and six months after the original altercation, on March 7, 1852, the coroner began taking depositions in the case. One deposition stands out as an echo of the dialogue above. Thomas Sayles, a porterhouse keeper, who must have been a friend of McCarty's, told how on the previous Monday night Dinan and a companion came to his house, "I suppose to see if I would fight him." Dinan's companion introduced Dinan to Sayles, who "asked him if he was the man who killed James McCarty."

> He said he was.
> I [Sayles] then took of [sic] my coat and asked him if he was able to fight me.

We [garbled] porter and Dennin [*sic*] was taken away.
The next morning Dennin sent over to know if I was going to fight him.
I went over with the person he sent.
Dennin was in the street in front of his house.
He asked me if I was ready to fight him.
I told him I would fight him on Thursday, the 4 inst.
On Thursday he came about 5 o'clock as I am told to fight me.
I was out of the house, hearing that a friend of mine was lying very
    low at Newark N.J. I had gone to visit him that day.

Dinan was clearly an aggressive terror in a group of men united by something we do not understand (there is a hint that it might have been a locale in Ireland), although James Donigan offered, "I did not know Dinan in the old country." Two hat manufacturers paid Dinan's bail. The trail ends there. We have glimpses of what could be an honor dispute, so much more common in the South, but among the elite. The use of seconds and the use of the word *satisfaction* suggest that elements of the duel could be found among New York's immigrants. What we do not know is if these elements had been appropriated just by these two groups of men or if they were more widespread.

TYPICAL HOMICIDE CIRCUMSTANCES

The relationship between killer and victim in known killings in New York City in the nineteenth century, with the number recorded for each type, are as follows:

acquaintances	237
spouses	211
business associates (e.g., bartender and patron)	84
working partners	57
family members	49
lovers	34
participants in political disputes	33
strangers	26
personal enemies	19

officials (e.g., police officer)   16
institutionalized cell mates   16
schoolmates   3

Since most murders within families or of intimate partners were likely to be so noted, it is reasonable to conclude that these include about 17 percent of all nineteenth-century New York City murders. About half of the individual New York City homicides examined here occurred under unrecorded circumstances—that is, there was neither definitive evidence that the victim and offender knew one another nor concrete hints about the circumstances precipitating the killing. This unknown category includes, for example, the McCarty killing just examined, even though it seems as though one might call this a duel or an intra-ethnic killing between near acquaintances or even between personal enemies. Nevertheless, the evidence is not definitive. One can infer from the McCarty case that killings by acquaintances probably were substantially higher than the count given here.

Most women victims (81 percent) and offenders (56 percent) were in the spousal and the family categories. As chapter 3 demonstrated, murders of women varied over the past two centuries in a loose relationship to overall levels of violence. The question as to whether spousal killings have increased or decreased seems, therefore, to be linked to all murders, rather than to changing family dynamics. Remarkably, in 1994, 14.4 percent of the known homicides in the United States occurred in either spousal or romantic relationships; this compares to 14.5 percent for New York City in 1800–1875. (For both eras, it is possible that filling in the large proportion of unknown relationships—40 percent in 1994—would change this ratio.) Because homicides were so much more common in the 1990s, this stable ratio also supports the notion that spousal violence varies by the overall amount of violence in society, rather than by large shifts in the nature of romantic relationships.[9]

One cannot conclude that the small proportion of killings—3 percent—clearly done by strangers in the nineteenth century is meaningful: the true figure could be huge, masked by the unreported relationships. Similarly, today's figure could be larger as well, but common sense and some evidence suggest that the unknown relationships reflect the known relationships and that stranger murders today are about 15–25 percent of the total.[10]

A much higher proportion of nineteenth-century killings were by inmates in institutions—typically in the almshouse, by workmates, and over political issues. The institutional killings of one inmate by another reflect the laxness of supervision in the nineteenth century compared to today.

KILLINGS AMONG ACQUAINTANCES

Nineteenth-century gender conventions almost guaranteed that lethal male disputes among friends and acquaintances would be common. "Skylarking" often led to killing. Historians have documented the narrow range of leisure options for urbanites, where bars provided the major public meeting spaces and male leisure sites.

Cornelius Mahoney (age twenty-seven, Irish) beat, kicked, and stamped to death his friend Edward Donovan (age fifty-two, Irish) on a Tuesday night, February 9, 1847.[11] As reported by the New York Tribune on February 15 and April 21, 1847, Mahoney, "a peaceable man, a friend of Donovan, . . . 'was more sorry for him than anyone else,'" according to Catherine Kelly, who lived with Mr. and Mrs. Donovan. Donovan had been drinking for a week. Mahoney had seen Donovan treating (buying drinks for) several men in a grocery earlier in the day. Knowing that Donovan was carrying a bank draft for eight sovereigns to be sent to Ireland, Mahoney took him home. There Donovan argued with his wife and "boxed her ears" twice. He announced that he would kill her even if he had to go to "State Prison" for ten years. Mahoney got him away from her and asked him if he meant this from his heart.

Donovan said that he did.

"I will not let you do it," Mahoney said. The two men fought, and in the course of their struggle Mahoney jumped on Donovan several times. Donovan succeeded in driving Mahoney out, throwing a bottle after him, and then heaved "himself on the bed."

"Call for my wife—I am done for," he told Catherine Kelly. Indeed he was. Donovan died on Friday.[12]

The ethnic groups that differed the most in killings by acquaintances were the Irish and the native-born Americans. Twenty percent of all Irish victims were killed by acquaintances, about 13 percent of non-Irish victims, and only about 9 percent of all Yankees. The data are not detailed enough to account precisely for these differences, yet it does seem that the major explanation comes from a combination of Irish drinking patterns and the differing role of male challenges in ethnic Irish male culture. Yankees, in the nineteenth century as well as today, tended to shrug off insults intended to trigger lethal male confrontations.

Sometimes "skylarking," male dominance, and the display of political violence all blended into an inseparable blur, fueled by alcohol. On the evening of September 27, 1843, prior to delegate selections for Tammany Hall, William Jones (about age forty), killed James Doyle, who must have been much younger.[13] Neither "drunk nor sober," they were skylarking when Doyle hit Jones with a "little blow," but Jones fell. Although Jones was physically unhurt from the fall, his dignity must have suffered. It may have suffered further when Doyle bought him a drink, saying, "old fellow, come up and drink." Jones at first refused (an insult to Doyle), saying that he could afford his own drinks, but finally agreed when others urged him. Jones then left the bar.

When he returned in fifteen minutes, Doyle was amusing the crowd by lifting a chair, his arm extended. From the doorway Jones hurled two or three paving stones at Doyle, exclaiming, "dawn [sic] you, now I have got you."

Michael Dean (a sailor, age thirty), cautioned Jones, "Suppose you had killed the man?"

"I had intended to kill him," Jones replied to Dean. Jones must have been satisfied when Doyle died later.

This case came to trial, and the jury, clearly concerned about the amount of punishment Jones would receive, consulted the judge on the level of charge. The jury selected the minimum, bringing in a fourth-degree manslaughter verdict (two years) and recommending the court's mercy.

WORKPLACE VIOLENCE

In the 1990s "going postal" became an offense of note, yet such killings within work settings were much more common in the nineteenth century.

We can reconsider the sad child murder involving two twelve-year-olds, Thomas Miller killed by William McElroy in a shoemaker's shop, discussed in chapter 4, as a workplace murder. Miller had been pestering McElroy, who used his awl to solve the problem. Such pestering probably reduced McElroy's productivity and income: harassment had serious daily consequences for these boys. The typical workplace killing involved two men (only two of the victims were women), the killers averaging a little younger, age twenty-seven, than their victims, age thirty-one. Irish and German immigrants dominated the numbers of workplace killers and victims, whereas native-born residents—about 54 percent of the city's population in 1850—made up a small group of workplace killers and victims—around 15 percent.

Some workplace killings occurred among sailors, reflecting that the city was a busy port. The sailor's life was brutal, much as Melville portrayed it in his popular early novels of the 1850s. On July 27, 1853, William Leslie, the third mate of the *Balmoral*, from Liverpool, got into a drunken fight with sailmaker Thomas Evans. The ship had been in port two weeks. He and Evans had spent the night drinking. On returning to the ship they got into a fight and Leslie threw Evans into the water, where he drowned.

The following summer, John Cochran and some other sailors beat the young Irish longshoreman Michael Coyne to death on the dock. As the *New York Times* reported the incident on August 2, 1854, the sailors' coastal steamer had arrived late at night, and by early morning the fight had broken out. Patrick Fallon, a thirty-year-old Irishman and ex-soldier in the U.S. army who lived nearby, testified that he heard someone yell "murder!" and saw Cochran come ashore barefoot, but armed with a capstan bar.[14] Coyne was already down, and Fallon tried to stop Cochran, who beat him and then turned back to Coyne.

"John, sure you will kill the man," Fallon said.

"Yes, and you too, you son of a b[itch]," Cochran replied.

After hitting Coyne, Cochran hit Fallon again and said, "I'll kill you too."

Fallon then ran, "crying out, 'Coyne is killed, Coyne is killed.'" No one came in answer to his call for help, so he went home.[15]

Melville makes clear that such fights could well have been related to shipboard tensions, as the sailor's life was dangerous, his sleep disrupted, and his on-ship behavior regimented by means of a strong dose of violence.

The close quarters and brutal maritime discipline were not unique causes of working anger. Even entrepreneurs in small operations turned their impulses into murder. On March 25, 1864, Patrick Brennan murdered his partner, Thomas McGowan, age thirty-three. McGowan, Irish, and Brennan, probably Irish, had a business selling portraits of the late Archbishop Hughes, who had died in January. Hughes had been a major figure in American and New York Catholic life, founding a wide variety of institutions, such as Fordham University, and he had tried to quell the Draft Riots only six months before his death. Brennan, angry with McGowan about his canceling an order, "seized a large piece of glass and struck McGowan on the left side of the head."[16] No brutalizing work regime can be used to account for this, as the two men were free from bosses and coworkers.

Moreover, this impulsive workplace violence did not rise out of the long-simmering anger and resentments that today turn workplace killers on their bosses, coworkers, and almost anyone else at the site. Rather, the more common nineteenth-century workplace violence stemmed from impulse, from indulging angry feelings, from almost childish needling and petty personal aggression. These men and boys were not failing to adjust to the growth of the regimented large-scale work site. Instead, they failed to get along with other people working in close quarters. Indeed, they would have benefited from the tight direction and clear sense of order brought by a bureaucracy. As Roger Lane and labor historians have observed, nineteenth-century cities and work sites required new kinds of personal self-discipline.[17] But for many newcomers, the "civilizing process" was remote from their daily lives.

POLITICAL VIOLENCE

When Americans think of political violence or murders, presidential assassinations or elections in politically troubled nations usually come to mind. On the other hand, when political scientists or historians write about political violence, they almost always mean one thing: mass violence—often riots by ordinarily nonviolent people—with broad political protest goals. Often the scholar's point is to show that "senseless" violence has a sense, something along the lines of giving "voice" to the "voiceless." Political violence was a familiar accompaniment to southern politics, keeping the one-party system sound, discouraging if not killing voters, and, toward the end of the nineteenth century, narrowing political participation to white men. Most American historians know about the political violence in antebellum Baltimore and in the reconstruction South, where voter intimidation and local terrorist acts were common.[18] New York City had election riots too, those of April 1834 perhaps the most locally infamous.[19]

Few historians have conceptualized violence to be a utilitarian tool, a part of normal northern politics, yet also the tool of criminals. But as the earlier discussions of weapons and gender have demonstrated, New York City's local politics had its own kind of violence in the nineteenth century. This violence differed significantly from assassinations, which are typically carried out by persons who have little to gain from them personally. This political violence also differs from the violence of riots, which are usually understood as mass actions by noncriminal or otherwise respectable members of society engaging in political protest. Political violence on the local level, on the other hand, involves the use of violence to gain power, either partisan or factional, to get a particular person or faction or party into office. This kind of violence, common in New York City, employed aggressive men using intimidation, assaults, and on occasion murder to eliminate rivals, to suppress rival factions, and to gain the minor spoils accruing to political office. The target practice and sword "play" of paramilitary political groups like the Fox Musketeers and the Brady Guards (discussed in chapter 3) combined the fun of drinking and shooting with the practical shading of political violence. It is hard to conceive now: armed bands of mainstream politically partisan men out target practicing. New York's elites dismissed these lower-class activities as childishly harmless, even effete, as in the cartoon that appeared in *Harper's Weekly* six days after the Stackpole murder (figure 3.1). The closest contemporary analogues would be the thoroughly marginal American militia movements of the late twentieth century or the dangerous private militias in emerging democracies.

Factional violence usually took place among the Democrats. When Tammany's support nearly assured a win, the contest among internal factions to get this support was significant.[20] And fighting or murder could intimidate a faction. It may be impossible now to reconstruct these fights; what seems to have been a simple gender- or ethnic-based challenge such as that between Dinan and McCarty (discussed earlier in this chapter) could well have had a factional political context of which I am unaware. Some political murders, such as that of Scannell and the two involving future mayor Richard Croker, seem to be over who within Tammany controlled the voting gangs (see chapter 3). These two men were affiliated with anti-Tweed factions in the Democratic party. Note the similarity of this factional violence to violence used for controlling drug sales or illegal liquor sales: the question is who has a monopoly of violence regulating this particular asset. The nineteenth-century New York City asset—political access—was not valued at all for policy considerations, but for money: jobs in particular and perhaps contracts or cash. As in illegal drug sales, the amount of money can be relatively small—most street-level drug sellers make only a modest amount of money yet live with the threat of lethal violence. Most of the political gains for political fighters, often called "shoulder hitters," came in the form of low-level jobs—street cleaning, for example.

Coroner Croker or his affiliates murdered John McKenna and Thomas Marra on election morning, November 2, 1874. The events, filtered through two highly partisan sets of accounts, come down to one group of about five Tammany Democrats, perhaps led by James O'Brien (ex–state senator or brother of an ex-senator), challenging another group of seven, led by Croker. O'Brien told Croker, "Get out; I don't want any repeaters around here," implying that the Croker group had intruded on alien voting territory. Croker or someone in his group began firing, killing McKenna and injuring Marra, not a voting gang member but attracted by the commotion, who died a month later.[21]

Figure 5.1. William John Hennessy, "At the Polls," satirical cartoon, *Harper's Weekly,* Nov. 7, 1857. An image of polling place roughhousing. Although police clubs are visible and two men are scuffling, one hardly gets the sense of the actual gun murders that occurred at election time. Note the hat in the gutter. The fighting dogs are a metaphor for the low male culture, a metaphor that reduces the violence to an even less threatening level. Courtesy Beinecke Rare Book and Manuscript Library, Yale University.

Just as the angry impulsive work world of the nineteenth century seems alien to us, so does this kind of political violence. Few have detailed the local political violence in New York City.[22] This political world was for white men only. But, "white" men included, for accidental reasons, what New Yorkers then perceived as widely varying races—the Irish, in particular. The maleness of this political world has been discussed in chapter 3, so here I wish to look at the political violence simply as a quantitative phenomenon. At least thirty-four murders (4 percent of all known) prior to 1875 were clearly political: 35 percent occurred in just two years, 1857 and 1858, with the next highest burst in 1874 (12 percent). Of the victims and killers whose ethnicity could be identified, a large proportion were Irish, but since most ethnicities went unmentioned, one must be careful about generalizing from this. Of the thirty-four incidents, in thirty-two either the killer's or the victim's ethnicity was mentioned; of these, seventeen appear to have been Irish and at least eleven were native-born.

Ireland itself had considerable local political violence, including a few murders, associated with elections, but historian K. T. Hoppen shows that this violence was tied to rural violence associated with religious and land conflicts.[23] The difference is that, like mob violence around American elections, the goals of political violence in Ireland were somewhat larger than one faction or another getting the rewards of office. New York City political murders were of a different kind: the violent men did not want change, they wanted office.

Street violence for control of an asset, whether political office or drugs, occurs in unregulated markets—usually unregulated because illegal. When the economic contestants cannot rely on the legal system to enforce claims, then violence and intimidation become the market regulators. From illegal liquor sales during Prohibition to fights about who stands where in illegal street vending, the violence is similar: economic advantage, even market monopoly, accrues to those who can marshal the most intimidation. One would expect, therefore, that when the courts or political parties successfully moderated factional political challenges, only then would the intimidation cease. No one, to my knowledge, has yet analyzed this particular kind of political violence, but the work of Scott James on federal intervention in elections clarifies this issue. He and Brian Lawson have shown how the Federal Election Law, designed to ensure voting rights for African Americans in the South, also featured intense electoral control of all elections involving federal offices in northern cities, especially in New York. This intervention involved prosecution for voting fraud and the supervisory presence of deputy U.S. marshals for two decades. (The data are collected in such a way that the details cannot be made more precise: expenditures grew from about $16,000 in 1884 to about $35,000 in 1892, just for special deputies for individual New York City elections.)[24]

As early as the election of November 8, 1870, the federal marshal had a force supervising the city's election. The published orders included these ominous words: "On the day of the election the deputy marshals are authorized to preserve order at the election, and to arrest for any offense or breach of peace in their view." Each assembly district had a chief deputy: of the twenty-one chiefs, eleven were mentioned by military rank. They supervised about one thousand deputies, one deputy for every 116 men voting. They arrested a large but unspecified number of men in a scene that sounds like the mass arrests during antiwar protests in the late 1960s. The *New York Times* reported that the federal building's "corridors constantly echoed with the tramp of prisoners arrested for violating the Congressional Election law. Numerous carriages were kept in readiness in front of the building for the purpose of conveying the prisoners to jail."[25]

Even with this very visible, even massive presence, there was not a complete and thorough legal control of the election market. For one thing, factional violence took place well before the actual election day. Perhaps the threat of such intervention combined with the bureaucratization of Tammany may have been all that was needed to reduce political murders in the long run. Thus, the famous arrest and trial of Tweed in the 1870s may have set the stage, even though the election of Richard Croker and his violent anti-Tweed faction followed. We can postulate that in the 1870s a long transition from intimidation began, which did not conclude for another fifty years. The federal election laws designed to introduce fair elections to the South may have accomplished their ancillary purpose in the North.

Certainly, by some point in the second half of the nineteenth century the concept that election days were dangerous times had disappeared. No longer would mothers warn their sons to stay home. Ann Barrett, a widow and the mother of twenty-four-year-old New York–born George, asked him in November 1854 not to go out "as it was election night." George had voted in the morning but, not heeding his mother, he went out that night to James McConnell's liquor store next door, possibly to continue voting. By eleven he was brought home, face bleeding, "face and eyes covered with dirt . . . groaning loudly till 5 o'clock" the next morning, when he vomited and died.[26]

VIOLENCE AND POLITICS
DURING THE COURSE OF ARREST

Arrests are not always nonviolent affairs. In 1992, most Americans became aware of violence during the course of an arrest when they watched the videotape of police officers beating Rodney King. According to the journalist Lou Cannon, had they seen the previous few seconds of video and the actions preceding that, they would have seen King violently resisting arrest. Had the arrest occurred in a more public setting, there might well have been a different chain of events. For example, when a highway patrol officer tried to arrest Marquette Frye for drunken driving in Los Angeles in 1965, his mother and neighbors tried to interfere, and the arrest quickly escalated to a community/police battle.

The same thing often happened during the nineteenth century. In what were then called "rescues," the friends of an arrested person tried to overwhelm the arresting officer as he struggled to drag the prisoner off to jail, sometimes a distance of several blocks.[27] Because this was all on foot and the police had no guarantee of support, many rescues were successful. Some, on the other hand, led to disaster.

On November 4, 1854, John B. Holmes, a twenty-five-year-old New Yorker, stabbed David Gourley, a thirty-three-year-old Irish police officer. Gourley died two days later.[28] The basic narrative account in the *New York Times* was of a rescue gone bad. The *Tribune*, on the other hand, mentioned that Holmes—a surveyor—was a "soft shell" Democratic candidate for alderman (the "soft shell" faction of the Democrats controlled the Tammany Society but had no clear political program). Officer Gourley had been dealing with a belligerent drunk, probably James Collis, a shoemaker. Gourley first tried to get him into his house and bed, then finally tried to arrest him and head to jail. Holmes, a neighbor living across the street, intervened to rescue the prisoner, fought with Gourley, and ultimately stabbed him to death. Officer Mike Sheehan, age twenty-two, Irish, then tried to arrest Holmes, and he, too, got cut.[29] Collis, who started the whole affray, seems to have escaped, and he was not even asked to testify.

The coroner held the inquest on November 6th in the city hospital's "Dead-house." At the inquest Holmes "bore the marks of the blows" from the police beating him during his arrest. The various testimonies reveal a tangle of relationships that make apparent that the murder involved ethnic politics as well as competing male challenges and a "rescue." About midnight on Friday, probably just after the circus at nearby Castle Garden and perhaps a political procession had ended, officers Sheehan and Gourley (not partners but friends) were chatting on Morris and Greenwich Streets when they heard a commotion down Greenwich. James Collis and others in a bar were quarreling about politics.

"Mike, I'll go up," said Gourley.

Soon after, he blew his whistle for Sheehan's help. Sheehan and Gourley ordered Collis to go into his residence above a bar at 56 Greenwich Street. Collis's wife pleaded with the officers to excuse her husband, saying by way of explanation that he had not had a thing to drink in six months. But Collis got angrier and told the police officers that he would show them what he could do. He went inside and came back out with a club. The officers asked what he was doing, and he said he was protecting himself from such "whelps" as they. At this point, things turned physical.

Gourley grabbed Collis by his cravat—a white neckerchief—and both men pushed into the hallway of the building. Sheehan, on the stoop, grabbed Collis's coat with his left hand as he held his nightstick in his right.

John B. Holmes and five or six others then pitched in. They came from Holmes's house across Greenwich at number 53, where he and his wife lived on the second floor.

"Don't strike that man," Holmes told Sheehan. "I am a citizen."

Someone knocked off Sheehan's hat and jumped on it. Holmes, behind Sheehan, cursed him and Gourley, and grabbed Sheehan's club.

Sheehan, still holding Collis, turned back to Holmes, saying, "Mr. Holmes, don't you know better than to do this, an educated man like you are? I have a prisoner and mean to arrest him."

Gourley by this time was "tussling" with two or more men and women in the hallway. Sheehan let go of Collis, and Holmes let go of Sheehan's club. Sheehan turned back to Gourley only to discover that someone had cut Collis's necktie loose, allowing him to escape.

Gourley turned to Holmes, threatening, "You have rescued my prisoner and I will sue you for it tomorrow."

Holmes's crew then retreated back across the street, mission accom-
plished. Holmes called Sheehan a "son of a b[itc]h," saying that he
(Holmes) had got Sheehan a place on the police force and that he would
"break" him. Sheehan did not give up, and, avoiding Holmes, he and
Gourley arrested one of his companions, James O'Calahan, a surveyor like
Holmes, for drunk and disorderly conduct.

As they returned to Greenwich Street from the station house in Trinity
Place, about two blocks away, Gourley told Sheehan that he wanted his
rescued prisoner and that his "side partner" (unnamed) would help him.
The three headed back down Greenwich Street.

"There is Holmes in the middle of the street. I shall go and arrest him,"
Gourley announced.

Holmes stood with two others, alderman Josiah W. Brown and Jacob
L. Smith, both young (ages twenty-eight and twenty-nine, respectively).
Brown, also a "soft shell" Democrat who sat in the number one seat in the
council chambers, was a merchant. Smith had worked with the United
States Steamship company until six months earlier. (Both claimed to be
native New Yorkers, yet Smith by 1858 was married to Sarah, who was
Irish, indicating clearly his integration into the immigrant community.)[30]

Holmes noisily called the police a "pretty set of suckers."

Officer Gourley approached Holmes, put a hand on his shoulder,
charged him with rescuing his prisoner, and told him that he had to come
to the station house. (He also may have whacked him with his club at this
point.)

"We'll take care of you for the elections, you son of a b[itc]h," Gourley
said (according to Holmes). (The election was on the following Tuesday.)

Officer Sheehan came up behind Holmes. But Holmes jumped around
Gourley and stabbed him with a ten-inch dirk. Gourley twisted and fell.

"Mike, he has stabbed me—I'm a dead man; oh! How it hurts."

Sheehan "sprang" at Holmes with his club, hitting him on the head three
times. He then tried to get Holmes's knife away, the knife slicing his hand.

Collapsed on the ground, Officer Gourley told Sheehan, "Take care of
little Billy [his son]."

Holmes escaped to his second floor apartment, where he collapsed on the floor, bleeding from his beating.

Sheehan must have called for assistance in the then traditional way: rapping his club on the sidewalk. Evidence of the compressed and silent night of the mid-nineteenth-century city, his rapping roused neighbors and brought more police officers running. Officer James Marshall arrived on the scene first.

"Holmes has stabbed me in the heart," Gourley told him.

A Dr. Monel then came to see Gourley.

"I am dying and my dying words are, 'John B. Holmes stabbed me'; what will my wife and family do, and my poor little Willy?" Gourley asked him.

Gourley survived to be carried back to the station house, where Jacob Smith found him lying on the floor.

"Jake, you know who did it," Gourley said to him.

Sheehan and three other police officers went up to Holmes's apartment. Holmes asked them to call for the politician Nicholas Dimond and for pen and paper so he could make out his will. His request was a strange linking of politics, histrionics, and fear: Dimond was a fifty-nine-year-old Irish laborer and a "hard shell" candidate for alderman (who lost). At some point, city council member Charles Gannon also visited Holmes. The police called in a doctor who pronounced him not in "dangerous" condition, so he was then arrested.

After visiting Holmes in his apartment, council member Gannon showed up at the station house, suggesting that Holmes, not Gourley, came first in importance.

"Charley, Mr. Holmes has stabbed me—won't you shake hands with me before I die?" Gourley pleaded of Gannon.

Later, Gannon asked Holmes why he had killed Gourley.

"It was Sheehan's fault," Holmes answered.

"What would you do if you were knocked down with a club? I don't know but I think as much of my life as anyone else," Holmes blustered to others.

Three days after Officer Gourley died, the city council voted to give Gourley's widow and five (or three) children $500—the equivalent of almost nine months' salary.

A week later two articles followed, noting Holmes's arrest, his release on $500 bail provided by Anthony J. Bleecker—a wealthy fifty-five-year-old New York–born auctioneer—and his rearrest. This occurred immediately on his release, after Holmes made what may have been a threatening remark about Officer Sheehan, saying to a friend, "There he is." Since we do not know how Holmes emphasized his words or who his friend was, the "threat" could have been real or innocuous. One thing is clear: Holmes had many powerful friends.[31]

Though incomplete, both the narrative details and contextual evidence suggest that this was a political murder as well as a "rescue." Since we do not know the exact political status of Collis—the drunk who precipitated this whole affair—or why he was worth rescuing from Officer Gourley, the exact political dimension must remain obscure. The police in 1854 were under the power of the mayor and the city council—the "forty thieves"— as the Tweed Democratic political regime handed out positions as political payoffs, often but not always to Irish immigrants. Holmes may not have been successful in gaining office but he was very clearly attached to both hard and soft shell Democrats, and he had had enough clout to get Sheehan a place on the police force a year and two months earlier.

Gourley died a few days before the elections in which notorious Fernando Wood became mayor. That at least two aldermen had shown up after candidate Holmes's arrest is not too surprising, since they had the power to release prisoners. But their presence suggests deeper complexity and now no longer recoverable relationships. Three years later, in 1857, the state legislature created a new, Republican (and perhaps Know-Nothing) metropolitan police department in order to undercut the immigrant influence in the city's Democratic regime. This new force literally had to battle the old one for its place.[32]

Were Sheehan and Gourley out of line and aggressively brutal? Only Holmes indicated so, claiming that both were drunk. Was Holmes protecting his neighbor or a "strong political friend" as the *Tribune* said on November 9th? Or were Sheehan and Gourley taking a factional side? One wonders how long Sheehan stayed on the police force after crossing so many politicians; there are too many Mike Sheehans in the 1860 census to find this one.

Was the Holmes intervention an example of an Irish politician controlling his forces? Holmes may not have been quite the person of distinction that he seemed to be in the *Times*'s account. Although he told census enumerators that he was a New Yorker and told Officer Gourley that he was a citizen, he told the coroner's jury on November 13 that he had been born in Mauritius (a British colony at the time). Holmes must have had an Irish accent or claimed an Irish ancestry, for he was also known as "Tipperary Jack." If the census listings are correct, Holmes's subsequent career is quite bizarre. One must wonder about his 1854 occupation, "Surveyor and Civil Engineer," given that by 1860 he was listed as a police officer and then in 1870 as a produce dealer.

Mary Holmes, who attended the inquest, was between fifteen and twenty-one years old at the time.[33] She, too, contributed to the family's dramatization of the incident.

"Oh! Don't murder him in this place. You're killing him," she cried out during the inquest.

In the late 1850s the city council was scrutinizing the police carefully. Every new officer hire was supposed to be reported by the police department, in order to curb excessive ethnic partiality. I cannot find John B. Holmes listed as a new hire, but there is a John W. Holmes hired in July 1857, who is most likely the same person.[34] That a police killer would quickly become a police officer indicates the nature of city politics as an asset—these men used political power and violence to control access to seven-hundred-dollar-a-year jobs just as drug dealers competed violently over urban turf in the late twentieth century.

Was Holmes ever prosecuted? Possibly, but the tragic shipwreck of the *Arctic*, in which 350 people perished, and the election riot in Williamsburg where two died pushed the whole affair out of the news.

HOLIDAY VIOLENCE

In the nineteenth century, holidays such as Christmas could be a time for murder, something almost as alien today as the notion of political murders. Holiday violence we now associate with automobile accidents, and we bracket these as accidents and hence outside the realm of human intention. Historians such as Paul Gilje and Stephen Nissenbaum have shown how early-nineteenth-century New York in fact had riots at Christmas.[35] These Christmas riots occurred until the mid 1830s, but the cessation of violence did not instantly follow the cessation of riots.

The holidays with the most noticeable excesses of killing were New Year's and the Fourth of July, followed by Christmas (and Irish Protestant-Catholic violence occurred on July 12–13—the Orange riots).[36] All three holidays involved drinking and group rowdiness, often with partisan political overtones on the Fourth. The duel in which Alexander Hamilton's son was murdered began with an earlier Fourth of July conflict. At least eighty-two people (sixty-eight of them men) died on or just after these holidays in the era prior to 1875, about 50 percent more than on ordinary days.[37] The historian Stephen Nissenbaum argues that New York City elites worried about this violence and in the early nineteenth century consciously set about transforming the nature of Christmas. People such as Clement Moore (author of the "Night before Christmas" poem) created a brand new "tradition," deliberately reshaping a rough public culture of drinking, mob behavior, and violence into a family-oriented, even religious, affair. The efforts of these reformers must not have succeeded until late in the nineteenth century, however, as Christmas murders continued well past the Civil War era. New Year's and the Fourth of July continued with their rowdiness even if with less personal violence into the twentieth century.

When known, the relationships of holiday killers and victims were somewhat less family based than killer-victim relationships in general: 8 percent of holiday victims were spouses, versus 12 percent of nonholiday victims. The victims were slightly more male, too, 85 percent of holiday victims versus 76 percent in general. These figures reflect the nature of nineteenth-century holiday violence: men on the loose, drinking and fighting. The *Times* editorialized, with a combination of anguish and moral correctness, about the execution of one such Christmas murderer, Bernard Friery. He had killed another "sporting man," Henry Lazarus, nearly a year and a half earlier. They had political connections, but it does not appear that the fight itself was political in nature. A twenty-one-year-old New Yorker, Friery's Christmastime "orgies" of violence attracted attention because of the unchecked danger his class—an "ordinary type of New-York rowdy"—posed. That it was a Christmas murder elicited no comment.[38]

It is now a commonplace among social historians that the late-nineteenth-century middle-class moral and feminist reformers reshaped the role of the family in the United States; the success of these reforms can be seen in diminishing holiday violence. By the mid twentieth century, the Fourth of July had become a family affair. Family picnics and government-funded fireworks displays suppressed noisy and aggressive male outbursts. Only New Year's remained a holiday for drinking and rowdiness, and even much of its violence had to do with drunken driving, not intentional fighting.

WHAT IS THE RIGHT OCCASION FOR MURDER?

From holidays and elections to carousing drunks, the elements of the murders discussed in this chapter reflect key features of most murders discussed in this book. Men fought over honor, assets, or power, passion to control others almost always their motive. Although the final moments of fights contained unexpected elements and uncontrolled impulse, the preconditions were dreadfully predictable. In contrast with spousal murderers, these men succeeded for the most part. Richard Croker became mayor. Joseph Kelly became the dominant male of that moment. Donovan succeeded in keeping Mahoney from killing his wife, though he lost his friend in the process. Holmes successfully "rescued" his neighbor from arrest.

One could hardly say that these cases showed the calculated use of violence, but they did show a rational if impulsive logic. The rationality of their violence was in part determined by the outcome—who died—and this clearly had to do with chance. So we can say that the risk came from unknowable consequences, but for certain kinds of contests, violence and the acceptance of its risk made sense.

In a larger sphere, these cases all show authority, if not legitimacy, being established. They also undermined the legitimacy of the state: in Max Weber's terms, the state reserves to itself the legitimate monopoly on violence. Here, the violence is not legitimate and even threatens the state's monopoly. Perhaps most striking is Holmes's becoming a police officer three years after killing one. To the political gangs the state was one means to money and resources; little questions of policy or big questions of political legitimacy were irrelevant to them. If produce sales or bartending were a better source of income, then they would turn to them. Mayor Richard Croker, similarly, used violence to get power for himself and his political faction, but he was not challenging the state itself.

These local, individually unimportant, actions formed a base for the strange relationship between the American political system and personal violence. The concept that the state must retain its legitimate monopoly on violence did not become an American practice. How could it?

Chapter 6 Race, Ethnicity, and Murder

The relationship of race and ethnicity to homicide can be a painful and sensitive topic. I have tried to incorporate racial and ethnic aspects of homicide throughout this book because these categories are not readily separated from others in the discussion of homicide, nor should they be. Yet it is still important to examine separately issues of race, ethnicity, and violence in a historical setting so that we may establish a perspective from which to view contemporary problems as well as understand the past.

Research on nineteenth-century Philadelphia by Roger Lane suggests that homicide patterns were not the same for African Americans as they were for whites. After the Civil War, white homicide rates declined while black homicide rates increased. Lane shows how racial discrimination created what was a structurally different city for blacks than for whites, including immigrants. He argues that these structural features account for the crime differences, creating different criminal worlds. Essentially, crime was more profitable for whites, whereas even in crime, discrimination blocked the more lucrative opportunities for African Americans and encouraged more violent, destructive offenses.[1]

For New York City, we can compare various newly arrived immigrants to African Americans. We know that African Americans faced increasing hostility from immigrants around the time of the Civil War and that all evidence points to declining economic opportunity in the late 1850s.[2] Historians have long noted the irony of the situation African Americans found in northern cities prior to the ending of slavery: free and able to pursue their own interests, such as religion, northern blacks were systematically excluded from occupations open to them in the slave South. Frederick Douglass, for example, was unable to obtain the same skilled work in northern shipyards as he had as a slave in Baltimore.

Although the limitations imposed on the homicide data—missing information in particular—frustrate fine-grained dissections, historical analysis makes clear some of the differences between the nineteenth and twentieth centuries. The identification of shifting race and ethnic patterns suggests that such patterns can continue to change, that a criminal offense sometimes considered to be beyond the reach of social control is not beyond the reach of social and historical circumstance. In some ways, the exact nuances of change are less significant than the discovery of change itself. Race and ethnic differences are not chiseled in stone.

THE SETTING

It is essential to understand some of the relevant population features of nineteenth-century New York City. Though very important, New York has never been a typical American city. Its great size, nearly ideal location, unrivaled port, and compact energy have always made it special. In the first three quarters of the nineteenth century, its population grew dramatically from about sixty thousand to more than a million. This astonishing growth made New York America's largest metropolis, with a polyglot immigrant population after 1840. Its early size alone makes the city worth studying, for although atypical, it was, by any kind of definition, *the* American metropolis. What it did and what happened there mattered for all Americans.

By 1834 the city's population had reached a quarter of a million, but it would not be until the last years of the 1840s that a transforming demographic event occurred: the flood of immigration from Ireland and Germany. In 1850 the city reached a half million, and on the eve of the Civil War, more than eight hundred thousand.

It may have had a foreign-born population as high as 20 percent in the 1820s, according to demographer Ira Rosenwaike.[3] In 1845, when the census began reporting birthplace tallies, the city had 135,000 foreign-born residents, about one-third of its population. By 1850 the figure had reached more than a quarter of a million; in 1860 it grew again to well over a third of a million—almost half the city's population was foreign-born. Virtually all of these figures for foreign-born must be understood as minimal counts, for there is ample evidence that children born in other countries often reported themselves as native-born when reaching adulthood. George Washington Matsell, New York's attention-grabbing police chief in the 1850s, caused a huge scandal by claiming to be a native New Yorker; one of his political enemies spent a month in England proving that he was born there to an Irish family.

The controversy about counting immigrants, the very poor, and racial minorities in recent censuses emphasizes that even today the proper enumeration of the poor remains difficult. Lane's detailed study of Philadelphia casts particular doubt on the 1860 census's accuracy in enumerating the African American population. Characterizing the census's enumeration in Philadelphia as "crudely unreliable," Lane argues that the census was a "barometer" of race relations, "an especially suspect enterprise from the black perspective." He points out that the northern city was a place for escapees to hide, that the Fugitive Slave Act certainly made free blacks afraid to give information to white officials, and that public discussion of forced emigration to Africa added even more threat to any census. Lane shows, for example, that the census missed six of twenty prominent black Philadelphians in 1870.[4]

Given that homicide rates are sensitive to how the population at risk—the denominator—is defined and measured, the demographic composition of the New York City African American population remains an important, unresolved, and perhaps even insoluble issue. New York State had abolished slavery by 1827. The city's African American population had a very different history from its immigrants—one of declension in size from 16,000 in 1840, to about 12,000 in 1860, to perhaps less than 10,000 in 1865. By midcentury, less than 2 percent of the city's population was black. This demographic trajectory, so different for the rest of the city's people, tells us much about the city's inhospitality to African Americans. Freedom, yes; friendship, no.

Traditionally, African American men had worked on the city's docks, in its shipyards, and in various service occupations. The new immigrants competed vigorously, and sometimes violently, for these jobs. This story culminated tragically in 1863 in the New York City Draft Riots. No matter how one interprets these riots, they always contain a base element of racism. Angered by the efforts to draft poor and immigrant workers, the city's white immigrant men quickly turned their initial political protest into a race war against African Americans. A large but never reliably established number of black residents died—many as victims of vicious public lynchings. Not too surprisingly, after the riots the city's black population decreased even faster. Novelist Peter Quinn brilliantly depicts the African American exodus.[5] Even though we can outline this demographic history of black New Yorkers, we cannot yet establish precise population measures, and we can expect that census enumerations were highly inaccurate. Thus, any construction of rates with at-risk denominators must be understood as estimates. If population counts are low, the calculated murder rates will be high.

The personal violence of the riots horrified most New Yorkers. But personal violence had been an increasing feature of city life well before 1863. The estimated per capita homicide rate had been increasing for several decades, reaching heights in 1863 that would not be reached again until 1971. By 1995, the rates fell below the mid-nineteenth-century peaks. This grim feature of the nation's largest metropolis went largely undiscussed in the nineteenth-century media.

TRENDS — FUNDAMENTAL OUTLINES

For a small population, such as the African Americans, many years often elapsed between homicides. Therefore, one or two missing observations can make the difference between a perceived crime wave and nothing: in nineteenth-century New York City, less than 4 percent of all offenders or victims were black. Thus the data in this chapter must be viewed with some caution.

The ideal graph would show every racial and ethnic group's homicide rate over time. For each group, this ideal graph would picture both the rates of homicide for males ages fifteen to forty-five, and then the outcomes of these rates as they combine in one total homicide rate. Only for African Americans and all others can we approach this, because the racial categorization for African Americans is by far the most consistent over two hundred years. Even an unidentified victim could be given a racial description, whereas ethnicity was both harder to establish and possibly less likely to be reported. Sometimes unidentified victims or floaters (bodies found in the river) were described as German, suggesting physiological or clothing characteristics that made Germans have a different appearance even in death.

Figure 6.1 contrasts white and black homicide rates. The rates here are for all white homicide victims per hundred thousand white males ages sixteen to forty-five, compared with the rates for African American male victims per hundred thousand black males ages sixteen to forty-five. These figures essentially capture the homicides by the age and gender group that does the most killing. In an ideal world, we would have these rates by offender, but for the nineteenth and most of the twentieth century we are fortunate to have good-quality information just on the victims.

In so picturing, the data compensate for the demographic differences in racial groups, though, to be sure, in the case of whites, some very different groups—Irish and Germans in the nineteenth century—are homogenized. Incomplete information makes ethnic-race comparisons difficult: my best estimate for the decade centered on 1860 sets the Irish homicide rate at 37.5 per 100,000 adult males, the German rate at 15.7, and the black rate at 32.[6] These estimates significantly refine the picture presented in figure

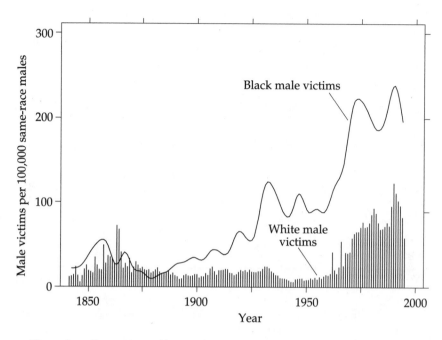

Figure 6.1. Comparison of homicide rates for blacks and whites: male victims per 100,000 males of the same race, aged 16–45, New York City, 1840–1995. Source: see appendix.

6.1. They demonstrate the high rates of African American and Irish homicides, and more generally support the notion that singularly high African American homicide rates are a twentieth-century phenomenon.

The graph in figure 6.1 displays the basic parallel in peaks and valleys between rates for African Americans and all others.[7] Although there are some important differences, examined below, this parallel serves as a reminder that despite all of the cultural differences, it is still one society, and that personal violence crosses all sorts of social divides. At each of the three major turning points—mid nineteenth century, 1930s, and early 1990s—both sets of rates changed together.

The twentieth-century difference in black and white rates is so large as to cry out for explanation and understanding. Much of the discussion of this issue, properly, has focused on relevant racial differences such as re-

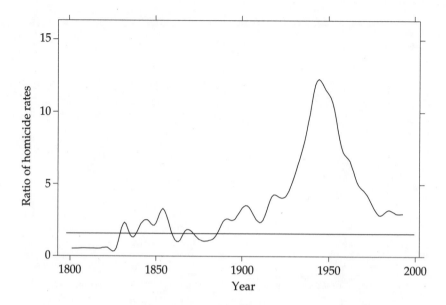

Figure 6.2.   Ratio of African American to white homicide victim rates, New York City, 1800–1995. The ratio is the rate of African American victims per 100,000 African American males aged 16–45, divided by the rate of white victims per 100,000 white males aged 16–45. One equals parity; a higher number means proportionally more African American victims. Source: see appendix.

gion, poverty, discrimination, and the violent heritage of slavery.[8] Here, the data can add a historical dimension: the twentieth-century increase in African American homicides. There is significant growth in the rates for African Americans emerging by the late nineteenth century, with an abbreviated decline during the Depression and a more recent decline beginning after 1988. This latter decline, which continues, represents a decline both in the race-specific differences and in the overall rate. Figure 6.1 shows that the major black-white disparity emerged and grew starting around 1925 and began to shrink after its 1950 peak. This reading is confirmed by examining the ratio between the two rates, the black rate divided by the white (see figure 6.2).[9]

Remarkably, the perception that homicide is a crisis located in the African American community was in certain ways more correct for the early and mid twentieth century than for recent times. The late nineteenth century had race rates at similar levels, with an enormous disparity emerging during and after World War I, peaking in the years between 1942 and 1949. This disparity is not a guide to overall levels of homicide; rather, it shows the *difference* between the homicide rates for two race groups. What could have been making the black rates so different from the city's white rates in the 1940s?

Arguably, the 1940s ushered in the new era of civil rights. The fight for civil rights occurred in a context of wartime mobilization and opportunity, but simultaneous discrimination. The civil rights initiatives often achieved success because the war so starkly highlighted racial discrimination. Progress, including economic opportunity, would come only later. Yet discrimination alone cannot serve as an explanation for personal violence. Nineteenth-century rates were low while discrimination most certainly was higher.

Was it migration within the United States? Three-fourths of New York City's total increase in African American population in the 1940s resulted from migration, much from the rural South.[10] In 1940 only 19 percent of the city's African American males aged sixteen to forty-five were native New Yorkers, contrasted with 61 percent of all white males, reflecting the enormous influx of black migrants from the South. By 1950 22 percent of African American men between the ages of sixteen and forty-five had been born in New York, as opposed to 68 percent of all white men.[11] To discover whether those non–New Yorkers actually caused the increased African American homicide rates would be difficult if not impossible at this remove. It remains a significant component of a likely explanation, however, analogous to the homicide burst among young Irish men a century earlier. Young males from a violent rural culture came to the city and increased their real income.[12] This led directly to skylarking, and too often skylarking led to murder.

RACE AND ETHNICITY

A question of initial interest is the nature of interracial homicides. These can give some insight into race relations and the nature of social rela-

Table 6.1 Offender and Victim Pairs, by Race and Ethnicity

	Victim					
Killer	*Native-born white*	*Black*	*Irish*	*German*	*Italian*	*Total*
Native-born white	27	3	11	4	0	45
Black	7	*31*	10	1	0	49
Irish	14	2	*126*	5	1	148
German	4	1	20	*41*	0	66
Italian	1	0	6	0	*11*	18
Total	53	37	173	51	12	326

SOURCE: see appendix.

tionships in nineteenth-century New York. It must be noted that even here relationships cannot be unambiguously interpreted: a low level of interracial violence could simply be the result of high degrees of social segregation.

Table 6.1 pairs the ethnic/racial identity of victims and killers for those homicides for which we have positive ethnic/racial information. Missing information reduces the total number of cases to 326, or about 18 percent of all killings. The highlighted diagonal shows that some ethnic/racial pairing was common across the range of murders.[13] The least paired, native-born whites, at 60 percent, may be somewhat erroneous because of missing information, the media being less likely to note that someone was native-born. Within other groups, 63 percent of African Americans were killed by African Americans, 85 percent of Irish victims were killed by Irish assailants, 62 percent of Germans by Germans, and 61 percent of Italians by Italians. This ranking makes an interesting point if the more isolated a group, the more likely that its murders would originate within its own ethnic boundaries. By this reasoning, native-born whites would be the least isolated and most numerous, while members of the smaller and more linguistically isolated recent immigrant populations such as the Italians should have been the most likely to work, play,

Table 6.2 Ethnic and Racial Identities in the General Population, New York City, 19th Century

Group	Percentage of population that was male, aged 16–45		
	1850	1860	1870
Native-born white	18	18	16
Irish	31	29	31
German	45	54	36
Black	26	24	26

SOURCE: see appendix.

and fight with one another. Instead, the Irish cluster much more tightly than the others.

These figures can be interpreted several ways, but the most straightforward has to do with opportunity: offenders and victims usually know one another, whether they are relatives, friends, workmates, or casual acquaintances. Even an interracial killing, such as the murder on October 20, 1844, of James Chapple (probably white) by Samuel Riley (black), is best understood this way. Chapple was a sailor and Riley the cook on board the docked brig the *Francis P. Beck*. In this context, and at this distance, we cannot know whether Riley and Chapple had a racial conflict or a workplace dispute. In either case, the interracial killing occurred between two men who worked together in close quarters for long periods of time.

If one considers the "at-risk" population among the city's population groups—that is, the at-risk portion of a group in the city's population as a whole—the varying rates of homicides become less shocking. Calculating the percentage of a group's population that was male and sixteen to forty-five years old yields bold differences.[14] Native-born New Yorkers had far fewer of their ranks in the murder-prone age groups than did African Americans, Germans, or the Irish. For both the Irish and the African Americans, demography alone would have doubled the homicide rates compared to native-born whites (see table 6.2).

At least four killings of blacks could be identified in the media as having possible racial motivations. These exclude the dozens of racially motivated killings during the Draft Riots of 1863, an exclusion necessary because all reports of the riots claim that many victims were secreted away at night. These four cases were identified by examining, where possible, the twenty-nine cases where the victim was black and the killer was not identified as black. It is easy enough to guess that these cases are not representative, but I present them to give an idea of the information available and the dynamics involved.

According to an account in the *New York Sun* on September 21, 1835, three African American men, John Van Winkle and his two employees, Joseph Lindsley and James Dewitt, had returned home to Anthony Street at 3 A.M. after cleaning a "sink," that is, a toilet pit. They had just washed up when their neighbor William Newman, an Irish immigrant who had been in the city six months, showed up drunk and aggressive. Dressed in a long-tailed coat and a black hat, perhaps Dead Rabbits gang attire, he announced that he had been "fighting with negroes in Catherine Lane" and that he meant to flog these men, too. Newman went into his apartment and took off the coat and changed to a straw hat: when he returned, the men had run down to Centre Street. There Newman caught up.

"D[am]n you, I have a pistol in my hand and will kill you," he threatened, and attacked Van Winkle.

"He has got a knife in his hand, take care boys," Van Winkle cried and ran up Orange Street while one of his companions ran for the watch. Unfortunately, Van Winkle was already stabbed and collapsed in a yard.

The watch showed up and found Newman carrying his "large dirk," but released him, unaware that Van Winkle was dying nearby. Van Winkle's friends found him and carried him back to his house in Anthony Street, where he died minutes later.[15]

Three days before Christmas, 1853, James Crumsley, white, murdered twenty-seven-year-old Edward Mathews, African American. Mathews left behind his wife, Elizabeth, and at least one small child. Mathews died when "a terrible conflict took place in the Fifth Ward, between a party of white men, who are of notorious character, and a gang of colored persons." This "riot" occurred after an African American, who had been assaulted by three of the white men, took shelter in a black oyster and liquor saloon at 55 Anthony Street run by Mathews, whence a group of blacks returned to avenge his injuries. According to the newspaper, Mathews "was a sort of leader among the colored residents of the Fifth and Eighth Wards, in consideration of his pugilistic abilities."[16]

African American witnesses testifying at the inquest only indirectly gave evidence of racial motivation. All involved made explicit that they understood the attack's racial dimension, if not cause. The tenor of the whole incident suggests that the attack involved racial dominance of the streets. Witnesses included Mathews's brother, Robert, and William Blames, both "public" waiters who "depend on being sent for" to work at dinner parties.[17]

The affair began innocently enough when Blames, drinking at the oyster bar, learned that it was 2 A.M. Concerned at the lateness of the hour, he decided to rush home. A group of three white "gentlemen" at the corner stopped him and asked, "What are you running for?"

Blames replied that he was going home.

Blames "was a damn lying black son of a bitch," said one of the "gentlemen." He pulled out a weapon.

Blames ran back to Mathews's bar.

"Bob, three white men at the corner want to kill me," he said to Robert.

The Mathews brothers and Francis Johnson ran out to defend or retaliate against the group of white men who had threatened Blames.

"You give me a chance to run while I shoot one of these fellows," Robert heard one of the white men say to the others.

It is unclear whether Edward was shot then or later in his bar, as shots continued to be fired while the groups sallied back and forth. At least one African American fired a shot. Several men were cut with knives. None of the African American witnesses seemed to know the attackers by name, or at least they did not mention it if they did. Their fearless demeanor probably did not deter their making an identification, but it is also possible that, like gang members today, they had so little confidence in the justice system that they knew better than to reveal names. They all knew exactly where to chase the attackers down, at another bar around the corner, the Ocean House.

The men from Mathews's oyster bar chased the whites into the Ocean House, 138 Church Street. By this time the noise had attracted the police, who chased away the African Americans, now a group of eight to ten. The police returned to Mathews's oyster bar to find him dead, "weltering in his blood." Following a blood trail back to the Ocean House, they arrested Crumsley, who himself was covered with blood.

(The strangest witness to this affray was one Susan A. Ledjum, who lived on the corner and watched from her second-floor bedroom window. Awakened by the rapping of the police clubs, she looked out the window, leaning out so far as to lift her feet off the floor. At the inquest, she mentioned her double bed and that she was married, her husband in Philadelphia on business. She recognized none of the combatants and could not discern their race.)

Ten years later, many race murders occurred during the Draft Riots. A month after the riots, an article describing the arrest of John McAlister, a forty-year-old Irish laborer, for the murder of a sailor, William Williams, indicates the nature of the race murders during the riots. The tone of the article, titled "Fiendish Murder of a Negro," captures the horrific incident. McAlister bashed in the head of Williams with a twenty-pound paving block in front of a crowd of "men, women and children, who coolly witnessed the fiendish act."[18] Police caught and arrested McAlister two weeks later.

Four years after the riots, in 1867, William Higgins and a gang of white men murdered Christian Bostwick in Higgins's liquor store.[19] Certain details of Higgins's background are unclear: the *Times* reported that he was a twenty-four-year-old New Yorker, but three years later the census lists a William Higgins similar in age (age twenty-six) and occupation ("drugstoreman") as Irish (in fact, only one of the city's nine William Higginses was a native-born New Yorker).

Higgins testified that Bostwick, a cook on a coastal steamer, refused to leave the store, so he beat him. According to the article, Bostwick was well

known among the "numerous colored population in the Eighth Ward."
Police arrested Higgins.

All of these cases include elements of a racial attack. Typically, the offender was backed up by other white men, and the victim's noted occupation hints that the murder could have involved latent conflict about occupation. The secondary literature for this era indicates that job "turf"
formed an important part of anti-black aggression in northern cities, and
these incidents seem to support that notion. On the other hand, the high
number of attacks that did not carry racial overtones requires that we be
very cautious. In table 6.1, the distribution of victims and offenders provides little evidence of a strong pattern of racially motivated killings.
Therefore I conclude that race motivation alone played a secondary role
in most homicides. Yet in such a small black community, the impact of
even a few unpredictable racial attacks must have been very deep. These
occasional yet lethal attacks, followed by the awful events in the Draft
Riots, imply that New York City's black residents always had to be alert
to sudden violence.

AN ISSUE OF JUSTICE

The study of the role racial bias played in the justice system is fraught with
complexity, even in the present era. During the period under examination
here, New York City changed from a slave to a nonslave city to one with
a fairly vigorous anti-Reconstruction political atmosphere. Throughout,
ethnic and racial hostility ran high, and most New Yorkers were white,
especially after the anti-black Draft Riots.

Immigrants, particularly the Irish and Germans, were more heavily involved in homicides than their numbers warranted, but as the city continued to fill with immigrants in the post–Civil War era, homicides per
capita decreased.

Race mattered in complex and shifting ways, and my discussion here
is based on the assumptions that white ethnicity (and class) played a
highly important role and that the experience of blacks contrasted with
that of all nonblacks is the fundamental starting point. Here the question

is about treatment by the justice system: what were the differences in arrest, trial, and punishment of black and nonblacks?

Blacks had nearly twice the likelihood of arrest and trial for homicides as nonblacks.[20] Race did not seem to affect the jury's decision to convict, however. (It is possible that missing information about trials—which is quite common—biases these results.) Because we have good records on executions, it is possible to examine at least the outlines of the role race played in the heaviest and rarest punishment meted out to offenders in nineteenth-century New York. For this portion of the analysis, the data on the beginning and end of the individual-level processes are better than those on the middle. That is, the original murder notation and any executions are more accurate than records of arrests, trials, and sentences.

Nineteenth-century New Yorkers tended to be opposed to capital punishment, in contrast to our perception of that era. Of the 1,700-plus nineteenth-century murderers, 3.4 percent (fifty-nine) were executed for their crimes. The proportion being executed diminished over time—every year that passed between 1800 and 1875 decreased the probability of execution by 3 percent. Even though a high proportion of arrests were made, there was erratic follow-up. Basically, it was easy to get away with murder, in part because when cases came to trial, juries were apt to give the offenders the benefit of the doubt. In a city filled with bars, rowdiness, and a good deal of physical violence, the all-important coroner's juries often placed themselves in the offender's situation and found the deaths to be accidental, the result of a friendly fight. Beginning in the decade of the 1820s, the loosely parallel relationship between executions and homicides ended—executions remaining at the same level as homicides spiraled upward. It is possible that this represents a measurement problem—the further back in time, the more difficult the recovery of homicides with no punished killer.

The one exception to such leniency for capital punishment came for African American offenders, who were six times more likely to be hanged than their white counterparts. Surprisingly, the race of their victims did not seem to matter much, however. Even this clearly biased system allowed 82 percent of the black offenders to escape the gallows versus 97 percent of all others, and executions became substantially less frequent for all every year.[21]

The suggestion here is that all offenders were treated rather casually by the lower tiers of the justice system, but from arrest on, African Americans had an increasing chance of further punishment, and at the stages of sentencing and carrying out the sentence the system became more harsh and racially discriminatory.

CONCLUSION

There are several conclusions to be drawn from this probe. New York was a violent city, even if not as violent as it is today. Perhaps more important is what it was not: a city with violence committed by people of color. It was a violent city of principally white persons, many of them recent immigrants. Had guns been as prevalent and powerful as they are today, how much more violent would this city have been?

The rate at which homicides occurred fluctuated considerably through this period, but it is important to note that it often dropped as precipitously as it rose: immigrants did not necessarily and always produce violence, as though by some law of pressure-cooking. Persons of color participated in this violent society. In every racially motivated incident, African Americans were the victims, not the perpetrators, of racially motivated attacks. None of these incidents can compare with the Draft Riots, of course, but they do illustrate that even in the safest of times African Americans lived in a dangerous city.

What does the declining racial disparity since 1950 and the actual late-twentieth-century overall decline portend? Will the mid twenty-first century look back upon racial disparities as things of the past? One can certainly hope so. New York City continues to change. By 1990, 51 percent of its African American males (compared to 56 percent of the white male population) had been born locally. This represents a very different kind of city than a half century ago and suggests that demographic and social change continue to reshape the city in somewhat unpredictable ways.

Finally, there are two broader implications. First is a message of hope: rates of violence can come down, even if we cannot yet identify mechanisms causing that to happen. Second is a message about research: we can learn a great deal from the past that will help us think about the present if we are willing to commit the energy to the task. It is worth doing. Coming to grips with contemporary crises as complicated and as ancient as interpersonal violence means coming to grips with a long human history.

anomaly disappear. Ask any knowledgeable person: that person already *knows* why the U.S. violence rates are higher. Because assumptions about violence—homicide in particular—and America's uniquely excessive experience with it run so deep, few have felt the need to develop ideas about it. Thus, there is too little serious questioning of the basis for America's uniqueness. Intellectual complacency feeds policy complacency. Why should violence be a policy concern, after all, if it is inherent, "natural," and virtually fundamental to the American character?

The starting assumption of this book was that none of these long-held beliefs was true, or at least none had been empirically verified. Although there is good evidence to qualify if not discard most of these beliefs, it is important to note that only a few studies of American violence have careful historical or comparative grounding.[3] One of these rare comparative violence studies begins by noting that crime research is "lamentably insular."[4] In order to avoid insularity, this chapter explicitly considers New York City as an international as well as a national and regional city; every step of the way, this chapter considers the background of murder in New York City in the larger Western world as well as in the United States.

FROM THE MONARCHY TO MODERNITY

In the last quarter of the twentieth century historical and comparative knowledge of homicidal violence grew from almost nothing to encompass an elaborate array of scholarly and popular studies. We now have better studies on homicide in the Middle Ages than were available on American homicide at the beginning of the 1900s. Through careful statistical work, we now have measures of homicide rates in the Middle Ages for many different locales in Europe. This work surprised everyone conducting it: rather than finding peaceful communities, scholars found high rates of personal violence wherever they looked, from Sweden and Finland to England and Holland.[5] Charming (we had imagined) medieval Oxford, England, produced rates of homicide more like the late-twentieth-century American city. Perfect, age-adjusted data on most medieval crimes is difficult to obtain, of course. There was very little movable property to steal, and crimes of violence occurred far from authorities. We often know less about population numbers than about criminal events. Because we usually begin our study of crime by looking at the number of occurrences per some population count, analysis of crime in the Middle Ages can become very tricky. Nevertheless, we do have a strong set of independent studies of homicide in the Middle Ages, all of which come up with rates much higher than our romantic notions would have caused us to imagine. These studies often have reversed common wisdom and much social science, which had assumed that the urban and industrial revolutions had destroyed the close-knit, intimate, communal, and safe world of the Middle Ages.[6]

Most Western nations went through an era of declining personal violence somewhere between the late seventeenth and the early nineteenth centuries. Overall, urbanization and modernization brought increased—not decreased—personal safety and freedom from violence to the ordinary person in the eighteenth century. And the nineteenth century—the age of industrialization—cemented a world where vicious personal attacks had become rare and noteworthy. There were exceptions, of course. Liverpool, for example, was a bit unusual in its midcentury violence burst.[7] Some European scholars, in particular Alfred Soman, argue that there has been a more general transition over the past six hundred years from crimes of violence to theft, an argument known to specialists as the *violence au vol* thesis.[8] This shift has taken place everywhere in the Western world—except in the United States.

Research on medieval England has established that rates of violence—especially homicide—were very high, as high as in the most violent American cities of the 1980s. Without the assistance of guns, neighbors killed neighbors, family members killed each other, and all who could took refuge at night in highly secured places. Laws expressed this concern about night, authorizing night watch in cities to apprehend people who were out without justification. Crimes committed at night earned harsher punishment than those committed during the day. People in the cities were lucky, for no such night watch could protect rural people. Cities were places of safety. Guards shut their gates firmly at nightfall.

One medievalist who has studied crime extensively, Barbara Hanawalt, writes of a society "in which men were quick to give insult and to retaliate with physical attack." She goes on to relate such a case:

> It happened at Ylvertoft on Saturday next before Martinmass in the fifth year of King Edward that a certain William of Wellington, parish chaplain of Ylvertoft, sent John, his clerk, to John Cobbler's house to buy a candle for him for a penny. But John would not send it to him without the money wherefore William became enraged, and, knocking in the door upon him, he struck John in the front part of the head so that his brains flowed forth and he died forthwith.

Note that the killer in the case was a clergyman. He and his clerk would have been "released to their bishop and tried in church courts where the punishment was penance," should they have been arrested.[9] Hanawalt concludes that such a violence-riven society is best compared to the American South in the late nineteenth century, when vicious personal violence was common. In any case, the evidence certainly contradicts the picture of happy communities and is a striking reminder that late-twentieth-century American cities were not uniquely bloodthirsty.

One synthesis of medieval research indicates that the thirteenth-century rates were high, the fourteenth century saw a "tremendous upsurge in violent crime," and then violent crime began a long period of decline.[10] Political scientist Ted Robert Gurr has brought together many different studies in what has become a famous graph. He estimated that medieval homicide rates were about 20 per 100,000. The curving line of descent to contemporary European rates followed what Gurr termed a "speculative curve" that pulled together many different places and times to suggest the broad trajectory of homicides. It is this trajectory that has stimulated much surprise and discussion among historians of crime. It shatters the easy assumption that the stress of modern life caused an increase in personal violence.

In the years since Gurr's important synthesis, many more studies have been done. They confirm his insights, adding a modicum of precision. In figure 7.1 I have put together these many new studies and spliced them to the North American data. American scholars have not yet generated data that would allow us to make the splices in 1700 or even 1750. This

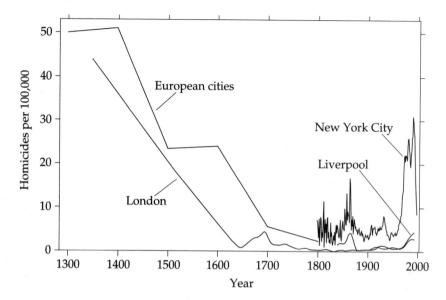

Figure 7.1. Medieval and early modern urban homicide rates in Europe compared with those of New York City. Cf. Gurr, *Violence in America*, 32–33. Sources: Pieter Spierenburg, "Long-Term Trends in Homicide: Theoretical Reflections and Dutch Evidence, Fifteenth to Twentieth Centuries," in *The Civilization of Crime: Violence in Town and Country since the Middle Ages*, ed. Eric Monkkonen and Erica A. Johnson (Urbana: University of Illinois Press, 1996), 63–108; Ted Robert Gurr, "Historical Trends in Violent Crime: Europe and the United States," in *Violence in America*, ed. Ted R. Gurr (Newbury Park, Calif.: Sage Publications, 1989), 21–54; Martin K. Schussler, "German Crime in the Later Middle Ages: A Statistical Analysis of the Nuremberg Outlawry Books, 1285–1400," *Criminal Justice History: An International Journal* 13 (1992): 1–60; and Heikki Ylikangas, *Five Centuries of Violence in Finland and the Baltic Area* (Helsinki: Hakapaino, 1998).

graph averages rates—a suspect if necessary procedure—and shows that rates were definitely declining when Europeans began colonizing North America. One cannot conclude that colonization came at a time of high personal violence, though it was higher in the seventeenth century than in the late eighteenth century, and that may have made a significant difference.

Since the Middle Ages, rural people—and this meant most people— stayed away from the paths and roads near their homes. They knew to avoid the night. Most ordinary people could not afford weapons; anything more than a staff was too valuable. The wealthy, on the other hand, fortified their houses and bought weapons, which they had the leisure to learn to use. By the seventeenth and eighteenth centuries armed gentlemen were common, armed commoners rare. Interpersonal violence, too, was declining, as figure 7.1 suggests.

Rates of violent crime slowly declined in Europe and England from the Middle Ages until by the mid nineteenth century they were at a level that remained low through the twentieth century. European historians of crime now attribute this slow transformation from a rural, violent world to an urban, less violent one to several things, but two interrelated factors seem to be the most important.

The first part of the new synthesis is standard Western history—the gradual spread of the state and its authority: the rationalization and bureaucratization of government, the spread of state organization outward from the towns into the countryside. In this process, habitually violent disputants began to be brought into the courts and prosecuted, and over a period of centuries this made a difference.

The second part is what Norbert Elias called the "civilizing process." Elias integrates the change in personal, impulsive violent behavior with the long sweep of Western European history and the growth of monarchies and the nation state. Standards of social behavior slowly began to be regularized in a way that made social interactions more predictable, and courtesy became customary. Starting in the most dangerous of social groups, the armed courtiers, these practices spread throughout society. Courtiers learned that it was bad manners to snatch food from one another at the table. People hit and grabbed less often. Such urban manners slowly spread and as they did, crimes declined. (This was indeed a slow process: masters still beat their servants, fathers their children and spouses for a long time after such behavior was not tolerated between neighbors and strangers.)

The United States, on the other hand, did not experience a decline in violence until the post–Civil War era, and in this New York City may have been unusually early for an American city. Other evidence shows high violence rates in the rural South in the 1880s, and in western cities as late as 1900.[11] What about the most violent section of the United States, the South?[12] Here the institution of slavery overwhelmed any more subtle social conditions such as demography. Put simply, slavery as practiced in the South required a high level of personal violence for whites to maintain dominance. The South had a deliberately weak state, eschewing things such as penitentiaries in favor of local, personal violence. The consequence: a high tolerance for violence continued through the twentieth century, although the nineteenth-century lack of penitentiaries had been more than compensated for.

This is the puzzle in its historical dimension: individuals brought their impulsive violent behavior under control—self-control—throughout Europe and its colonies most closely resembling the United States, Australia and Canada. Did European colonies in North America start out more violent than the nations of origin? Where did the United States go wrong? Why did it follow such a different path? When did this begin? All evidence points to the formative national years, the time between independence and the Civil War, which unified a highly split nation. From the work of Norbert Elias we know that even a nicely fitted demographic explanation is not enough. We cannot pretend that the demographic differences between Liverpool and New York accounted for the whole story—they actually would not, for murder is not a natural occurrence, a weed appearing every so many thousand persons. Rather, it is the culminating event in a series of interactions, some over years, some over seconds. Murder is the result of individual actions, interpretations of those actions, and then reactions. These all occur in a cultural context tempered by broad political and state-based forms, practices, and patterns. Pieter Spierenburg has reminded us that the American state formation process differed from that of European nations, affecting its criminal punishment structure. If we consider also that the whole criminal justice system was taking shape in the mid nineteenth century, we must use this development to understand the emergence of very different national violence patterns.[13]

In Europe's North American colonies the European patterns probably continued, but there were multiple complicating factors. Cities and civilizers were far away. The center of the colonial empire was distant both in real terms and in psychological ones. The colonies were in some ways like the distant areas or borderlands of the more rural European nations such as Sweden. Areas far from the center of the state were typically more violent. Many of the colonists had rejected some of the controlling institutions of the Old World, such as state churches and sumptuary laws. The slowly created rules of behavior in the Old World did not work as well among people of very mixed cultural-political origins. The New World's system of social relations included personal violence codified as slavery. For all of these reasons, the state itself had less authority. And the colonies were less urbanized; because crime was more likely to be rural, this meant more crime.

Certainly the association of wealth and weaponry translated to the American colonies and to rituals of violence. Colonial settlers who came to North America found that they could own more land and personal goods than they had owned in England. These goods may have included weapons, although the work of Michael Bellesiles suggests that few Americans actually wanted to spend their scarce resources on them.[14] Personal ownership of weapons by ordinary people became enforced by the use of militias rather than standing armies. Requiring a less sophisticated tax system or governmental apparatus than the standing army, the local militia put the burden of military readiness on individuals, who had to own weapons.

Normal institutional practices crystallized in other nations when their social expectations for personal violence were low. The United States, by contrast, went through its era of centralization and unification with high levels of personal violence the norm. If we conceptualize the period between American independence and the Civil War (1780s–1860s) as a period of state structure building, then that same high-violence era set the basic platform of social expectations and practices.[15] It is irrelevant that the high violence did not come from some special national character, but rather from a demographic imbalance toward young and middle-aged males.

Curiously, this era does not have a name or names accepted by historians, who used to divide it into the "early national period," the "age of Jackson," the "antebellum era," and the period of the "Civil War and Reconstruction." Between independence and the Civil War's end, the United States set in place its fundamental law and form of government. This era, which culminated with the end of slavery, saw an unusual federal system emerge, in which individual regional political units, states, delegated almost all forms of taxation and crime control to subunits of the states, counties and—on occasion—cities, which became the actual bureaucracies executing most criminal law.

Cities administered criminal law through constables and the night watch. From the 1840s through the time of the Civil War, cities innovated and created their own uniformed police, modeling them as best they could on the English precedent. Of course, because the American police were local creations, they differed fundamentally from their English model, which originated in the national government. By the 1870s most larger cities had adopted uniformed police, though some small cities tarried another decade or so. From the beginning the additional cost of policing caused considerable resistance to the reform. But the form was set: state legislatures defined criminal behavior, usually borrowing whole from English common law. City police or county officials—the sheriff, also copied from England—caught criminals and jailed them in, usually, county-run jails. Prosecution was done by either county or, more rarely, city attorneys, or, in the case of New York City murders, the county coroner, all in felony courts run by counties. Jurors, including those of the coroner, were drawn from voter pools, which by the 1830s were composed of all white males over age twenty-one.[16] On conviction, offenders were executed by county officials or imprisoned in state-run penitentiaries. The federal government rarely dealt with crime. There was, after all, only a handful of federal crimes—treason, for example.

Federalism gave the United States a highly decentralized state system, variable in form and quality, and closely tied to the locale. Much has changed, of course, since the mid nineteenth century, but the basic contours of criminal justice have not. State legislatures still define crime and punishment, city and county governments still administer the law, and reluctant local voters still comprise the jury pool. There is still no one way to organize a police department in the United States: several voluntary templates were produced in the decades after 1920.[17] At the end of the twentieth century, for example, the Los Angeles County Sheriff's Department patrolled an urban—even an "inner-city"—population of more than one million.

All of this loosely articulated system with its segmented authority crystallized during an era of high personal violence and grudging social tolerance.[18] What would have happened if it had been set during an era of personal peace? Would it have been less tolerant, more vigorous in dealing with violence? Would the social tolerance have differed? American society and its criminal justice system—a portion of the state—all came together in a personally rough world, which excluded the goal of achieving a peaceful one. Sometimes Americans noticed this: reread *Huck Finn*, for example, and one can see Mark Twain coating each painful and coarsely violent interaction with humor—how else to deal with cruel and abusive men like Huck's father, who himself was murdered, shot in the back in a thieves' den?

From a federation of independent states to its post–Civil War unity, the United States had had an unusually high rate of violence in large part because of the demographic consequence of immigration—lots of men. In addition, immigration, including the forced migration of slaves and freed people, had bequeathed to this nation in formation a population of great ethnic and racial diversity. Religious freedom, meaning the absence of a state-supported church, coupled with the opening of the franchise to all white men, had the unforeseen consequence of allowing religiously and ethnically diverse voters and jurors to participate in local government. The consequence cannot be stressed too much: by their own standards these white men were not a homogenous group at all, but instead were of completely different races. Late-twentieth-century Americans liked to think of their society as diverse, by which they meant that racially distinct groups had to coexist; the same condition obtained among what now seem homogenous white men in the mid nineteenth century.

This racial distinctiveness did not preclude integration, on the other hand, for many of the homicide incidents in New York reveal interracial groups mixing for leisure, as well as fighting. The entry of Irish men into politics was met with nativist violence as well as internal bureaucratic resistance. In 1855 New York City saw the murder of a nativist political tough, "Butcher Bill" Poole, by Irish political fighter and former police officer Lewis Baker. At the same time, police chief George Washington Matsell was busy defending his own nativity, and charges of his pro-"foreign" (i.e., Irish) racial hiring preferences convulsed the city council.[19] Nineteenth- and early-twentieth-century racial categories distinguished between Irish Catholics, Irish Protestants, Germans, Italians, and Yankees as well as between the categories remaining today: Africans, Asians, and Native Americans, and each of these groups made similar internal distinctions. Dickens noted of New York in 1841 or 1842, even before the city had its biggest flood of immigrants: "foreigners abound in all the streets . . . they pervade the town."[20] The gangs of midcentury New York were, from their own point of view, race based—the Dead Rabbits were Irish Catholic, for example. In a famous murder just after the Civil War, the victim, Albert Richardson, was a Yankee, and the offender, Daniel McFarland, was Irish: this was an enormous racial difference, one understood by all involved.[21] Making the case more racially complex, however, was the political culture, for McFarland was a Republican, a rare quirk for a New York City Irishman, and one that may have made the jury more sympathetic to him.

In a society composed of multiple ethnic groups there is always a high probability of mutual misunderstanding, of misinterpreting the order present in the behavior of others as chaos or disorder. Rather than assuming that the problem of intergroup conflict is automatic, it is important to understand that for the heterogeneous society to function, high levels of tolerance of apparent disorder are essential. The United States, since the 1840s if not from the beginning, has had to function with an apparent degree of disorder and difference. Tolerance was essential to public space and life, even if the notion of religious tolerance had not been instilled earlier.

Once we understand the code we can see these divisions in racial caricatures. A genre painting, *The First Mayor of Pittsburgh*, by David Blythe (c. 1860), shows a lower-level criminal court in Pittsburgh in the early to mid nineteenth century. This painting gives us a rare glimpse of the criminal justice world (see figure 7.2).[22] The painter has included background detail seldom if ever presented in crime-related lithographs of the period.

The scene is deliberately coarse. The judge, a stereotypical Protestant Yankee, pages through his legal manual. The police constable, an Irish caricature, club (and hat) in hand, is simianlike in his cringing brutality. The offender, a pitiful creature in rags, is clearly more terrified by the police constable, on whom his eyes stay focused, than by the judge or the murky jury. The jury shows intense interest—this is their entertainment. By contrast, two loungers seem to be sleeping on the bench in front of the jury box. A newsboy smoking a cigar seeks to find customers in the room, even as the officer testifies. In this scene, only the judge and his books embody the authority and dignity of the law. For the jurors and—through the newsboy—the media, the law is a source of entertainment. The offender appears as victim and the law enforcer seems more beast than man.

This picture expresses American criminal justice practices of the nineteenth and twentieth centuries. Justice was crude in all aspects, and it daily confronted deep racial divides. A reluctant and negative tolerance had to characterize this world, and this tolerance included ignoring high levels of physical violence. Tolerating a Catholic, for Protestants, was only a little more of a stretch than letting a possible murderer escape punishment. How could one be sure about values when groups with ancient animosities had to share political power as well as public space? Perhaps it is no wonder, then, that juries seldom convicted, judges and governors happily pardoned, and executions were rare.

The crystallization of American local government practices and rules came, then, at a moment of high religious as well as racial diversity, a moment when what we now deem "white male" had begun to shift and encompass a broader racial and religious spectrum.[23] The previous expansion of the franchise meant that it was too late to keep these people who were newly defined as white males out of government. They were an essential part of it.

How does a nation state work with such a violent and diverse society? Other nation states depended on ethnic unity, imagined or real, on some kind of elite solidarity and consistency, on a single state religion, and on the successful state monopoly on violence.[24] This latter needs a bit of explaining. Max Weber articulated the concept of the state monopoly on violence. His point is clear enough: as a basis for enforcing its legitimate

Figure 7.2. David Blythe, *The First Mayor of Pittsburgh* (painting). Blythe captured here one of the few images of a mid-nineteenth-century criminal courtroom. Courtesy Carnegie Museum of Art, Pittsburgh; gift of the Richard King Mellon Foundation.

claim to power, the state must have the means of violence reserved to it and not to individuals or rival groups within the state.[25] The criminal law makes this clear: criminal charges typically read, "the State of ——— v. John Doe." In a republic, the charges can sometimes be replaced with "The People," but in this case the people have vested their inherent power in the state. Crime is an illegal act by an individual person or persons against the state, not against other individuals, as we imagine. The criminal offender's actions usurp state power: only the state legitimately can take a person's life or property.

Private vengeance competes with the state monopoly on violence, so the modern nation state must suppress it. This is not accomplished by some sort of formal act, for the most part, but by a much longer developmental process whereby individuals willingly give up their implicit power to the state. The yielding of individual violence has occurred over a long period since the Middle Ages, through a series of typically small actions. The disappearance of private vengeance in toto was a large development, but it occurred in the context of much more subtle processes. Norbert Elias wrote about this transformation in *The Civilizing Process*, in which he showed how a whole range of behavior, from violent impulsive acts to table manners, slowly moved toward the regular, predictable social order of the modern era. This process, an effect of the rise of monarchies and courtly societies and their subsequent replacement by the nation state, lay beneath the slow decline in the impulsive personal violence that had characterized medieval society. Elias showed that the pacification of personal behavior was a precondition of the complex modern state, and that this slow spread of impulse control, once done, was so mutually beneficial to all that it has become a significant social value.

The continuing and increasing European-American differences in interpersonal violence since the early nineteenth century cannot be attributed purely to demography. The post–Reconstruction era American practices of personal violence and tolerance of it persisted through very different times. It is important to note that the United States in the post–Civil War, post-unification era possibly had slightly lower homicide rates than it had in the prewar era outside of New York City, but this long era of relative stability had a homicide rate much higher than that of England.[26] To repeat the argument: the timing of the high-homicide era made an enormous difference to American violence and the state's response to it. Its continuation represents a kind of equilibrium: we and our political structure are accustomed to it.

And what of American character, what Hector St. John de Crèvecoeur in *Letters from an American Farmer* (1782) called "this new man"? Who cares? In the mid nineteenth century there were so many men that their character hardly mattered. Men aged fifteen to fifty-five made up more than 30 percent of New York City's population, 20 percent more than in Liverpool, another similarly rough port city. This simple and accidental demographic difference partially accounted for New York City's higher violence rate. We do not need to worry about whether or not there was such a thing as this "new man" to see that personal violence was not uniquely American, but that the particular circumstances under which the nation learned how to run itself required a high degree of tolerance for many things, and that these, incidentally, included violence.

This assertion, that Americans unconsciously made a trade-off between tolerance and violence, would not have shocked English political leaders like the Earl of Dudley, a Tory MP, who, for example, resisted the creation of the Metropolitan Police (London) for fear that the police would impinge on English liberty. After a brutal multiple murder in 1811 in London's East End and the subsequent outcry for protection, he commented, "I had rather half a dozen people's throats should be cut in Ratcliffe Highway every three or four years than be subject to domiciliary visits, spies, and all the rest of Fouche's [Napoleon's infamous minister of police] contrivances."[27] For the English, police equaled French political spies, yet the English ultimately led the Americans in creating a uniformed police.

But the trade-off was actually more complex, for it implies that a vigorous, harsher crime control system in itself would have lowered violence levels. Here the ideas of Elias can help, for he has shown how the control of violent and impulsive behavior came in a thousand tiny ways. Looking back at Blythe's painting (figure 7.2), we can see forms of disorder and impulsiveness on a smaller scale than that of murder. The newsboy peeks in the door, interrupting the "solemn" judicial proceeding, and only two people seem to notice—one a juror. The cowering defendant is about to be frightened backward into a bench lounger (or another defendant), who may be sleeping. More to the point, the police constable rather than the judge draws the terrified defendant's attention. The scene gives a visceral realization of NYPD officer "Clubber" Williams's supposed observation that there is more justice in a nightstick than in a statute book.[28]

How different would this picture have been in England? In *Cops and Bobbies* Wilbur Miller develops ample evidence that it would have differed significantly. He demonstrates that from the 1830s and 1840s on, New York City police followed a path fundamentally different from that of London's Metropolitan Police, their explicit template. In the United States the power of the police resided in their individual presence and potential for violence—"street justice"—whereas in England the police understood themselves as representatives of the state, of a larger and more abstract presence. As created, the English police saw themselves as representing the English constitution. This is not to say that they were incapable of violence, but as opposed to their American imitators, from their origins the English police considered themselves an integral part of the justice system.[29] This difference in style as well as substance permeated the United States and has partially persevered. No wonder Blythe's police officer looks like a thug and exerts a clear personal dominance over the quivering defendant. The aggressive police officer on the beat was of a piece with a more lax, uneven, and individualistic prosecution and punishment process. Although English executions diminished in the first half of the nineteenth century, the huge number of felons punished by transportation to Australia kept the system highly punitive and feared.

As early as the mid nineteenth century, American police correctly understood themselves as actually administering justice, punishment as well as arrest. Given the arrested felon's likelihood of acquittal, one can see why. Police officers justify violence during an arrest as a substitute for the punishment an offender may not receive. This deep divide between the theory of the American justice system and its reality may still pervade American police work.

Moreover, as the Blythe painting so vividly illustrates, the courts had good reasons as well as bad to mistrust the police. Who, from the painting, would one rather meet in a dark alley, the pathetic offender or the beastly police officer? And if we imagine the criminal as victim, as this one surely appears to have been, then why would any jury convict?

It is out of this raggedy court scene that our thinking about American violence should begin. No grand passions, no well-oiled pistols, no easy moral divisions, but adult men unwittingly laying the foundation for a violent future. The evidence I have gathered for New York City indicates that although about half of all murderers were arrested, less than half of these were tried, and about half of these were convicted. Of this handful (10.7 percent) convicted, three-fourths were sentenced to less than seven years in prison, and a large but difficult to measure proportion of these were pardoned. Of the 107 murders committed in the city between 1799 and 1821, thirty-four offenders were given a sentence, but only nineteen people actually served time. Of these nineteen, one was executed, three died in prison, and at least ten had their sentences commuted with an average time served of a year and a half.[30] By the 1880s New York State published a table as a guide to the amount of sentences typically commuted, usually at about 25 percent of the time to have been served.[31] One more recent study of criminal sentencing in nineteenth-century New York, Philadelphia, and Boston confirms that "leniency" was the "central element" of the criminal court system in all three cities.[32] Throughout the nineteenth century, as the practices that define the nation state were instituted and bureaucratized, an elaborate mechanism for tolerating personal violence became articulated. Juries sympathized with the offenders, not with the judges, prosecutors, or police.

Although the United States and England make excellent comparison nations for several obvious reasons, one should remain alert to salient differences. Their similar legal and law enforcement systems, as well as the more obvious colonial and demographic ties, allow the focus to be on behavior, not on legal and political detail. But the United States lagged England in many important respects, urbanizing and industrializing some fifty to one hundred years later and getting uniformed police thirty to fifty years later. Equally important, the United States never federalized its policing functions. The states continue to be reluctant to cede criminal justice powers to the federal government, so that at the end of the twentieth century genetic identification remained controversial rather than accepted as a tool for criminal identification as it is in England.

The United States led England in other important respects, opening the white male franchise some half century before England did and, in a linked development, opening the jury system to non-elite men relatively quickly in the same period. The *New York Times* commented in 1854 that in England the jury was gradually becoming "extinct" in civil cases, and its status seemed unsure in criminal ones.[33]

It is difficult to make a clear contrast of punishment in the two countries: England seems to have been more likely to hang in the pre-1800 era, and certainly it had the ability, unavailable to the United States, to transport felons to Australia. On the other hand, the United States did have a famous (if ineffective) penitentiary system from the early nineteenth century on. The problem is that few offenders ever saw the inside of it. Impressionistic evidence suggests that English offenders were much more likely to be punished, and that the option of transportation made punishment harsh. Vic Gatrell estimates that 7,000 were executed in England between 1770 and 1830, far fewer than the shocking 75,000 executed in the century between 1530 and 1630. In the decade of 1821–1830, England executed 672. By this time, national homicide rates for England were probably well below those in the United States, and most English executions were for much less serious property offenses, not for personal violence.

The United States, in contrast, executed at least 1,580 people between 1770 and 1830, and 379 in the 1820s. When adjusted for population differences, the execution rates in England were about twice as high as those in the United States—that is, until the 1830s, when England slowed considerably (347 murderers executed between 1837 and 1868).[34] The United States continued to increase its executions, their rate not peaking until a century later, in 1930. In other words, state violence in England followed a path virtually opposite to that in the United States. During the era when the American system came together, at least some were highly aware of the differences with England. An editorial in *Harper's Weekly* (February 14, 1857, p. 97) pointed out that "when we framed our institutions" the vicious English justice system hanged men "like onions" and in consequence Americans have gone to the "absurd extreme." The editorial pronounced American criminal justice a "ludicrous farce."

Executions should be conceptualized as the response of a weak or at least poorly articulated state to particular problems, whether political dissidence, as was common in late-twentieth-century nations, or to crime. Weak and ineffective states usually cannot control crime, but those offenders who do get caught are punished harshly. Thoroughly legitimate and articulated state systems seldom resort to executions. The trajectory of executions in England is particularly telling here. In the eighteenth century, parliament continued to add to the list of particular offenses punishable by death, but the actual criminal justice apparatus was a ramshackle affair. Executions diminished for many other reasons, but they did so as the creation of a thorough policing system appeared. In essence, the state had traded executions away for an actual justice system.

New York City's execution count may be directly compared to London's. For the first thirty years of the nineteenth century, London's execution count was four times that of New York City's. Then the two cities abruptly reversed positions. For the 1830s, New York's count was twice London's, and after that London's dropped to nothing. In the context of New York City's much greater homicide rate, the city punished extraordinarily lightly. As William F. Kuntz observed for the period after 1830, "New Yorkers were extremely reluctant to execute those convicted of capital offenses."[35]

England's incredibly harsh system persisted after its homicide rates had fallen, but then came to a sudden end. The United States slowly increased its punishment via execution well into the twentieth century. The English justice system—with a nationally authorized police—implemented in the early nineteenth century did not depend on executions. Rather, an integrated and consistent national police spread throughout the countryside as well as cities, while in the United States city police developed on a slow and ad hoc local basis, creatures of penny-pinching local municipal governments.

In the middle of the nineteenth century, a whole armada of daily practices began to shore up violence rates that had originated in simple demographic differences. These all contributed to violence rates very different from the host nations of most Americans, including those committing the violence. Newly mass-produced guns in the mid nineteenth century became popular male consumer items. Politically open coroners' positions and coroners' juries tolerated violence. Trial juries continued this tolerance. A loose accountability became accepted as normal and became embedded in the lower levels of state practices as well as in social practice. This continued through the late twentieth century, when district and federal attorneys only prosecuted cases deemed serious and police followed the same lead, all citing lack of resources.

American personal violence occurred in a context in which the risk of violent and sudden death was high from other directions as well. Horrific accidents often swamped the feeble capacities of the state; for example, shipwrecks just offshore drowned hundreds. Both the site of this study, New York City, and the kind of death studied, the wrongful killing of one person by another, obviously preclude shipwrecks. But a few barroom murders shrink beside the horror of more than three hundred persons dying, as happened when the *Arctic*, bound for New York from Liverpool, collided with another ship in October 1854, or when river steamers burned to the waterline, the passengers either drowning or burning just offshore. In the decade of the 1850s alone, nearly ten thousand people died in fifty-six marine disasters involving American or British ships.[36] The presence of such constant disaster may have swamped concerns about the comparatively rare homicide.

TWO NATIONS: THE DIVERGENCE
OF THE UNITED STATES AND ENGLAND

Figure 7.3 displays the national homicide rates for the United States and the United Kingdom for the twentieth century. These two very different lines need some brief methodological discussion. Although homicides are the best comparative indicators of personal violence, they may not relate to other forms of serious violence—since we only have a good measure of historical homicides, we are not really in a position to claim that they index assaults, for example. A further difficulty may blur international differences: if one reporting locale systematically reduces murder to the ac-

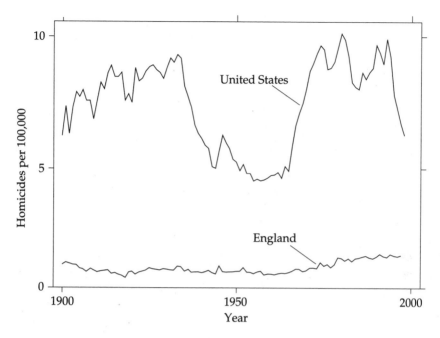

Figure 7.3. Homicide rates for the United States and England, 20th century. Source: see appendix.

cidental category, undercounts result. I have tried to correct for such possibilities throughout this book, but even the best data are still vulnerable to definitional error.

Three things may be observed about the initial U.S./U.K. comparison:

First, twentieth-century U.S. rates average something like ten times those of England. (The multiples have ranged from as little as six to as high as nineteen during the century.) The difference has declined recently from its worst, during World War I and then again in the 1970s; at the end of the twentieth century, the differential was at its lowest, "only" five times as high. The high violence rates of Americans are not new, at least not new to the recent twentieth century.

Second, there is a loose correlation between the two national rates, although almost invisible in figure 7.3 because of the differences in scale. This correlation increases substantially when World War I years are removed.

The traumatic drain of English men to war reduced homicides abruptly, while the limited U.S. involvement in the war made little difference to its rates.[37] In the 1940s and early 1950s, England's rate did not decrease nearly so much as did that of the United States, but clearly some global, or at least transatlantic, forces were affecting both nations simultaneously.

Third, differences between the United States and England—as well as the rest of the industrial world—apparently emerged prior to the twentieth century, perhaps even before it is possible to measure the differences. To extend the U.S./U.K. comparison backward in time becomes more difficult prior to the twentieth century, given the lack of national reporting for the United States and probably incomplete reporting for England. Therefore, to refine this probe of differences, I return to the more limited geopolitical units, New York City for the United States and London and Liverpool for England. New York City and London were the biggest cities in their nations. Both were big even by twentieth-century standards, and therefore both can be considered important in themselves even if they turn out to be unrepresentative of their nations.

For the twentieth century, the city comparison looks almost exactly like the national one, with the dramatic exception of the 1970s through 1990s, when New York City's homicide rates soared. The city rates correlate more tightly than do the national ones.[38] They differ by a similar factor for the twentieth century, a mean multiple of 8, but by a higher factor when the nineteenth century is included: 15.

Not too surprisingly, London's rates are very low, even for the nineteenth century, and it takes a step back to the seventeenth and eighteenth centuries before one can see high rates for London. Figure 7.4 shows the very long term comparison for the two cities. The picture is important for one reason: London did have high homicide rates in the seventeenth and early eighteenth centuries, suggesting that the international historical comparison is not preposterous. But the picture also indicates that London had become very different from its colonies by the mid eighteenth century, prior to the time at which the American data can be used. (London also differed from the rest of England. The homicide rate for all of England was considerably higher in the nineteenth century, about twice that of London for those years when it was nationally reported.)

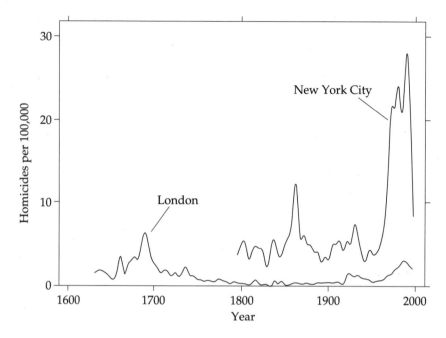

Figure 7.4. Homicide rates for London and New York City, 17th century to the present (smoothed). Source: see appendix.

Liverpool turns out to be a better city to contrast with New York City, at least as far as homicides are concerned, with Liverpool's mid-nineteenth-century rates nearly equal to those of New York City (and as high as early modern London's). (Note that rates for an earlier period in Liverpool seem to be unrecoverable, an instance of the historian's dilemma: full information for the wrong place, incomplete information for the right one.) Figure 7.5 shows the two cities over time. Late-twentieth-century high homicide rates in Liverpool mirror New York's, although at a lower level. Of greater interest, however, is the set of high rates in mid-nineteenth-century Liverpool. These rates nearly match those of New York.

Subjectively this is understandable. Liverpool was a new industrial port city, growing rapidly and filled with impoverished immigrants. Not far from the Manchester depicted by Charles Dickens in *Hard Times* and by Mrs. Gaskell in *Mary Barton*, the city's gritty reputation has persisted

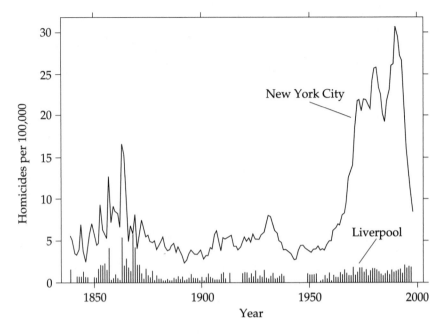

Figure 7.5. Homicide rates for Liverpool, 1838–1997, and for New York City, 1838–1998. Note that Liverpool has several data gaps. Source: see appendix.

until today. Even before the arrival of Irish immigrants fleeing the famine, the city was, as one historian observes, "at the head of every list of in-dices of bad living conditions."[39] As in some late-twentieth-century sub-Saharan African nations, half of the children born in Liverpool in the mid nineteenth century did not live to age five. With the mass influx of Irish immigrants, the city became a site of Protestant-Catholic violence simi-lar to late-twentieth-century Belfast.

Yet Liverpudlians in the mid nineteenth century had the idea that Amer-icans were particularly brutal and violent. The Liverpool *Mercury* often ac-cused American sea captains of excessive violence.[40] At least one Ameri-can sailor actually wrote of his experience with just such a cheating and brutal captain. The sailor, Herman Melville, wrote of his 1839 voyage to Liverpool ten years later in his novel *Redburn*. The nineteen-year-old Melville had seen things in Liverpool very differently from the *Mercury*.

The city's callous indifference to its poor horrified him. He wrote of the disturbing instance when he tried to find help for a starving woman and her two children. He could get no one to hear his appeal and they died. Melville creates a feeling for the city's violent ambience by casually mentioning the murder of a prostitute—"a woman of the town"—by a "drunken sailor from Cadiz" in the context of telling the more amazing (to him) story of a street balladeer. Mightily impressed with the balladeer's skill, Melville mentions how he watched "the murderer carried off by the police before my eyes, and the *very next morning* [emphasis added]" the balladeer was singing the story and "handing round printed copies of the song, which, of course, were eagerly bought up by the seamen."[41]

Melville's description of the sailor's part of Liverpool parallels the more famous description of the Five Points area of New York by Charles Dickens in *American Notes*, published seven years earlier. Dickens wrote: "Debauchery has made the very houses prematurely old. See how the rotten beams are tumbling down, and how the patched and broken windows seem to scowl dimly, like eyes that have been hurt in drunken frays." Melville wrote: "the pestilential lanes and alleys . . . are putrid with crime and vice; to which, perhaps, the round globe does not furnish a parallel. The sooty and begrimed bricks of the very houses have a reeking, Sodomlike, and murderous look."[42] This he absorbed during the course of a six-week visit while his ship took on cargo.

Melville also distinctly set London, which he had briefly visited, apart from Liverpool and New York City. "As we rattled over the boisterous pavements . . . all the roar of London in my ears . . . I thought New York a hamlet, and Liverpool a coal-hole."[43] He recognized that London's size, elegance, and level of civility made it a city of a wholly different character.

A careful examination of the joint high-homicide years in Liverpool and New York—the late 1860s in particular—reveals crude parallels between the two cities and in two years almost identical rates.[44] This has never happened since.

Could the relative similarity of New York City's and Liverpool's murder rates be due to the cities' demographic compositions? As early as 1854 the *New York Times* speculated that of the four main "material" influences on the "desire" to commit crime—age, sex, seasons, and climate—age equaled energy. This energy peaked at twenty-five, as evidenced by the number of crimes per age group, said the *Times* (November 23). In historical violence research we are usually unable to ask such questions. If they are very lucky, historians can establish the rate of homicides per 100,000 persons, even though we know we should look more precisely at the population's age and sex structure. For example, we would predict that a population with a heavy proportion of young men would be more homicidal than one of children or older women. Age- and gender-specific rates measure more precisely the relevant demographic features of violence, but for most early modern populations such figures are unavailable.

Nineteenth-century New York City had a flat distribution of offenders' ages when adjusted for population at risk, as figure 4.2 showed. This contrasted with the late-twentieth-century distribution, which peaked much more sharply at age twenty. Age data for mid-nineteenth-century Liverpool allow a transatlantic contrast with New York, Liverpool charting a route intermediate between nineteenth- and twentieth-century New York's. Liverpool's age rate rose to a peak at twenty-five, then slowly tapered off. At the maximum, its age rate was three times that of New York's.

The New York City rate per total population was higher than that of Liverpool even though Liverpool's young men were more violent. Therefore, it must be the case that New York City's low proportion of children gave it the high per capita rate for the mid nineteenth century. That is, whether because of lower birth rates or the swelling of the adult male population due to immigration, the city had more men in the age group likely to commit murder. Although sociologist Rosemary Gartner is careful to remind us that "demography is not destiny," it did set a pattern in New York and presumably much of the rest of the United States.[45]

The higher age-specific rate for males indicates that, all else being equal, Liverpool should have had a *higher* homicide rate than New York City. That it did not is purely due to demographic differences. New York City's fifteen- to fifty-five-year-old males accounted for 30.5 percent of its population, but in Liverpool these men made up only 24.9 percent of the population. It was primarily the 20 percent more males in the New York population that made it so comparatively dangerous. (Today, for New York City, the proportion of such males is 27.4 percent.) The often-used notion of American character and violence, prevalent since H. Rap Brown's 1960s utterance that "violence is as American as cherry [*sic*] pie," may have much more to do with demography than with anything more exotic.

Urban migrants raised the median age of the population. This was as significant as the effects on the gender balance. When there are few children, a population has a different character, both in constructing rates and in actual orientation. It should be clear by now that the demographic structure of migrants and immigrants can sharply boost any locale's proportion of young men. That these men arrived in a city filled with opportunities, however meager they may seem to us, and that these opportunities led to higher real incomes, which in turn translated into more leisure-time drinking, is so obvious as hardly to need reiterating.[46]

Establishing reliable crime data for the North American colonies is more difficult than for European nations in the same early modern era, and as yet there is no truly usable data series with which to make clear comparisons. An educated guess would put the trends in crime between Europe and North America as about the same down to the end of the eighteenth century. That is, crime probably generally decreased in North America as it did in Europe and England. But trends do not capture the whole story, as crime was probably higher in North America for the demographic reasons mentioned above. By the time comparable data get better, as for example for certain places during the nineteenth century, crime in North America is higher than in Europe.

Figures 7.1, 7.4, and 7.5, comparing the homicide rates in three major cities—New York, Liverpool, and London—over a very long time period, confirm that something unusual happened in American big-city crime in the last part of the twentieth century, a surge in homicides of greater total magnitude than ever occurred in the past two centuries.

A careful look at these figures also confirms that the United States is not alone: London has had an increase in homicide rates since the end of World War II, but it is still vastly more peaceful than New York City. Note that if we were to examine the rates of London alone, using a full vertical scale, then the surge in London homicides would appear much more dramatic than it does in comparison to New York. But the picture also shows that things have been bad before, particularly in the mid nineteenth cen-

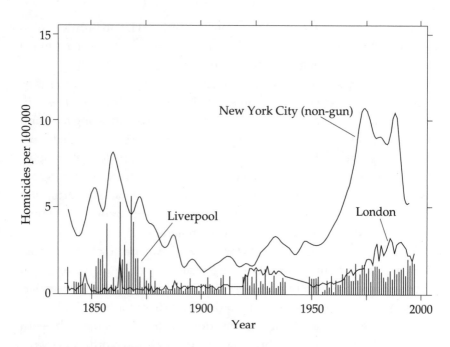

Figure 7.6.   Homicides per 100,000 residents: homicides by all weapons for London and Liverpool, non-gun homicides for New York City (smoothed), 1838–1995. Source: see appendix.

tury. Had social theorists known the shape of this visual big picture they might have been careful to dissociate crime and urbanization, for in the period of New York City's explosive growth and greatest disorder, from the end of the Civil War to World War I, homicide rates declined.

The key to the U.S.-European differences clearly lies elsewhere. The most obvious start is with guns. Figure 7.6 shows the New York, Liverpool, and London homicide rates plotting only non-gun deaths for the United States. The figure employs a severe, even unrealistic, assumption: what if guns were to be extracted from New York City and if those gun-using murderers did not substitute another weapon? Answer: the city would still lead Liverpool and London, but not by such an enormous factor as it does with guns.

Over the two centuries, and giving the English the added advantage of any guns they could obtain, New Yorkers still managed to outstab and outkick Liverpudlians by a multiple of 3 and Londoners by a multiple of 5.6. (With guns added back in, the multiples leap to 5 and 9.4, respectively.)

As is apparent in figure 7.6, the shifts over time in these severely altered homicide rates still parallel one another, those of New York and Liverpool in particular. This parallel clarifies one issue. There are some basic forces driving homicide rates, whether in England or in the United States.

Figure 7.6 underscores another issue: high American violence is not simply a matter of weapon availability. Yet weapon availability did make a huge difference, for it nearly doubled the American excess of violence. To clarify the ongoing debate: Would gun control to the point of elimination save lives? Obviously. Would the United States then join other industrial nations? Even without guns, the United States would still be out of step, just as it has been for two hundred years.

Conclusion

In the seemingly tame 1950s, the violence rates of both New York City and the United States were far below their norms, as low as two previous low eras: the turn of the twentieth century and the 1830s. Yet in these quiet eras, the rates were still far above the norm for most of the Western world. At these most quiet of times in the United States, whether we compare New York City with London, or the United States as a whole with England, the U.S. murder rates were six or more times higher than the English rates. It is only in the late 1990s that the differential dropped below a factor of five. American-Canadian differentials dropped to a similar low (in 1997) of 3.5; in 1950 the U.S. rate was six times that of the Canadian one. In other words, a return to the Ozzie and Harriet days would be good only in comparison to the nasty past and nastier present; it would not be good in comparison to Canada or Europe. Therefore, we should be prepared to remind ourselves that even in the best years the United States has had an abysmal violent crime record compared to that of similarly privileged nations.[1]

The controversial part of this book is its insistence that the current explanations are not enough, that our violent country has basically good reasons for its violence (tolerance, emphasis on individual freedom, and an adversarial justice system, for example), and that consciously to change will require subtle, consistent, and serious efforts. These efforts have to avoid losing the good (tolerance of peoples and ideas) while changing the bad (the criminal as victim, the justice system as offender, tolerance of dangerous consumer items such as guns). Like remodeling a beautiful old house with a flawed floor plan, our remodeling must be done both while we live here and in such a way as to preserve the good in the overall structure. More difficult, we undertake this remodeling with very limited understanding.

We can learn something from the historical cycles in violence: as violent crime drifts downward now, we must be aware that in similar eras in the past, it has always eventually turned upward again. The basis for understanding our violent present lies in the past (hardly a startling assertion from an historian—only the opposite would be). The work to keep driving violence rates lower must continue as vigorously as feasible, or we will certainly hit another turnaround. How do we keep the rates going downward? How do we avoid complacency and an expectation that because things are going our way, we know why?

First, we start with the good sense to know that violence is complex and multicausal, and that no one has all of the answers. Cycles suggest that violence is like an epidemic, one offender having "caught" it from another. All kinds of personal violence rose and fell together in New York's past two centuries. For instance, in figure 3.3 it is apparent that the per capita murders of women track the per capita murders of men, even in times such as the 1970s and 1980s, when there is wide agreement that the homicide epidemic was caused in part by street killings of strangers or in drug-related transactions, almost always involving males killed by males. So why did violence against women also increase in this period, even if somewhat less dramatically? Similarly, almost all serious urban riots occurred during periods of high or rising homicide, as did the Civil War. What reasonable theory relates these?[2]

Second, given that our understanding is still in its infancy, we should pursue every action plan, not just one. Yes, offenders should be caught and punished. Yes, offenders should be treated. Yes, violence prevention programs in churches, schools, homes, rape crisis centers, fraternities, and youth clubs should be supported. Yes, early childhood intervention and treatment is a good idea. Yes, we should implement simple-minded ideas such as manners training and television propaganda on kindness. Yes, we should teach that self-respect cannot be taken away by others and that honor systems are potentially dangerous. Yes, weapons control is important.

Is it not strange that in current policy, prevention and punishment are politicized and opposed? Conservatives emphasize punishment, liberals prevention. Anyone truly serious about violence prevention would not make such a policy separation. No research supports it, nor does common sense. Would we listen for a minute to a politician who proposed fire prevention and not fire-fighting, or vice versa? Or disease treatment but not prevention?

History does not teach us which is the best violence policy, nor should we expect it to do so. It teaches us that we have had enormous violence waves in the past and probably will again in the future. It teaches us not to assume that one particular weapon is the culprit, but it also teaches us that the cultural acceptance of weapons can have very bad consequences. It teaches us that age, race, and ethnicity can play large but temporary roles in violence. These cannot be ignored, but they must be seen as changeable. Finally, we must accept the fact that violence is primarily a problem of men; we may never sort out the whys, but men certainly must accept their responsibility. If men take charge of anything, it must be of the notion that real men don't kill, that self-respect means shrugging off an insult, and that the better manliness accrues to him who does not fight. Other countries have done this, and so can the United States.

Comically inept and blundering little incidents suddenly left victims bleeding to death on the streets of nineteenth-century New York City. Sticks and kicks, stylish swords, rocks, guns: weapons of all rank caused minor disputes to result in sudden—or agonizingly slow—deaths. Or, sometimes, what may have been a long pattern of anger and abuse ended with a final push. Yet, whether it was the long-term spouse abuser or the sudden flare between two friends, the fundamental asymmetries stand out. A trivial action causes a big reaction, and a life ends. Most stupidity and error are easily corrected and forgotten; homicides are the outcome of rare, irreversible actions.

Every homicide scholar wonders at how these trivial and unpredictable stories add up to larger social patterns. If one read only the reconstructed scenarios in this book, one might well conclude that randomness and accident dominated. On the other hand, if one looked only at the quantitative data, one might as easily conclude that social, political, and economic "forces" drove the rates. Homicide raises the fundamental problem of social science: the free and unfettered acts of individuals predictably snap into patterns. Add together enough drunken barroom fights, angry husbands, children with rocks, and young men with Glocks or sword canes, and we have wave patterns that could be mathematically modeled.

The challenge, both for thinking and feeling, is to keep both—the stories and the patterns—in sight. There is no reason that we have to accept a homicide rate greater than zero, but after two hundred years the deeply troubling evidence is that in the United States we will have four times as many people murdered as we should, when viewed in a bigger context. The American heritage may take centuries to correct. This can cheer us, however, if we rein in our expectations for quick success and look at homicide as a history that we can overcome, but not right away. The challenge for the twenty-first century is to keep pushing for lower rates even when it seems as though this is happening automatically. The long-run evidence indicates that rates may turn back up; our goal should be to keep them heading down and, if they do turn the wrong way, never to give up.

Appendix on Sources

My basic approach to data collection and use has been to get the best estimate of annual counts and the most complete possible information on individual homicides. I have used records to cross-check and complement one another as much as possible. For example, the original account of a homicide might not have had both offender's and victim's ages, but later accounts—say, of the trial—might give the offender's age. Or in cases occurring near decadal census years, a census search using CD-ROM indexes of household heads might turn up an occasional age or birthplace.

Annual counts—whether total homicides per year or more specific kinds of homicides per year—come from multiple sources. For post-1930 data, the FBI's *Uniform Crime Reports* or *Supplementary Homicide Reports* are the starting point. I have supplemented these with other official counts, ranging from those of the New York City Police Department to those of the City Inspector in the early nineteenth century. When there are discrepancies, I have opted for the source giving the higher count on the assumption that missing information is almost always going to bias toward an undercount. Thus, for example, I have discovered six individual murders for 1814, and the City Inspector says that there were seven; I use the City Inspector's count in the annual tabulations, but use the six individual records for supplementing the counts by kinds of weapons used. For most years prior to 1976, I have had to use multiple sources—from police reports to vital statistics reports—in order to get the more specific kinds of annual rates, such as by the gender of the victim or by the kind of weapon used.

A question always arises in homicide research: to use murder and manslaughter combined or only murder? I use the combined number because charge bargaining often blurs this legal distinction. I think recent (post-1980s) data combine manslaughter and murder, as there is no manslaughter reporting, whereas in the pre-1950 era murder tallies excluded manslaughter, which was listed separately. I exclude accidental homicides, infanticides, and killings of children under age five except when evidence in individual cases makes clear that these were murders: such deaths were often not reported as homicides. I have excluded the cases of women who died during the course of an abortion, which was often counted as murder. I also exclude deaths of riot victims, killings of offenders during the course of arrest, and legal executions. There are good grounds not to make these exclusions, but for the sake of consistency in reporting I hold to this standard. Those wishing to modify my data may retrieve them from the Inter-University Consortium for Political and Social Research (ICPSR) archives and do so.

U.S. rates are from Paul C. Holinger, *Violent Deaths in the United States: An Epidemiologic Study of Suicide, Homicide, and Accidents* (New York: Guilford Press, 1987), augmented with Douglas Lee Eckberg, "Estimates of Early Twentieth-Century U.S. Homicide Rates: An Econometric Forecasting Approach," *Demography* 32 (Feb. 1995): 1–16, which gives estimates for years before 1933.

LONDON

Basic counts for the early modern period to the 1830s can be drawn from Thomas Birch, *A Collection of the Yearly Bills of Mortality, from 1657 to 1758 In-*

clusive. Together with Several Other Bills of an Earlier Date. To Which Are Subjoined I. Natural and Political Observations on the Bills of Mortality: by Capt. John Graunt . . . Reprinted from the Sixth Edition, in 1676. . . . (London: Millar, 1759); John Marshall, *Mortality of the Metropolis: A Statistical View . . . Bills of Mortality* (London: J. Marshall, 1832); Secretary of State for the Home Department, *Criminal Statistics: England and Wales* (with various supplements reporting data for offenses by police district) (London: H.M. Stationery Office); Great Britain, Home Office, *Summary Statements of the Number of Criminal Offenders Committed to the Several Gaols in England and Wales. . . .* (London: s.n., 1834). Individual London murders and counts can be supplemented with Arthur L. Hayward, ed., *Lives of the Most Remarkable Criminals* (1735; reprint, London: Routledge, 1927), covering offenders executed 1722–1735. London executions can be annualized from table 1, V. A. C. Gattrell, *The Hanging Tree: Execution and the English People, 1770–1868* (Oxford: Oxford University Press, 1994), 616. For London and Middlesex, 1815–1821 (murder *and* manslaughter), see *War Office Summary of the Number of Criminal Offenders Committed to the Several Gaols in England & Wales* (microform, Goldsmiths'-Kress). For a discussion of London Bills, see David Glass in *London Inhabitants within the Walls, 1695,* London Record Society Publications vol. 2 (Leicester: London Record Society, 1966), xxxv–xxxvi.

Howard Taylor, "Rationing Crime: The Political Economy of Criminal Statistics since the 1850s," *Economic History Review* 51 (1998): 569–590, argues that the costs of prosecution caused English crime rates to stay artificially low in the second half of the nineteenth century. Even the finding of murder by a coroner's jury was so affected. This is a serious critique of the English data, which is more plausible for crimes other than murder. Only careful reconstruction of individual-level homicide data, augmented by capture-recapture tests, can confirm his argument. If he is correct, it may explain the higher rates I have for Liverpool in the mid nineteenth century, where the data were drawn from newspapers.

Population statistics come from John Landers, *Death and the Metropolis: Studies in the Demographic History of London, 1670–1830* (Cambridge, Eng.: Cambridge University Press, 1993), 179; E. Anthony Wrigley, *People, Cities, and Wealth: The Transformation of Traditional Society* (Oxford: Blackwell, 1987), 162; and Roger Finlay and Beatrice Shearer, "Population Growth and Suburban Expansion," in *London, 1500–1700: The Making of the Metropolis,* ed. A. L. Beier and Roger Finlay (New York: Longman, 1986), table 1 (p. 39) and table 5 (p. 49).

LIVERPOOL

Liverpool counts for murder (not manslaughter) for 1838, and London counts for 1838–1839 combined are in Great Britain, General Register Office, *Third Annual Report of the Registrar-General for England and Wales* (London: H.M. Stationery Office, 1841), 59–60. Only this report contains murders; later ones fold murder into all deaths by violence. For a discussion of this source, see Naomi Williams, "The Reporting and Classification of Causes of Death in Mid-Nineteenth Century England," *Historical Methods* 29 (spring 1996): 58–71. The population basis for Liverpool reporting in *Criminal Statistics: England and Wales* changes several times down to the present (most recently using the Merseyside police district), and my rate calculations may on occasion be based on the incorrect population denominator.

Paul Laxton and Joy Campbell, *Homicide and Manslaughter in Victorian Liverpool: A Research Report* (Liverpool: n.p., 1997)—a privately printed study—draws individual cases from the Liverpool Chief Constable's Reports, 1842–1845, the Liverpool Coroner's Court, 1852–1865, and the *Liverpool Mercury,* 1839–1846.

NEW YORK

Individual Level

Individual data for 1798–1862 are drawn from the coroner's inquests, which are held by the New York City Municipal Archives, and from daily newspapers—down to 1874—that reported incidents. For some years, the inquests are included in New York Superior (or General Sessions) Court Minutes. Many years have been summarized and published by the genealogist Kenneth Scott. Coroner inquests vary in completeness. I have used information on 1,781 homicides prior to 1875. By roll no. 93, 1868–1873, the inquest cases seem to be only those that did not go somewhere (e.g., the offender was not known, hence no prosecution).

The question of whether or not these sources give accurate counts is significant. I assume that I have only created a lower estimate and that there must be murders, both officially discovered and undiscovered, that I have missed. For the years 1784–1867 I have been able to use two sources, the coroner's inquests and newspapers (or a prison list, 1784–1820), to compare, name by name, which victims are listed in both sources and which in only one. Using these three numbers—those listed only in the coroner's inquests, those listed only in the newspaper, and those listed in both—I have used an estimation technique known as "capture-recapture" to estimate the homicides not in either source. (See Douglas Eckberg, "Stalking the Elusive Homicide: Dual Enumeration Techniques and Post-Reconstruction South Carolina Killings," paper presented at the Social Science History Association annual meeting, November 20, 1998, Chicago; Eric Monkkonen, "Estimating the Accuracy of Historic Homicide Rates: New York City and Los Angeles," *Proceedings of the 1999 Homicide Research Working Group Annual Meeting* [forthcoming].) The annual added homicides vary from 3 to 13 percent more than my initial counts, with a weighted mean of 8 percent. There is no way to assess if this level of undercount was consistent across time, or if it is a reflection of my own methods of data gathering with the human error involved. Prior to doing these tests, I was guessing that my data undercounted by 5 percent.

For 1968–1976, individual data are from Marc Riedel and Margaret Zahn, *Trends in American Homicide, 1968–1978: Victim-Level Supplementary Homicide Reports* (computer file), compiled by Center for the Study of Crime, Delinquency, and Corrections, Southern Illinois University, Carbondale. ICPSR ed. (Ann Arbor: Inter-University Consortium for Political and Social Research [producer and distributor], 1994). For 1976–1992, data are from James Alan Fox, *Uniform Crime Reports [United States]: Supplementary Homicide Reports, 1976–1992* (computer file). ICPSR version (Boston: Northeastern University, College of Criminal Justice [producer], 1994; Ann Arbor: Inter-University Consortium for Political and Social Research [distributor], 1994). Post-1992 data have been regularly updated from the ICPSR website.

These basic sources have been supplemented with the following.

Other Manuscript Sources

District Attorney (New York County), New York County District Attorney Indictment Papers, 1790–1822; New York Superior (or General Sessions) Court Minutes, which include coroner's inquests; New York City police office/police court docket books; Special Justices Watch Returns Felony Register. All in the New York City Municipal Archives.

Jacob Hays, *An Account for Prisoners Received into the New York State Prison* (c. 1822), Museum of the City of New York. Searched by Jane Roddy.

"A General List of All Persons Indicted and Convicted in the City and County of New York from the End of the American Revolution to the Year 1820," roll N-YR 1015, Queens Borough Public Library, Long Island Division, book 15, vol. 15. Gathered by Jeffrey Kroessler.

Executions in the United States, 1608–1991: The Espy File (ICPSR 8451) is a computerized file of most executions in the United States and includes data on the offenders and the nature of their offenses. Archived at the ICPSR.

Newspapers

New York Times (after 1853); *New-York Daily-Tribune; New York Gazette* for the 1750s; *The New-York Weekly Museum,* no. 19 (Sept. 20, 1788) to no. 156 (May 7, 1791); *Daily Advertiser, Courier American Citizen* (Mar. 10, 1800–Nov. 19, 1810); *New York Morning Post, Evening Post Commercial Advertiser* (1795–1825); *Daily Advertiser* (1786–1805); *Commercial Advertiser* (1800–1820); *Pennsylvania Gazette* (1728–1765), searched on CD-ROM.

Other Published Materials

Alfred Trumble, *The New York Tombs. Its History and Its Mysteries. Life and Death in New York's Famous Prison* (New York: Richard K. Fox, 1881).

Pamela Haag, "The Ill-Use of a Wife—Patterns of Working-Class Violence in Domestic and Public New-York City, 1860–1880," *Journal of Social History* 25 (1992): 447–477.

Paul A. Gilje, *The Road to Mobocracy: Popular Disorder in New York City, 1763–1834* (Chapel Hill: published for the Institute of Early American History and Culture by the University of North Carolina Press, 1987).

New York (N.Y.), Common Council, *Manual of the Corporation of the City of New York* (New York: 1842–1870).

Kenneth Scott, *Coroner's Reports, New York City, 1843–1849* (New York: New York Genealogical and Biographical Society, 1991); Kenneth Scott, *Coroner's Reports, New York City, 1823–1842* (New York: New York Genealogical and Biographical Society, 1989); Kenneth Scott, "Early New York City Coroner's Reports," *New York Genealogical and Biographical Record* (Apr. 1988): 76–79, (July 1988): 145–150, (Oct. 1988): 217–219, (Jan. 1989): 18–20, (Apr. 1989): 88–92; Kenneth Scott, comp., *Rivington's New York Newspaper: Excerpts from a Loyalist Press, 1773–1783* (New York: New York Historical Society, 1973); Kenneth Scott, "Prisoners of the Provost Marshal, 1783," *New York Genealogical and Biographical Record* 104 (Jan. 1973): 1–15; Kenneth Scott, comp., *New York City Court Records, 1684–1760: Genealogical Data from the Court of Quarter Sessions* (Washington, D.C.: National Genealogical Society, 1982).

Thomas M. McDade, *The Annals of Murder: A Bibliography of Books and Pamphlets on American Murders from Colonial Times to 1900* (Norman: University of Oklahoma Press, 1961).

Augustine E. Costello, *Our Police Protectors: History of the New York Police from the Earliest Period to the Present Time*, 2nd ed. (New York: the author, 1885), 419ff.

American Antiquarian Society, *Index of Marriages and Deaths in the New York Weekly Museum, 1788–1817* (Worcester, Mass.: American Antiquarian Society, 1952).

Charles Sutton, *The New York Tombs: Its Secrets and Its Mysteries. Being a History of Noted Criminals, with Narratives of Their Crimes, as Gathered by Charles Sutton . . .* , ed. James B. Mix and Samuel A. Mackeever (1874; reprint, Montclair, N.J.: Patterson Smith, 1973).

Julius Goebel Jr. and T. Raymond Naughton, *Law Enforcement in Colonial New York: A Study in Criminal Procedure (1664–1776)* (1944; reprint, Montclair, N.J.: Patterson Smith, 1970). From their footnotes, I have extracted all the murder cases that appear to be from New York City, especially if taken from the General Quarter Sessions of the Peace for the City and County of New York.

For one 1870 murder I drew information from Ted Collins, ed., *New York Murders* (New York: Duell, Sloan & Pearce, 1944).

Thomas Duke, *Celebrated Criminal Cases of America* (1910; reprint, Montclair, N.J.: Patterson Smith, 1991).

A Brief Narrative of the Trial for the Bloody and Mysterious Murder of the Unfortunate Young Woman, in the Famous Manhattan Well. Taken in Short Hand by a Gentleman of the Bar (New York?: s.n., 1800), Early American Imprints, first series, no. 37039.

James Hardie, *An Impartial Account of the Trial of Mr. Levi Weeks, for the Supposed Murder of Miss Julianna Elmore Sands: At a Court Held in the City of New-York, March 31, 1800* (New York: printed and sold by M. M'farlane, no. 29 Gold-Street, 1800).

Annual Counts

For 1870–1954, I used the annual counts of the coroner, compiled and reported by the Department of Health; after 1954, I used the annual counts from the FBI as compiled by the New York City Police Department. The best sources of the public health data are Haven Emerson and Harriet E. Hughes, *Population, Births, Notifiable Diseases, and Deaths, Assembled for New York City, New York, 1866–1938, from Official Records* (New York: DeLamar Institute of Public Health, College of Physicians and Surgeons, Columbia University, 1941), and Haven Emerson and Harriet E. Hughes, *Supplement, 1936–1953, to Population, Births, Notifiable Diseases, and Deaths, Assembled for New York City, New York, 1866–1938, from Official Records* (New York: DeLamar Institute of Public Health, College of Physicians and Surgeons, Columbia University, 1955). Costello, *Our Police Protectors*, 116–117, has some summarized arrest data for 1845–1850. On pp. 158–159 Costello gives Oyer and Terminer and General Sessions trials for murder and manslaughter, 1841–1857. If my individual data sum is higher, I use it. Information on weapons is from individual records prior to 1874, from New York City Department of Health *Annual Reports* for 1873 and 1908–1931, from New York City Police Department *Annual Reports* for the 1930s (note that the New York City Police Department total in the 1930s is different from the coroner's total, so I have taken the proportion of murders using guns given in the New York City Police Department reports); from New York City Police Department, Crime Analysis Unit, Office of Management Analysis and Planning, *Homicide Analysis: New York City, 1984* (New York: n.p., n.d. [c. 1989]), table 102, for 1958–1967; and from individual-level FBI *Supplementary Homicide Reports* data after 1967.

For gender and age, most post-1874 data are from Emerson and Hughes, *Population*, and Emerson and Hughes, *Supplement*.

I have used data supplied to me by Philip C. McGuire and Arthur Haimo of the New York City Police Department to supplement gender data for the years 1961–1968 and 1993–1995; these data seem to give a somewhat higher percentage of women victims because the data include child murders and infanticides, which are typically evenly divided by gender of victim. For the missing years 1956–1960 in the police data, I have used New York City, Department of Health, *Vital Statistics by Health Areas*, also using these to supplement black victims for 1955–1957 and 1961–1962, and weapon type for 1956–1957 (these may give a slight overcount, given that this source gives an overcount of 2–14 percent compared to the New York City Police Department for 1958–1960).

Source for annual conviction counts: *Annual Report of Secretary of State on the Criminal Statistics*, often bound with New York (State) *Assembly Documents*. *Assembly Documents* for 1867, vol. 13, no. 240, includes a complete retrospective to 1832. Summary counts for 1791–1801 are taken from Thomas Eddy, *An Account of the State Prison or Penitentiary House, in the City of New-York* (New York: Isaac Collins, 1801). See also *Second Annual Report of the State Historian of the State of New York* (Albany, N.Y.: Wynkoop Hallenbeck Crawford, 1897), 356.

Arrest data for 1846, 1849, 1850, and 1851–1854 are drawn from police reports in Board of Aldermen of the City of New York, *Documents* 22 (New York, 1855). Homicide arrests for 1854 are from ibid., 6–8, reprinted in Edward K. Spann, *The New Metropolis: New York City, 1840–1857* (New York: Columbia University Press, 1981), 483. For 1884, arrest data are from *Annual Report of the Board of Police Justices of the City of New York for the Year Ending October 31, 1884* (New York: Martin R. Brown, 1885), 4. Prior to 1884, the coroner arraigned homicide suspects; hence few or no arrests appear in the police justice reports. *Annual Report of the Board of Police Justices of the City of New York for the Year Ending October 31, 1876* (New York: Martin R. Brown, 1877), 8: "But, from longtime usage in this city, some of the Coroners (perhaps sustained by public impressions) seem to be of opinion, that all cases of homicide come specially under their jurisdiction, even to the extent of interfering with, obstructing, and in some instances, reversing the action of Police Magistrates having the cases in charge." Arrest data from the 1920s and 1930s are drawn from New York City Police Department *Annual Reports*. Other arrest data are drawn from Eric

Monkkonen, *Police in Urban America, 1860 to 1920* (New York: Cambridge University Press, 1981).

In the mid twentieth century, the coroner and the New York City Police Department differ on the number of homicides (e.g., for 1953 they give 314 and 350, respectively). I think this is because the New York City Police Department count includes vehicular homicide until 1978. When I have coded from the newspaper or coroner's inquests, I have excluded vehicular homicide, which means that it may be included for 1870–1953, the years drawn straight from Emerson and Hughes, *Population,* and Emerson and Hughes, *Supplement.*

For percentages of gun and knife use: before 1875, the source is the individual-level data. For 1925–1933, data are from New York City Police Department *Annual Reports.* For 1931–1936 and 1939, data are from New York (N.Y.) Department of Health, *Annual Report: New York City's Health.* This report is also used for black homicide victims, 1909–1954; note that these counts do not include infanticides and are not age-separated. For black victims pre-1909, I used Emerson and Hughes, *Population,* and Emerson and Hughes, *Supplement,* which include infanticides and seem to have low numbers in the 1880s–1890s.

The City Inspector, an office that became the Department of Health in about 1866, was apparently expected to record ages and causes of death. In the report published in 1810 (p. 5 and preface) there is a suggestion that these data came from Bills of Mortality based on actual internments. The 185? (Yale) text suggests that at this point the cause of death came from the coroner, but whether this had always been the case is unclear. New York (N.Y.) City Inspector, *Annual Report* (New York, 1830–1864). An index to deaths for the 1850s held in the New York City Archives seems to be compiled from internment records; this may have been the basis for the City Inspector's Reports and would indicate internments, not coroner's records, as the basis for the reports. The City Inspector was a political appointment, with a million-dollar annual budget, and apparently the replacement battle pitted reformers against Tammany (Stephen Smith [Health Commissioner, 1868–1875], *The City That Was* [New York: Frank Allaben, 1911], 41–42). The reformers won.

I have been able to find published City Inspector's reports for 1804–1809 (by City Inspector John Pintard), 1816, 1818; at Yale, City Inspector's reports for 1831, 1849, 1850, 1860, and 1863—which has a retrospective summary to 1854; for 1820, a summary in the *New York American* (Jan. 22, 1921), "Annual

Report" [of City Inspector] for New York city/county (with "3 killed or murdered, 1 of manslaughter"); and at the New York Municipal Reference Library, City Inspector's reports for 1854, 1855, 1856, 1857, and 1853–1865 inclusive. It is unclear what the differentiation between "killed or murdered" and "manslaughter" was—a coroner's jury decision, perhaps. Because the City Inspector only tabulated, I cannot compare the names of decedents to see where the sources of differences lie. For 1816 and 1818, the report did include the month of death; in each case my individual data were less than the official counts, and the monthly comparisons suggest that the City Inspector and I agreed, but that I had missed a death each year that he (George Cuming, a medical doctor and professor at Columbia) had recorded.

Full citations: New York (N.Y.) City Inspector, *Annual Report* (New York, 1830–1864). Also bound in New York (N.Y.) Board of Aldermen, *Documents* (New York, 1830s–1860s). New York (N.Y.) City Inspector's Office, *A Comparative Statement of the Number of Deaths in the City of New-York During the Years 1804, 1805, 1806, 1807, 1808 and 1809* (New York: Southwick & Pelsue, 1810), Early American Imprints, second series, no. 20884. New York (N.Y.) City Inspector's Office, *Report of Deaths in the City and County of New-York for the Year, 1816*, published by order of the Common Council (New York: Thomas P. Low, 1817), Early American Imprints, second series, no. 41609. New York (N.Y.) City Inspector's Office, *Report of Deaths in the City and County of New-York for the Year 1818*, published by order of the Common Council (New York, 1819). *Table of the Mortality of the City of New York, Comp. from the Records of the City Inspector's Dept., Comprising the Full Period from Jan. 1st, 1804, to Dec. 31st, 1855, Inclusive* (New York, 1855?) (located in the National Library of Medicine); for 1810–1817, the City Inspector seems not to have reported murders.

Population

In reporting homicides, the convention is to per capitize by 100,000 population. This convention is designed to give a sense of the size of the population out of which killers and their victims originate; obviously, raw numbers of killers and victims mean little without compensating for the size of the base population.

To produce reasonably comparable time graphs, I use as the denominator two different figures: the standard 100,000 population and 100,000 men between the ages of sixteen and forty-five. (I use forty-five rather than, say, forty or fifty-three because before 1850, the census only allows us to use the age forty-five cut-off.) Pre-1880 population estimates come from published U.S. and New York state censuses. These have been augmented with the individual-level samples in IPUMS (see next paragraph) and the individual indexes to the census for 1800 and 1810 sold under various titles by Broderbund. Such technical luxuries were unavailable to scholars prior to 1994.

Scholars of New York City are fortunate to have the work of the demographer Ira Rosenwaike, who has assembled and criticized all official population statistics for the city in his *Population History of New York City* (Syracuse, N.Y.: Syracuse University Press, 1972). I have used his data whenever possible, supplementing it with the more recently available samples of individuals known as the IPUMS (Integrated Public Use Micro Sample) created at the University of Minnesota and with the CD-ROM indexes to the census created for genealogists and marketed by Broderbund.

Typically, we have reasonably accurate counts of population only when the decadal U.S. census is taken. If no other information is available, population for the intervening years has been estimated by simple linear interpolation. Often I have been able to modify these estimates by taking account of known sudden and dramatic population changes, for example, the British occupation in 1776 and then abandonment in 1783; the cholera epidemics of 1795, 1798, 1832, 1849, and 1854; and the influenza epidemic of 1918—all hard, sharp, and loosely measurable effects on the city population. For the eighteenth century, Rosenwaike has reported the best contemporary population estimates. The Draft Riots, too, may have had dramatic effects on the city's population by terrorizing the African American population into flight. I have tried to account for such changes by using linear interpolation from known points, reducing or adding population appropriately.

State censuses were performed in the mid-decadal years from 1825 to 1875. In addition, the City Inspector reported a census for 1805 (which, incidentally, rounded to 76,000 my interpolated estimate). New York (N.Y.) City Inspector's Office, *A Numeration* [miscatalogued from *Enumeration*] *of the Inhabitants of the City of New-York* (New York: s.n., 1806), Early American Imprints, second series, no. 10998. Although the accuracy of all pre-1900 censuses is open to question, it is ironic that there were more censuses prior to 1880 than since. Specific age estimates: For 1800 and 1810, the CD-ROM indexes give age categories for men and women, allowing a count of sixteen- to forty-five-year-old males (the indexes for other census years do not contain the age/sex information). For 1830 and 1840, the U.S. Census gives rough age/sex breakdowns, with somewhat finer ones for 1860–1890 and 1910–1990. For 1850 and 1900 the IPUMS samples allow proportional counts of any age/sex group. For 1865 and 1875, the New York state census gives age/sex breakdowns.

To estimate New York City males age sixteen to forty-five for the years 1746, 1749, 1756, and 1771, ages are taken from "Statistics of Population," 1647–1774, 465–474, and for 1703, ages are tallied from "Census of the City of New York," 395–405, in E. B. O'Callaghan, *The Documentary History of the State of New-York; Arranged under Direction of the Hon. Christopher Morgan, Secretary of State*, vol. 1 (Albany, N.Y.: Weed, Parsons & Co., 1850–1851). To estimate the number of men age sixteen to forty-five for 1790–1800, I use a linear interpolation of 22.7 percent rising to 23.4 percent of the 1790/1800 populations.

We can use 1850, a year of the first IPUMS samples, to compare the age distributions of a sample of 4,514 individuals to those reported for the 1820 census, the nearest tabulation. They seem to be reasonably similar, and the 1820 ratio has been used to estimate the distributions for 1703–1771, reducing the age sixteen to forty-five group by the same proportion as the known 1820 ratio. (The 1800 census does not report ages for slaves, whereas 1820 reports black and white ages in a comparable manner.) Individual-level, detailed population counts were created from samples in IPUMS: S. Ruggles and M. Sobek, *Integrated Public Use Microdata Series: Version 2.0.* (Minneapolis: Historical Census Projects, University of Minnesota, 1997; http://www.ipums.umn.edu/). Additional population data are from the sources in New York (N.Y.) Board of Health, *Annual Report of the Board of Health of the Department of Health of the City of New York* (1906), 2:1008–1011. In 1890 the U.S. census counted 1,513,501 and the police census counted 1,710,715.

For table 6.2, Jane Roddy kindly allowed me to tabulate her total samples of New York City African Americans in the 1850, 1860, and 1870 manuscript censuses.

Table A1.1   Time from Assault until Death, New York City, 1859

Hours elapsed	Number of deaths	Percentage of total deaths	Cumulative percentage of deaths
1	12	25.0	25.0
2	2	4.2	29.2
5	1	2.1	31.2
6	1	2.1	33.3
12	2	4.2	37.5
18	2	4.2	41.7
24	8	16.7	58.3
30	3	6.2	64.6
36	2	4.2	68.7
48	1	2.1	70.8
72	6	12.5	83.3
120	4	8.3	91.7
144	1	2.1	93.7
168	1	2.1	95.8
240	1	2.1	97.9
720	1	2.1	100.00
Total	48		

Changes in Medical Care

Chapter 2 opens up the issue of weapons changes and mortality, but what about changing medical practice? That issue, unfortunately, cannot be resolved here. Even now, access to medical care can sometimes determine whether or not an assault becomes a murder (William G. Doerner and John C. Speir, "Stitch and Sew: The Impact of Medical Resources upon Criminally Induced Lethality," *Criminology* 24 [1986]: 320). Other than observing that the spread of antibiotics in the early twentieth century and the growth of trauma centers in the post–Vietnam War era no doubt affected mortality from wounds, there is one potential way to assess the intersection of medical technology and increased weapon lethality—time from assault until death. That would be a separate study, requiring original information gathering and some educated guesswork, but doing it would allow one to estimate the proportion of victims dying within a short time—say thirty minutes after an assault—versus those who linger. In the past a large number of victims lingered for days or even weeks, whereas today most victims either succumb to their wounds almost immediately or else survive because of medical intervention (see table A1.1).

Even if one were to establish that 50 percent of the victims in the past would have survived with modern medicine, the results would be difficult to interpret. Would offenders have become more vicious in order to compensate for the likelihood that their victims would survive if taken to the hospital?

Images and Archiving

The figures were found using the illustration search engine developed for *Harper's Weekly*, HarpWeek.

The primary data for this project will be archived at the Inter-University Consortium for Political and Social Research, Ann Arbor, Michigan.

Notes

INTRODUCTION

1.   Throughout this book, I use the customary rates per 100,000, and I use the terms *homicide* and *murder* interchangeably.

CHAPTER I

1.   Horace E. Flack, "Congestion in Cities," in *Cyclopedia of American Government*, ed. Andrew C. McGlaughlin and Albert Bushnell Hart (New York: Appleton, 1914), 1:380–381, citing Lawrence Veiller.
2.   Alfred Blumstein and Richard Rosenfeld, "Explaining Recent Trends in U.S. Homicide Rates," *Journal of Criminal Law and Criminology* 88 (1998): 1175–1216.
3.   Arrests are a better guide to actual murders than trials, convictions, or even the nineteenth-century census vital statistics, but none are as good as coroners' reports or local vital statistics. Sources: U.S. Census Office, *Report on the Social Statistics of Cities in the United States at the Eleventh Census: 1890* (Washington, D.C.:, Government Printing Office [hereafter GPO], 1895); U.S. Bureau of the Census,

Statistics of Cities Having a Population of over 25,000, 1902 and 1903, bulletin 20 (Washington, D.C.: GPO, 1905); U.S. Department of the Interior, Census Office, *Report on Crime, Pauperism, and Benevolence in the United States at the Eleventh Census, 1890,* part 1, *Analysis* (Washington, D.C.: GPO, 1895–1896). For 1996–1997, FBI *Uniform Crime Reports* (Nov. 23, 1997) (U.S. Department of Justice [hereafter USDOJ], FBI, Washington, D.C. 20535), internet file on cities of more than 100,000 inhabitants.

4. Compared to other cities with populations greater than 25,000, in 1903 it was twenty-first, in 1890 tenth, and in 1996 sixty-seventh. Of course, there were more cities with reported murder data in the population greater than 100,000 group in 1996 (188) than in 1890 (28), which makes the comparisons problematic. Correlation of New York's size and homicide rate in the twentieth century: $r^2 = .09$.

5. Emile Durkheim, *Suicide: A Study in Sociology,* trans. John A. Spaulding and George Simpson (London: Routledge & Kegan Paul, 1952), 353. Although *Suicide* appeared in French in 1897, it did not appear in English until 1951. The lack of an English translation until the mid twentieth century plus the lack of emphasis in Durkheim's throwaway comment on homicide may explain why this empirical critique of the correlation between urbanization and violence has had so little impact.

6. G. de Beaumont and A. de Tocqueville, *On the Penitentiary System in the United States and Its Application in France: With an Appendix on Penal Colonies, and Also, Statistical Notes,* trans. Francis Lieber (Philadelphia: Carey, Lea & Blanchard, 1833), xx–xxii.

7. Adna Ferrin Weber, *The Growth of Cities in the Nineteenth Century: A Study in Statistics* (New York: published for Columbia University by the Macmillan Co., 1899), 407, 442.

8. Big city correlation: $r = .2$; smaller cities: $r = -.14$.

9. Roger Lane, "The Social Meaning of Homicide Trends in America," in *Violence in America,* vol. 1, *The History of Crime,* ed. Ted Robert Gurr (Newbury Park, Calif.: Sage, 1989), 55–79, 65.

10. Noted by Roger Lane in a pioneering article, "Crime and Criminal Statistics in Nineteenth-Century Boston," *Journal of Social History* 2 (1968): 157–163.

11. Weber, *Growth,* 459–468, contrasts New York City's denser wards with sections of other Western cities, notably with London's Bethnal Green, but confidently shows how the density decreases as an area ages, calling the whole process "city-building." Like most progressives of his time, Weber saw in the rise of suburbs the hope for alleviating crowding (475).

12. See Kenneth T. Jackson, "100 Years of Being Really Big," *New York Times,* Dec. 28, 1997.

13. The notion of an underclass has such historical ambiguity that it is almost impossible to employ in an empirical analysis. For essays on the historical context in the United States, see Michael B. Katz, ed., *The "Underclass" Debate: Views*

from History (Princeton, N.J.: Princeton University Press, 1993). The lack of a relationship between unemployment and many kinds of crime probably comes as a surprise to many people: see James Q. Wilson and Philip J. Cook, "Unemployment and Crime—What Is the Connection?" *The Public Interest* (spring 1985): 3–8; Philip J. Cook and Gary A. Zarkin, "Crime and the Business Cycle," *Journal of Legal Studies* 14 (Jan. 1985): 115–128.

14.   Counts of murder victims by gender allow us to estimate whether the end of Prohibition lowered murder rates:

Year	Women	Men
1928	66	336
1929	91	334
1930	86	408
1931	113	475
1932	119	460
1933	103	438
1934	92	366

Note that even in Chicago, the estimates of murders related to the "Beer Wars" and other gang killings to control the illegal liquor trade amounted at most to 10.7 percent of all murders, 1923–1926.

Based on the 2,001 total Chicago murders in Chicago Board of Health, *Report of the Department of Health,* vital statistics (Chicago, 1932), p. 1138; and 215 gang murders for all of Cook County reported by Illinois Association for Criminal Justice, *Organized Crime in Chicago,* by John Landesco, with a new introduction by Mark H. Haller (Chicago: University of Chicago Press, 1968), p. 97.

15.   New York (State) Legislature, Senate Committee on Police Dept. of the City of New York, *Report of Special Committee Appointed to Investigate the Police Department of the City of New York, Transmitted to the Legislature January 18, 1895* [Lexow Committee] (Albany, N.Y.: J. B. Lyon, state printer, 1895).

16.   Edith Abbott, "The Civil War and the Crime Wave of 1865–70," *Social Service Review* (June 1927): 212–234. I must point out that I earlier presented evidence that strongly contradicted this theory, but ignored it because the idea was so compelling: Eric H. Monkkonen, *Police in Urban America, 1860–1920* (New York: Cambridge University Press, 1981), 77 and 81.

17.   The literature on this topic is enormous. For historians, the starting point is George Rudé, *The Crowd in History: A Study of Popular Disturbances in France and England, 1730–1848* (New York: Wiley, 1964).

18.   The turn-of-the-century trough shown here parallels one previously identified by comparing murder arrest data for the largest U.S. cities, 1860–1920, which showed a bottom reversal point in 1893. See Eric H. Monkkonen and Catrien Bijleveld, "Cross-Sectional and Dynamic Analysis of the Concomitants of Police

Behavior," *Historical Methods* (spring 1991): 16–24. These data graph a decline from the Civil War and an increase from 1893 until 1920. The sixty-year series was not long enough to capture the repeated cycles of homicide.

19. This is not an entirely crazy idea. In 1998 George Edward Tita chaired an American Society of Criminology panel, "In Search of Diffusion: Methods for Identifying Changes in the Spatial and Temporal Distribution of Homicides," which discussed the spread of homicide and violence from one neighborhood to another.

20. Arthur M. Schlesinger Jr., *The Cycles of American History* (Boston: Houghton Mifflin, 1986), 25, 420. Plotting the homicide rates against Schlesinger's cycles or against those proposed by David M. Gordon, Richard Edwards, and Michael Reich in *Segmented Work, Divided Workers: The Historical Transformation of Labor in the United States* (New York: Cambridge University Press, 1982), 9, has virtually no predictive power.

21. The literature on the issue-attention cycle is extensive, from Anthony Downs, "The 'Issue-Attention Cycle,'" *The Public Interest* 28 (1972): 38–50, to Frank R. Baumgartner and Bryan D. Jones, *Agendas and Instability in American Politics* (Chicago: University of Chicago Press, 1993).

CHAPTER 2

1. Andie Tucher narrates this astounding affair in *Froth and Scum: Truth, Beauty, Goodness, and the Ax Murder in America's First Mass Medium* (Chapel Hill: University of North Carolina Press, 1994), 99–107, 193–195. Tucher points out that this trial had a political element: the Colts associated with Whigs, the police and the prosecution with Democrats. The Colts had a strange history of personal involvement with weapons: Samuel's son Caldwell was murdered with a gun in 1894. R. L. Wilson, *Colt, an American Legend: The Official History of Colt Firearms from 1836 to the Present* (New York: Abbeville Press, 1985), 154.

2. Robert J. Cottrol points out that semiautomatic pistols became functional by World War I: "Hard Choices and Shifted Burdens: American Crime and American Justice at the End of the Century," *George Washington Law Review* 65 (March 1997): 515–516.

3. Fred L. Israel, ed., *1897 Sears Roebuck Catalog* (reprint, New York: Chelsea House, 1976), n.p. Roger Lane has found one Philadelphia murder case in which the (unintentional) killer announced: "Hear my Bull Dog bark!" *Roots of Violence in Black Philadelphia, 1860–1900* (Cambridge, Mass.: Harvard University Press, 1986), 146.

4. At the time, handguns were a three-million-dollar business. Cited in H. C. Brearley, *Homicide in the United States* (1932; reprint, Montclair, N.J.: Patterson Smith, 1969), 74.

5. Roger Lane, *Violent Death in the City: Suicide, Accident, and Murder in Nineteenth-Century Philadelphia* (Cambridge, Mass.: Harvard University Press, 1979).

6. Gordon B. Minnis, *American Primitive Knives, 1770–1870*, with photography by Daniel Fox (Bloomfield, Ont.: Museum Restoration Service, 1983); Yvan De Riaz, *The Book of Knives* (New York: Crown, 1981); Joseph Beeston Himsworth, *The Story of Cutlery, from Flint to Stainless Steel* (London: Benn, 1953).

7. Harold L. Peterson, *American Knives: The First History and Collectors' Guide* (New York: Scribners, 1958), 200, 208. Personal conversations with a Culver City gun store owner and the New York Police Department (NYPD) museum chief.

8. William J. Burtscher, *The Romance behind Walking Canes* (Philadelphia: Dorrance, 1945), 59. Gun dealers have told me that a very high-tech, very lethal, and illegal (because of concealed-weapon laws) sword cane is available today.

9. *New York Times*, Dec. 3, 1855.

10. For a clear explanation of the rather complex manufacturing and patent issues surrounding early American handguns, see Roy C. McHenry and Walter F. Roper, *Smith & Wesson Hand Guns* (Harrisburg, Pa.: Stackpole, 1958), 1–32.

11. Alden Hatch, *Remington Arms in American History* (New York: Rinehart, 1956), 105–112. The kind of Colt weapon most commonly associated with the name, the Single-Action Army, was introduced in 1873.

12. Wilson, *Colt*, 362–364.

13. The gun type is mentioned in the *New York Times*'s Nov. 26, 1869, article, which also includes the account of the earlier assault. See Hatch, *Remington Arms*, 358, for a description of the Zig-Zag gun. For a full narrative of this melodramatic story, see George Cooper, *Lost Love: A True Story of Passion, Murder, and Justice in Old New York* (New York: Pantheon House, 1994), 14. For a full analysis of the Sickles and McFarland affairs, see Hendrik Hartog, "Lawyering, Husbands' Rights, and the 'Unwritten Law' in Nineteenth-Century America," *Journal of American History* 84 (June 1997): 66–96.

14. *New York Times*, Dec. 21, 1874.

15. *New York Times*, Nov. 22, 1863. It is hard to find these people in the manuscript census, raising the question of their "prominence." There is a Eugene Keteltas, age forty-six in 1850, who is a lawyer, but if he is William's father, William is not in the household, nor could I find him. William is in the 1854 city directory, with no occupation listed. Could William have been the grandson of the feisty Republican politician William Keteltas? See Alfred F. Young, *The Democratic Republicans of New York: The Origins, 1763–1797* (Chapel Hill: University of North Carolina Press, 1967), 476–495.

16. *New York Times*, May 10, 11, and 19, 1864.

17. Note that the percentages quoted vary due to missing information on the other variables—ethnicity and gender, for instance.

18. Michael A. Bellesiles, "The Origins of Gun Culture in the United States, 1760–1865," *Journal of American History* 83 (1996): 425–455. He argues that the Civil War, the rise of mass manufacturing, and efforts by the state governments to make

militias arm themselves resulted in much-increased ownership by the 1870s. He buttresses some of his argument with out-of-date murder statistics, but the work he has done on gun culture makes a significant contribution to our knowledge of weapons.

19. Coroner's inquest, May 25, 1821. District Attorney (New York County), New York County District Attorney Indictment Papers, 1790–1822.

20. John Marshall, *Mortality of the Metropolis: A Statistical View of the Number of Persons Reported to Have Died, of Each of More than 100 Kinds of Disease and Casualties within the Bills of Mortality, in Each of the Two Hundred and Four Years, 1629–1831: Accompanied with a Variety of Statistical Accounts, Illustrative of the Progress and Extent of the Amount Expended for the Maintenance of the Poor* . . . (London: printed for J. Marshall, 1832). Data cited from unpaginated fold-out table, "An Account of the Number of Deaths." Supplemented with Thomas Birch, ed., *Collection of Yearly Bills of Mortality, 1657–1758* (London: Millar, 1759).

21. *Tribune*, Dec. 25, 1858.

22. "*Harper's* was aimed at the middle and upper socio-economic classes, and tried not to print anything that it considered unfit for the entire family to read." (John Adler, Statement of the Publisher, on HarpWeek website: http://app.harpweek.com/DataCode/Menu.asp).

23. I have been unable to identify either the editor, J. S. Vincent, or the journal, the *New Era*. There were several publications with this title in 1865.

24. Douglas S. Weil and David Hemenway, "Loaded Guns in the Home: Analysis of a National Random Survey of Gun Owners," *Journal of the American Medical Association* 267, no. 22 (June 10, 1992): 30–33. Other surveys find somewhat different distributions, but they are not national. In Michigan, two-thirds of households own guns: A. P. Rafferty, J. C. Thrush, P. K. Smith, and H. B. McGee, "Validity of a Household Gun Question in a Telephone Survey," *Public Health Reports* 110, no. 3 (May–June 1995): 282–288.

25. These proportions are extracted from the individual data set. Corroborating antebellum data may be extracted from the reports of the City Inspector (the forerunner of the Department of Health), which may have been compiled, in turn, from cemetery reports, somewhat unreliable. The ratio of gun murders to knife murders for 1854 through 1857 combined was .89.

26. George T. Strong, in his diary in 1838, noted that his father confirmed a recent article claiming that Burr had practiced, saying that he had visited Burr's residence, where he saw a "board" set up as a target. Strong's father did not actually see the target practice and, as a Whig, he disagreed with Burr's politics. Allan Nevins and Milton Halsey Thomas, eds., *The Diary of George Templeton Strong*, vol. 1, *Young Man in New York, 1835–1849* (New York: Macmillan, 1952), 82. A similar remark is quoted by Arnold A. Rogow, *A Fatal Friendship: Alexander Hamilton and*

Aaron Burr (New York: Hill & Wang, 1998), 255. Burr was at the time vice president, and Sean Wilentz points out that he was not impeached, either—in fact, he presided over a judicial impeachment (Sean Wilentz, "It Depends on How You Define Murder," *Los Angeles Times*, Nov. 22, 1998).

27. Rogow and others suggest that Hamilton committed suicide by duel. See Rogow, *Fatal Friendship*, chapter 11, for a summary of the various interpretations of both men's characters and a discussion of the cloud under which Burr lived for the rest of his life.

28. The oration that got Philip Hamilton killed: George I. Eacker (d. 1804), *An Oration Delivered at the Request of the Officers of the Brigade of the City and County of New York, and of the County of Richmond: Before Them, and the Mechanic, Tammany, and Coopers' Societies, on the Fourth of July, 1801, in Commemoration of the Twenty-fifth Anniversary of American Independence* (New York: printed for William Durell, 1801), 23 pp. Early American Imprints, second series, no. 430.

29. This gun is now owned by the Chase Manhattan Bank. Analyzed in Merrill Lindsay, "Pistols Shed Light on Famed Duel," *Smithsonian* 7/8 (Nov. 1976): 94–98, cited by Rogow, *Fatal Friendship*, 326.

30. Neither Eacker nor Price appears in biographical dictionaries of the period, nor does Eacker appear in the 1800 manuscript census.

31. Robert M. Goodwin, *Trial of Robert M. Goodwin, on an Indictment of Manslaughter for Killing James Stoughton, Esq., in Broadway, in the City of New-York, on the 21st Day of December, 1819. Tried at the Court of General Sessions of the Peace Held in and for the Body of the City and County of New-York. Including the Arguments of Counsel and Opinions and Orders of the Court on a Motion to Bail the Prisoner, Previous to His Trial, after the Finding of a Coroner's Inquest of Wilful Murder, and a Verdict by a Grand Jury of Manslaughter. And a Further Motion to Bail on the Petit Jury Being Polled and Disagreeing in Their Verdict, and Being Final Discharge at the Close of the Session, after a Trial Which Lasted Five Days, Having Began on the 14th and Ended on the 18th Day of March, 1820. And Also a Motion to Bail on a Writ of Habeas Corpus Before His Honour the Mayor, at His Office in the City-hall. And a Like Motion Before His Honour Chief Justice Spencer, at His Chambers, with His Opinion and Order to Admit the Prisoner to Bail. Taken in Shorthand by William Sampson* . . . (New York: G. L. Birch & Co., 1820–1821).

32. See Peterson, *American Knives*.

33. *New York Times*, Dec. 20, 1865.

34. Case reconstructed from Superior [or General Sessions] Court Minutes and Coroner's Inquest. District Attorney (New York County), New York County District Attorney Indictment Papers, 1790–1822.

35. Phillip L. Walker, "Wife Beating, Boxing, and Broken Noses: Skeletal Evidence for the Cultural Patterning of Interpersonal Violence," in *Troubled Times: Violence*

and Warfare in the Past, ed. D. Martin and D. Frayer (Langhorne, Pa.: Gordon and Breach, 1997), 145–175; see also Elliot J. Gorn, *The Manly Art: Bare-knuckle Prize Fighting in America* (Ithaca, N.Y.: Cornell University Press, 1986).

36. The difference is best seen in the correlation coefficients (r) of the homicide rate and non–gun/knife weapons before and after 1932/1933, which show the virtual reverse of the relationship as they switch from .21 to –.83.

37. Geoffrey Canada, *Fist, Stick, Knife, Gun: A Personal History of Violence in America* (Boston: Beacon Press, 1995).

38. Note that this statement cannot be backed with evidence: Are attempted murders by knife more successful than those by pistol? Possibly, but how could we prove this?

CHAPTER 3

1. *New York Tribune,* Nov. 20, 1858. Stackpole was probably an Irish immigrant, a brother of the only Stackpole in the 1850 manuscript census, Agnes, an Irish immigrant, age 20; Agnes became Ann in the 1860 census. Could they have been related to Patrick Stackpole, who had killed his child a month earlier, in October 1858? David Fox, 42, native-born father of at least three children, was a carman. The probability of this murder also being an ethnic conflict is high, if not absolutely verifiable.

2. Richard B. Felsen, "Big People Hit Little People: Sex Differences in Physical Power and Interpersonal Violence," *Criminology* 34 (1996): 433–452.

3. Martin Daly and Margo Wilson, *Homicide* (New York: A. de Gruyter, 1988). For an excellent theoretical overview, see Nancy A. Crowell and Ann W. Burgess, eds., *Understanding Violence against Women* (Washington, D.C.: National Academy Press, 1996), 49–72. For a useful overview of the various theories, see Jacquelyn W. White and Robin M. Kowalski, "Male Violence toward Women: An Integrated Perspective," in *Human Aggression: Theories, Research, and Implications for Policy,* ed. Russell G. Geen and Edward Donnerstein (San Diego: Academic Press, 1998), 205–212.

4. Deborah Blum, *Sex on the Brain: The Biological Differences between Men and Women* (New York: Viking, 1997), 175.

5. Richard E. Nisbett and Dov Cohen, *Culture of Honor: The Psychology of Violence in the South* (Boulder, Colo.: Westview, 1996).

6. Geoffrey Canada, *Fist, Stick, Knife, Gun: A Personal History of Violence in America* (Boston: Beacon Press, 1995).

7. David Kennedy, Anne M. Piehl, and Anthony A. Braga, "Youth Violence in Boston: Gun Markets, Serious Youth Offenders, and a Use-Reduction Strategy," *Law and Contemporary Problems* 59 (1998): 170.

8. Here r = –.38.

9. Here r² for percentage of women with the total homicide rate when overall rates are less than 10 per 100,000 is .04; for more than 10 per 100,000, .20, with a negative slope.

10. George F. E. Rudé, *The Crowd in the French Revolution* (Oxford: Clarendon Press, 1959), may have been the earliest influential work on the rational crowd.

11. For an excellent summary of the city's riots, see Paul Gilje's entry, "Riots," in *The Encyclopedia of New York City*, ed. Kenneth T. Jackson (New Haven: Yale University Press, 1995), 1006–1007. A recent work in progress on New York politics by Tyler Anbinder shows that "Dead Rabbits" probably was not the name of an actual gang, but a name created by the media applying the phrase—which meant tough dude—to groups of young men who may or may not have been gang members. Unfortunately, I discovered my repetition of this error only after completing this manuscript. I wish to thank Professor Anbinder for sharing this discovery with me.

12. For a recent analysis and list of deaths in the Draft Riots, see Iver Bernstein, *The New York City Draft Riots: Their Significance for American Society and Politics in the Age of the Civil War* (New York: Oxford University Press, 1990).

13. *New York Tribune*, Nov. 9, 1874.

14. For a discussion that sets violence against women in a class context, see Pamela Haag, "The 'Ill-Use of a Wife': Patterns of Working-Class Violence in Domestic and Public New York City, 1860–1880," *Journal of Social History* 25 (spring 1992): 447–477. Haag argues that aggression against wives was an aspect of property control by men.

15. *New York Times*, June 24, 1864.

16. *New York Times*, July 3, 1864.

17. In New York City in the post-1975 era, 52 percent of young or old victims were male versus 82 percent male for victims between ages eleven and seventy-five. In the United States as a whole a similar balance held for old or young victims: 51.67 percent were male.

18. For an excellent summary, see Peter Hoffer and Natalie Hull, *Murdering Mothers: Infanticide in England and New England, 1558–1803* (New York: New York University Press, 1981); on pp. 54–55 they argue that prosecution of infanticide varied with hostility toward women, as in witchcraft trials.

19. There is an early medical dissertation on the subject that gives instructions on autopsies to determine if the infant was born alive. John B. Beck, *An Inaugural Dissertation on Infanticide . . .* (New York: J. Seymour, 1817). See also Hoffer and Hull, *Murdering Mothers*.

20. *New York Tribune*, Nov. 19, 1859.

21. Mentioned in Thomas McDade, *The Annals of Murder: A Bibliography of Books and Pamphlets on American Murders from Colonial Times to 1900* (Norman: University of Oklahoma Press, 1961). Trial transcript in William Sampson, *Murders: Re-*

port of the Trial of James Johnson, a Black Man, for the Murder of Lewis Robinson, a Black Man . . . : Also, the Trial of John Sinclair, a German . . . for the Murder of David Hill . . . (New York: Southwick and Pelsue, 1811), Early American Imprints, second series, no. 23446. Quotations from pp. 8, 17.

22. Sampson, *Murders,* 8, 17.

23. *New York Times,* Oct. 5–6, 1854.

24. Alfred Henry Lewis, *Richard Croker* (New York: Life Publishing, 1901).

25. This is a simplified and cleaned-up version of this vicious conflict. Details of both affrays are in the *New York Times,* Nov. 4, 1872.

26. See Timothy J. Gilfoyle, *City of Eros: New York City, Prostitution, and the Commercialization of Sex, 1790–1920* (New York: Norton, 1992).

27. *New York Daily Tribune,* Dec. 19, 1854. For a discussion by a psychologist of the role of scripts in aggression, see L. Rowell Huesmann, "The Role of Social Information Processing and Cognitive Schema in the Acquisition and Maintenance of Habitual Aggressive Behavior," in *Human Aggression,* ed. Geen and Donnerstein, 73–110.

28. Lincoln Steffans, *The Autobiography of Lincoln Steffans* (New York: Harcourt, Brace, 1931), 248.

29. Here I employ the late-twentieth-century meaning of *disrespect.* Anthropologists and historians consider this to be dishonor, for respect comes from within whereas honor is conferred by others. Hence, one's honor can be attacked, but not one's respect.

30. This incident is taken from the coroner's inquest, New York Superior [or General Sessions] Court Minutes (1811), which include coroner's inquests for this year, and from District Attorney (New York County), New York County District Attorney Indictment Papers (1811).

31. In late-twentieth-century New York City (1994), the proportions are 4 percent and 17 percent of the pathetic 12 percent where relationship is noted. Almost none of the FBI's *Supplementary Homicide Report* data have relationship coded. Pearson chi²(1) = 1.9038, Pr. = 0.168.

32. Marvin Wolfgang, *Patterns in Criminal Homicide* (Philadelphia: University of Pennsylvania Press, 1958), 125.

33. *New York Tribune,* Oct. 19, 1858.

34. Anne Parrella, "Industrialization and Murder: Northern France, 1815–1904," *Journal of Interdisciplinary History* 22 (1992): 627–654, poses thoughtful analytic questions about intimate partner murder, showing the basic "paradox" that murder ultimately fails when its object is control.

35. Pearson chi²(1) = 0.0254 Pr = 0.873, n = 216. The Coleman case is detailed in William Francis Kuntz II, *Criminal Sentencing in Three Nineteenth-Century Cities: Social History of Punishment in New York, Boston, and Philadelphia, 1830–1880* (New York: Garland, 1988), 544.

36. *New York Times*, Dec. 8, 1855. Elliot J. Gorn, *The Manly Art: Bare-knuckle Prize Fighting in America* (Ithaca, N.Y.: Cornell University Press, 1986), 409–410.

37. *New York Times*, Mar. 12, Dec. 3 and 8, 1855.

CHAPTER 4

1. *New York Times*, Aug. 30, 1856.

2. Of course, social scripts can also steer people toward violence, if cues interpreted as aggressive or threatening require an escalating and violent response. This is how cultural rules can produce more violence, rather than less.

3. Estimates from Kathleen Maguire and Ann L. Pastore, eds., *Sourcebook of Criminal Justice Statistics 1995*. U.S. Department of Justice, Bureau of Justice Statistics (Washington, D.C.: GPO, 1996), tables 3.133 and 6.72.

4. "Boys Plead Not Guilty in Toddler's Murder," *New York Times*, May 15, 1993. "Two Boys Convicted of Killing Toddler," *Facts on File* 53, no. 2766 (Dec. 2, 1993): 901. Robert Thompson and Jon Venables, who murdered two-year-old James Bulger, were both age ten. See the review essay by Tony Jefferson in *British Journal of Criminology* 36, no. 2 (spring 1996): 319–323, of David James Smith, *The Sleep of Reason: The James Bulger Case* (London: Arrow, 1995), a book that covers many cases of child murderers.

5. Allan Abrahamse, "The Coming Wave of Violence in California," draft report (Santa Monica: RAND, 1995). There are two ways to examine the age of murderers: the first, which I use here, is to compare the age of young killers with the age of all other murderers; the second is to compare the age of the killers with the age of the whole population. The latter is important but requires fairly complete age reporting for the offenders, which I do not have. See David P. Farrington, "Age and Crime," in *Crime and Justice: An Annual Review of Research,* vol. 6, ed. Norval Morris and Michael Tonry (Chicago: University of Chicago Press, 1986), 189–250. For the most recent decline in the younger age groups, see Alfred Blumstein and Richard Rosenfeld, "Explaining Recent Trends in U.S. Homicide Rates," *Journal of Criminal Law and Criminology* 88 (1998): 1175–1216.

6. As a comparison that hints at accuracy we can look at age heaping (the tendency to round to certain numbers) in New York City in the nineteenth century and in the 1990s (see table N4.1). What this shows is a continued tendency to give an age as twenty when, logically, there must have been more nineteen- and twenty-one-year-olds than reported.

The missing ages of killers may cause biases in both the early New York City data as well as in the FBI's Supplementary Homicide Reports for the city. There are strange parallels in the patterns of the missing ages, but these should not be seen as proof of similar biases. The parallels: when looking at victims younger than age twenty, the FBI data has 41.2 percent of the offender ages recorded; my

Table N4.1   Heaping in Reporting of Ages of Young Killers, New York City

	Number of killers	
Age	*1990s*	*1800s*
19	680	16
20	990	24
21	561	16

SOURCES: 1800s: see appendix; 1990s: FBI, *Supplementary Homicide Reports.*

nineteenth-century sample has 40 percent. For victims older than age twenty, the FBI has 31 percent recorded, my data 38 percent. Further, when correlating the nonmissing pairs of victims and killers, for victims of age twenty the r is .21 for the FBI, .20 for me. For victims younger than age twenty there is a difference, my data showing no correlation, the FBI a –.15 correlation.

The reasons for the missing ages differ: for my data, it is most often that the killer is identified but no age given; for today, the killer is less likely to be identified.

7. See Sean Wilentz, *Chants Democratic: New York City and the Rise of the American Working Class, 1788–1850* (New York: Oxford University Press, 1984). See Patricia Cline Cohen, *The Murder of Helen Jewett: The Life and Death of a Prostitute in Nineteenth-Century New York* (New York: Knopf, 1998), for an account of young people on their own in New York City in the 1830s.

8. *New York Times,* Mar. 26, Apr. 4 and 5, 1859.

9. Lawrence M. Friedman, *Crime and Punishment in American History* (New York: Basic Books, 1993), 163. For a summary of English law from Anglo-Saxon times to 1933, see A. W. G. Kean, "The History of the Criminal Liability of Children," *The Law Quarterly Review* 211 (July 1937): 364–370. Kean shows how the age of culpability moved between about seven and about fourteen with little regularity.

10. *New York Times,* Oct. 1 and 4, 1853.

11. *New York Times,* Nov. 23, 1857.

12. *New York Times,* Nov. 9, 10, 13, 16, and 23, 1857.

13. *New York Times,* Oct. 21, 1853.

14. *New York Tribune,* Jan. 11 and 12, 1849; 1850 MS census, sixth ward.

15. *New York Times,* Oct. 19, 1855. *New York Tribune,* Oct. 19 and 22, 1855.

16. New York County Coroner's Inquests, roll 93.

17. *New York Tribune,* Oct. 16, 1873; *New York Times,* Oct. 17, 1873. The only family in the 1870 census manuscript with a similar name was that of sixty-three-year-

old Charles Dockett, Irish, twenty-second ward, r. 1012, p. 191, who lived with his wife, Rosanna, age fifty-three, and son, Charles, age twenty.

18. New York County Coroner's Inquests, roll 93, July 31, 1871.

19. Trial transcript in William Sampson, *Murders: Report of the Trial of James Johnson, a Black Man, for the Murder of Lewis Robinson, a Black Man . . . : Also, the Trial of John Sinclair, a German . . . for the Murder of David Hill . . .* (New York: Southwick and Pelsue, 1811). Early American Imprints, second series, no. 23446, p. 32. Anthon, incidentally, may have been the father of one of the lawyers who defended John Colt (see chapter 2). See Anne Parrella, "Industrialization and Murder: Northern France, 1815–1904," *Journal of Interdisciplinary History* 22 (1992): 627–654, for a historical reflection on the meaning of murder.

20. Sampson, *Murders*, 29.

21. Ibid., 27, 30.

22. Ibid., 20.

23. *New York Times*, Mar. 8, 1869. This is one of the *Times*'s earliest pieces that uses the turgid language and description typical of the penny press.

24. If we set the age threshold a bit higher, to those age twenty-one or younger, the shift is more dramatic: 32 percent dropping to 11 percent and then rising back to 21 percent after the war.

25. William Osborn Stoddard, *The Volcano under the City, by a Volunteer Special . . .* (New York: Fords, Howard & Hulbert, 1887). James M. McPherson, *Battle Cry of Freedom: The Civil War Era* (New York: Oxford University Press, 1988), shows that immigrants were underrepresented in the Union military.

26. This dialogue exemplifies what historians call the political culture of the nineteenth century: men who defined much of their public cultural life through political participation. See Daniel Walker Howe, *The Political Culture of the American Whigs* (Chicago: University of Chicago Press, 1979); Jean H. Baker, *Affairs of Party: The Political Culture of Northern Democrats in the Mid-Nineteenth Century* (Ithaca, N.Y.: Cornell University Press, 1983); and Joel H. Silbey, *The American Political Nation, 1838–1893* (Stanford, Calif.: Stanford University Press, 1991).

27. *New York Times*, Nov. 12, 1863.

28. The Espy data set has missed some executions of New York City murderers: Thomas Byng, 1727; James [Thomas?] Eager, 1844; William Harper, 1845; Richard C. Jackson, 1835; James Johnson, 1810; John Johnson, 1823; William Saul and Nicholas Howlett, 1852; Diana Sillick, 1816; John Frederick Sinclair, 1810. This is an undercount of about 18 percent.

29. Alan F. Abrahamse, "Demography and Youth Violence in California," in *Lethal Violence: Proceedings of the 1995 Meeting of the Homicide Research Working Group*, ed. Marc Riedel and John Boulahanis (Washington, D.C.: USDOJ, n.d.), 3–14; and Alfred Blumstein, "Youth Violence, Guns, and the Illicit-Drug Industry," *Journal of Criminal Law and Criminology* 86 (fall 1995): 10–36.

30. David T. Courtwright, *Violent Land: Single Men and Social Disorder from the Frontier to the Inner City* (Cambridge, Mass.: Harvard University Press, 1996); Roger D. McGrath, *Gunfighters, Highwaymen, and Vigilantes: Violence on the Frontier* (Berkeley: University of California Press, 1984); and Clare McKanna, *Homicide, Race, and Justice in the American West, 1880–1920* (Tucson: University of Arizona Press, 1997).

31. For three-fourths of the nineteenth and twentieth centuries, very good data allow us to plot the population proportion of men age sixteen to forty-five who were born abroad or who were simply migrants from within the United States. These values follow the murder rate's peaks and valleys, though they do not vary enough to account for them completely. Nor do the data from the decadal censuses capture any quick surges or the probable drop caused by war. In 1850, slightly less than 28 percent of the city's population was composed of non–New York–born men age sixteen to forty-five (about 16 percent of the city's population was immigrant men). This figure declined until 1960, when it reached a nadir in these men, 4 percent and 3 percent of the city's population, respectively. By 1990 their presence had tripled, to 11 percent and 9 percent.

If we focus on the direction of change rather than on the actual percentages, by assuming that the high point of 1850 had been preceded by a sharp uptake, then could this be the significant feature? In essence, the city continually filled with more and more men in the mid nineteenth century and in the post-1950s. U.S. social historians have discovered and marveled at the mobility of ordinary Americans in the nineteenth century, using terms such as "churning" to describe a society in motion. Such mobility was not in itself harmful and may have even created an ebullient, energetic society. But its eddies and currents could create cities with pools of men. These men were often in families, and even those apparently adrift stayed near former neighbors and kin. Some, however, composed what historian John Schneider identified as the "bachelor subculture," which came to include men who in the twentieth century lived on skid row. The research in this area is enormous, beginning with Stephan Thernstrom's classic *Poverty and Progress: Social Mobility in a Nineteenth-Century City* (Cambridge, Mass.: Harvard University Press, 1964) and continuing through the recent work of economic historian Joseph Ferrie; see, for example, J. P. Ferrie, "Up and Out or Down and Out—Immigrant Mobility in the Antebellum United States," *Journal of Interdisciplinary History* 26 (summer 1995): 33–55. Peter R. Knights's work has shown how men often ended up near close kin, even though far from their original homes: see *Yankee Destinies: The Lives of Ordinary Nineteenth-Century Bostonians* (Chapel Hill: University of North Carolina Press, 1991). See John C. Schneider, "Tramping Workers, 1890–1920: A Subcultural View," in *Walking to Work: Tramps in America, 1790–1935*, ed. Eric Monkkonen (Lincoln: University of Nebraska Press, 1984), 212–234. During the significant pre–Civil War period, the increasing male population helped lay the foundation for the American state system to follow.

32. The discussion of age rates in this section is based on my more detailed analysis, "New York City Homicide Offender Ages: How Variable? A Research Note," *Homicide Studies* 3, no. 3 (August 1999): 256–269.

33. Richard E. Nisbett and Dov Cohen, *Culture of Honor: The Psychology of Violence in the South* (Boulder, Colo.: Westview Press, 1996), 45–48.

34. Robert W. Fogel, "New Sources and New Techniques for the Study of Secular Trends in Nutritional Status, Health, Mortality, and the Process of Aging," *Historical Methods* 26 (winter 1993): 5–43.

35. Richard Steckel's work on age at leaving home captures an excellent measure of all the nutritional and family structure changes as they drive one major social variable: when children actually leave home. He estimated, for the northeastern United States in the mid nineteenth century, a median age of departure for males of 28.3 years. This contrasts with an estimated median time of departure for 1900 of 23.2, declining to 21.2 by 1980. Richard H. Steckel, "The Quality of Census Data for Historical Inquiry—A Research Agenda," *Social Science History* 15 (winter 1991): 579–599; Richard H. Steckel, "The Age at Leaving Home in the United States, 1850–1860," *Social Science History* 20 (winter 1996): 507–532. David A. Stevens, "New Evidence on the Timing of Early Life Course Transitions: The United States, 1900 to 1980," *Journal of Family History* 15 (1990): 163–178.

36. Data are drawn from the IPUMS samples for the City of New York (IPUMS). This calculation has the advantage of actually sampling individuals. The years 1960 and 1970 have no city codes in the IPUMS samples and therefore include the whole state. Based on 1990, this introduces a bias, as New York City had nearly 30 percent more at-risk population than did the rest of the state: 5.07 percent for the non–New York City region, 6.57 percent for the city. I have therefore multiplied the 1960 and 1970 estimates to correct.

37. Schneider, "Tramping Workers"; and Courtwright, *Violent Land*.

38. Neither calculate age rates, only per total population. See McKanna, *Homicide, Race, and Justice,* and McGrath, *Gunfighters, Highwaymen, and Vigilantes*.

CHAPTER 5

1. Were these two men brothers? There are four Joseph Kellys and four Charles Kellys just as heads of households in Brooklyn in 1860, making name linkage too risky.

2. *New York Times,* Aug. 29, 1866. Because Brooklyn was still a separate city at this time, this case is not included in the database or statistics in this book.

3. Carolyn Rebecca Block, "Lethal Violence in the Chicago Latino Community," in *Homicide: The Victim/Offender Connection*, ed. Anna Victoria Wilson (Cincinnati: Anderson, 1993), 277.

4. Roger Lane, *Roots of Violence in Black Philadelphia, 1860–1900* (Cambridge, Mass.: Harvard University Press, 1986), 104.

5. Carolyn Rebecca Block and Christine Martin, *Updated Graphs, Major Trends in Chicago Homicide: 1965–1995* (Chicago: Illinois Criminal Justice Information Authority, Jan. 2, 1997).

6. This episode and the dialogue are reconstructed from the coroner's inquest of April 24, 1851. The clerk made several errors, substituting key nouns and confusing the names of victim and offender.

7. For a very useful analysis of duels, which primarily examines German dueling from the point of view of masculinity and state building, see Ute Frevert, *Men of Honour: A Social and Cultural History of the Duel*, trans. Anthony Williams (Cambridge, Eng.: Polity Press, 1995). For a recent lighthearted look at duels, see B. Holland and P. DeSeve, "Bang! Bang! You're Dead—Dueling at the Drop of a Hat Was as European as Truffles and as American as Mom's Apple Pie," *Smithsonian* 28 (Oct. 1997): 122.

8. I have drawn Dinan's age, ethnicity, and occupation from the 1860 census manuscript, introducing the possibility of mislinkage and error. That hatmakers bailed him, and that his victim was about his age and of the same ethnicity, makes the linkage seem reasonable. There may be a William Dinan in the 1850 manuscript census, but the writing is illegible. An advertisement for the benefit appears in the *Tribune* on Sept. 8, 1851. Quotations are from the coroner's inquest, March 7, 1852.

9. A definitive assessment of this is not possible here, because to do it correctly, one would have to compare the ratio of spousal and romantic killings to the number of such relationships, not to the total population. To do this, the bias caused by missing information also would have to be carefully adjusted, probably more easily done for the nineteenth century than for the twentieth.

10. See Marc Riedel, "Counting Stranger Homicides: A Case Study of Statistical Prestidigitation," *Homicide Studies* 2 (May 1998): 206–219.

11. Mahoney may not have been this age: the only Cornelius Mahoney in the 1850 census is by then age thirty, Irish, and blind, so it may have been a different man. The other age and ethnicity information on these two is from noncensus sources.

12. *New York Tribune*, Feb. 15, 1847, and Apr. 21, 1847.

13. *New York Tribune*, Mar. 26, 1844.

14. The information on Fallon is from the census manuscript.

15. *New York Times*, Aug. 2, 1854.

16. *New York Times*, Mar. 25, 1864.

17. Roger Lane, *Violent Death in the City: Suicide, Accident, and Murder in Nineteenth-Century Philadelphia* (Cambridge, Mass.: Harvard University Press, 1979).

18. Eric Foner, *Reconstruction: America's Unfinished Revolution, 1863–1877* (New York: Harper & Row, 1988), has the most clearly focused discussion of such violence. For a local southern example, see William Ivy Hair, *Carnival of Fury: Robert Charles and the New Orleans Race Riot of 1900* (Baton Rouge: Louisiana State University Press, 1976). For Baltimore, and antebellum riots generally, see David Grimsted, "Rioting in Its Jacksonian Setting," *American Historical Review* 77 (Apr. 1972): 361–397. I have not been able to find any discussion of such local northern political violence. There is a vast and sophisticated literature on voting fraud that mainly focuses on how the illegal votes might or might not mask the counts of true votes used for subsequent historical analysis. This literature does not seem to consider that violence would be used to protect the assets at stake in elections.

19. See Paul A. Gilje, *The Road to Mobocracy: Popular Disorder in New York City, 1763–1834* (Chapel Hill: published for the Institute of Early American History and Culture by the University of North Carolina Press, 1987), 138–142.

20. In testimony on the Poole murder in 1855, mention is made of one Cy. Shay, who was known as the "fighting man of the Whig Party in California," an indication that not all violence was Democratic. And Poole himself was a nativist Know-Nothing, an enemy of the Irish and the Democrats. His killer, Lewis Baker, age thirty in 1855, supposedly was Welsh.

21. Covered by the *New York Tribune*, Nov. 5–Dec. 2, 1874.

22. Czitrom Daniel, "Underworlds and Underdogs—Big Tim Sullivan, and Metropolitan Politics in New-York, 1889–1913," *Journal of American History* 78, no. 2 (Sept. 1991): 536–558.

23. K. T. Hoppen, "Grammars of Electoral Violence in Nineteenth-Century England and Ireland," *English Historical Review* 109 (June 1994): 597–620. Election mobs "were a case of labourers and cottiers invading the neatest urban polling place armed with the weaponry of their rustic quarrels and pursuing agrarian disputes by other means" (618).

24. Scott C. James and Brian L. Lawson, "The Political Economy of Voting Rights Enforcement in America's Gilded Age: Electoral College Competition, Swing States, and the Implementation of the Federal Election Law" (manuscript, 1998). Expenditure estimates calculated from data on p. 20.

25. The *New York Times*, Nov. 6, 1870, published the marshal's orders, which did not enumerate the actual deputies, only their chiefs. An article on Nov. 8 says that "about" one thousand deputies had been sworn in on Nov. 7. An article on Nov. 9 refers to the "tramp" of arrested prisoners' feet.

26. *New York Times*, Nov. 11, 1854. Ann, widow of Hugh Barrett, may have been the same Ann Barrett in the 1860 manuscript census. If so, she was Irish, as were her two younger daughters. George was not present in this household, so he may

have not been of the same family, but the hints are that he was, and simply was not there for the enumeration in 1850. This would make him Irish, also.

27. Roger Lane has a graphic description of such a rescue in Boston, in *Policing the City: Boston, 1822-1885* (Cambridge, Mass.: Harvard University Press, 1967), 188-189.

28. My account of the Gourley murder is based on the coroner's inquest, reported in the *New York Times*, Nov. 7 and 9, 1854, and articles scattered through the *Times* and *Tribune* in the subsequent days. I have not been able to find the ultimate outcome of Holmes's arrest, perhaps an example of careful political suppression. The last article seems to be on Dec. 1, 1854.

29. Source: manuscript census, 1850. In 1850 Sheehan was a clerk living in a boarding house. His ethnic connections to the police may have come from the adjacent household, where dwelt James McGrath, an Irish police justice, or from three households away, where dwelt Thomas Duncan, an Irish policeman.

30. Source: manuscript census, 1850 for Brown, 1860 for Smith.

31. *New York Times*, Nov. 29 and Dec. 1, 1854.

32. The city's politics in this era can be followed in Edward K. Spann, *The New Metropolis: New York City, 1840-1857* (New York: Columbia University Press, 1981), chapters 12 and 13. The story of the literal battle between the two police forces in April is ably told by James F. Richardson, *The New York Police, Colonial Times to 1901* (New York: Oxford University Press, 1970), 82-109.

33. Information drawn from the manuscript census for 1860 and 1870. I could not find Gourley or Holmes in the 1850 census, possibly because both would have been too young to be enumerated as household heads and therefore not in the CD-ROM indexes to the census. Mary told the census enumerators that she was age thirty-seven in 1870, and age twenty-one in 1860, making her actual age difficult to guess.

34. New York (N.Y.) Common Council, *Manual of the Corporation of the City of New York* [Valentine's Manual] (New York, 1859), 149.

35. Stephen Nissenbaum, *The Battle for Christmas* (New York: Alfred A. Knopf, 1996), 49-99, describes the riotous behavior that slowly came under scrutiny and control in New York City in the period 1820-1850; Gilje, *Road to Mobocracy*, 253-260, describes the "Calathumpian" misrule on New Year's Day in the city. He also describes Christmas riots in 1806 that were Protestant attacks on Catholics, resulting in one murder.

36. For the Orange riots, see Gilje, *Road to Mobocracy*, 134, and Michael A. Gordon, *The Orange Riots: Irish Political Violence in New York City, 1870 and 1871* (Ithaca, N.Y.: Cornell University Press, 1993): see appendixes I and II for lists of the dead. In the interest of accuracy, reluctantly I must report that three other days during the year had high levels, but none seem to have been connected with holidays:

Feb. 25, June 13, and June 16. These and the holiday days all had seven or more murders prior to 1875: more than two standard deviations above the mean of three per day.

Gordon enumerates eight deaths in the 1870 riots, sixty in 1871. His lists show that most deaths were from gunshot wounds from militias—which, though his numbers are certainly wrong, I hesitate to enumerate as murders. Therefore, in the interests of consistency I ignore these deaths in the annual counts, as I do for the 1863 Draft Riots. Readers may mentally add about 10 percent to 1870 and double 1871 if they wish.

37. The number may have been higher: Bernard Friery, for example, was a Christmas killer but because his victim lingered, it has been more difficult to discover the connection to the holiday.

38. *New York Times*, Aug. 16, 1866.

CHAPTER 6

1. Roger Lane, *Violent Death in the City: Accident, Suicide, and Homicide in Philadelphia, 1850–1900* (Cambridge, Mass.: Harvard University Press, 1979); Roger Lane, *Roots of Violence in Black Philadelphia, 1860–1900* (Cambridge, Mass.: Harvard University Press, 1991); Roger Lane, *William Dorsey's Philadelphia and Ours: On the Past and Future of the Black City in America* (New York: Oxford University Press, 1991).

2. Graham R. Hodges, *New York City Cartmen, 1667–1850* (New York: New York University Press, 1986).

3. Ira Rosenwaike, *Population History of New York City* (Syracuse, N.Y.: Syracuse University Press, 1972), 39.

4. Margo J. Anderson, *The American Census: A Social History* (New Haven: Yale University Press, 1988); Lane, *Roots of Violence in Black Philadelphia*, 59–60.

5. For the most recent work on the riots, see Iver Bernstein, *The New York City Draft Riots: Their Significance for American Society and Politics in the Age of the Civil War* (New York: Oxford University Press, 1990). His bibliographical essay (341) summarizes the extensive literature on the riots. Peter Quinn, *Banished Children of Eve* (New York: Viking, 1994).

6. Missing data on the ethnicity of the victims or offenders—unreported in 42 percent of cases—hamper the comparison of ethnic to racial groups for the mid nineteenth century. Here victim race and ethnicity are used, with offender race and ethnicity substituted in cases where the victim variable is missing. These estimates are inflated for the Irish and Germans assuming that the missing information was equal for all whites. For African Americans, I assumed that all black victims were reported, or at least were most likely identified as black. Because there were only sixteen reported black victims between 1855 and 1864, an omission of

just one would raise the reported rate by 6 percent. I omitted two black victims of white offenders. Horace V. Redfield, *Homicide, North and South: Being a Comparative View of Crime against the Person in Several Parts of the United States* (Philadelphia: J. B. Lippincott, 1880), 103–104, found higher white than black homicide rates for the South. To test for possible errors caused by the small numbers of blacks, I have estimated the black homicide offender rate for the period 1845–1874. In this period there were forty-four black offenders, but ethnicity or race was identified for only 35 percent of all killers. The number of black offenders rises to fifty-six if I assume that all black victims with unidentified offenders were killed by blacks. Using this as the figure to calculate rates, and using the average adult population from 1850, 1860, and 1870, yields a value of 30 for African American offense rates. A similar calculation for the Irish-born yields 28.5.

7. The r^2 is .55.

8. Darnell F. Hawkins, ed., *Ethnicity, Race, and Crime: Perspectives across Time and Place* (Albany, N.Y.: State University of New York Press, 1995); J. A. Phillips, "Variation in African-American Homicide Rates: An Assessment of Potential Explanations," *Criminology* 35 (Nov. 1997): 527–559.

9. Douglas L. Eckberg examines this ratio for the twentieth-century United States in "Early Twentieth-Century Black and White Homicide: Was There Divergence?" (paper presented at the American Society of Criminology annual meeting, Chicago, Nov. 1996). His figure 2 corresponds to the twentieth-century values for New York City, with the difference that New York's lower-ratio era was much lower than for the United States as a whole. A sharp reader might complain that my figure 6.2 shows the emergence of the disparity before 1925, but this is an artifact of the smoothing of the line; a more focused picture shows clearly that 1925 is the demarcating year. The horizontal line at 1 in figure 6.2 indicates exact parity in homicide rates.

10. Rosenwaike, *Population History,* 140.

11. Source: calculated from IPUMS sample for 1950. The non-native New York African American men actually reported greater annual incomes than the New Yorkers: $2,150 versus $2,074 per year. Even greater income disparities obtained in the 1930 census: $640 versus $471. The newcomers to the city made considerably more than the natives.

12. This is shown dramatically by Fox Butterfield, *All God's Children: The Bosket Family and the American Tradition of Violence* (New York: Alfred A. Knopf, 1995).

13. Pearson chi^2(16) = 487.8040 Pr = 0.000; Cramer's V = 0.6334 gamma = 0.7375 ASE = 0.049; Kendall's tau-b = 0.6026 ASE = 0.046. This table drops all ethnicities with fewer than eighteen occurrences, e.g., French at eight offenders.

14. Done from the IPUMS samples of 1850–1870, which are randomly drawn individuals.

15. *New York Sun,* Sept. 21, 1835.

Table N6.1 Liberal Race Identification

Variable	Odds ratio	Std. err.	z	P > z	LR chi²(1)	Prob > chi²	Pseudo r²	Number
Arrested	1.79	0.45	2.3	.02	5.59	0.018	.002	1773
Tried	1.75	0.54	1.78	.08	3.22	0.073	.003	856
Convicted	0.66	0.28	−0.98	.33	0.99	0.319	.0019	378
Executed	4.13	2.91	2.01	.04	3.67	0.056	.024	163

16. *New York Times*, Dec. 22, 1853; coroner's inquest; manuscript U.S. census for 1850.

17. There is a Blames family, African American and New York–born, in New York City in the 1850 manuscript census, but it does not include William. The surname was also reported as Blanes or Blamy.

18. *New York Times*, Aug. 1, 1863.

19. *New York Times*, Jul. 24, 1867.

20. This note reports the results of logit analyses of the likelihood of arrest, trial, conviction, and execution for blacks versus all others. It updates and modifies the analysis made with a smaller data set and reported in Eric H. Monkkonen, "Racial Factors in New York City Homicide, 1800–1874," in *Ethnicity, Race, and Crime*, ed. Hawkins, 99–120.

Table N6.1 reports four different estimates on the declining numbers of those arrested, tried, convicted, and executed (in the right-hand column). These analyses were done with the assumption that African Americans would be more likely to be noted than others, so that when unreported, a person's race was coded as white; similarly, if no arrest, trial, conviction, or execution was discovered, it was assumed that they had not occurred. An odds ratio of less than one for the killer's race indicates that being African American reduced the probability of an event occurring, which happened only in the convictions. Being African American doubled a person's chances of arrest and trial, but not conviction. It quadrupled the person's likelihood of execution.

Table N6.2 tries to ascertain whether the race of the victim affected the execution of African American offenders. Estimates of the odds ratios resulted in no statistically significant relationships, implying that although jurors were four times more likely to execute black offenders than white offenders, the victim's race did not matter.

21. Pearson chi²(1) = 52.5143 Pr = 0.000 likelihood-ratio chi²(1) = 27.3599 Pr = 0.000 Cramer's V = 0.1748; gamma = 0.7836 ASE = 0.066; Kendall's tau-b = 0.1748 ASE = 0.049.

Table N6.2   Executions of Black Offenders, by Race of Victim, New York City, 19th Century

	Offender executed?		
Victim's race/ethnicity	*No*	*Yes*	*Total*
Native-born white	6	1	7
Black	26	5	31
Immigrant	12	1	13
Total	44	7	51

CHAPTER 7

1. Portions of this chapter are from Eric H. Monkkonen, "Searching for the Origins of American and European Violence Differences" (paper presented at the Elias Centenary Conference, December 18–20, 1997, Amsterdam).

2. Alfred Blumstein and Richard Rosenfeld, in "Explaining Recent Trends in U.S. Homicide Rates" *Journal of Criminal Law and Criminology* 88 (1998): 1175–1216, note that New York City contributed 10 percent of the nation's murders, a large enough proportion to dominate the trajectory of the national rates. Franklin E. Zimring and Gordon Hawkins, in *Crime Is Not the Problem: Lethal Violence in America* (New York: Oxford University Press, 1997), say that the United States' high violence "is a third world phenomenon occurring in a first world nation" (52).

3. Recent good exceptions include Fox Butterfield, *All God's Children: The Bosket Family and the American Tradition of Violence* (New York: Alfred A. Knopf, 1995), and Roger Lane, *Murder in America: A History* (Columbus: Ohio State University Press, 1997).

4. Dane Archer and Rosemary Gartner, *Violence and Crime in Cross-National Perspective* (New Haven: Yale University Press, 1984), 3.

5. Iceland may have been an exception. See Jesse L. Byock, *Medieval Iceland: Society, Sagas, and Power* (Berkeley: University of California Press, 1988). For Oxford, see Carl I. Hammer Jr., "Patterns of Homicide in a Medieval University Town: Fourteenth-Century Oxford," *Past and Present* (1978): 3–23.

6. Ted R. Gurr, who edited *Violence in America* (Newbury Park, Calif.: Sage Publications, 1989), was one of the first social scientists to show that there is more than an antiquarian interest that propels this quest. He has surveyed a large body of research that indicates that our current high homicide rates and rates of other crim-

inal violence are a relatively recent phenomenon. See Eric A. Johnson and Eric H. Monkkonen, eds., *The Civilization of Crime: Violence in Town and Country since the Middle Ages* (Urbana: University of Illinois Press, 1996), for a collection of essays on Europe from the Middle Ages through the early modern period.

7. Johnson and Monkkonen, *Civilization of Crime*, 9. Finland showed an early-nineteenth-century increase in murders: see Heikki Ylikangas, "What Happened to Violence," in *Five Centuries of Violence: In Finland and the Baltic Area*, ed. Mirkka Lappalainen (Helsinki: Academy of Finland, 1998), 20.

8. Alfred Soman, "Deviance and Criminal Justice in Western Europe, 1300–1800: An Essay in Structure," *Criminal Justice History* 1 (1980): 1–28.

9. Barbara A. Hanawalt, "Violent Death in Fourteenth- and Early-Fifteenth Century England," *Comparative Studies in Society and History* 18 (July 1976): 311–312; private communication, Apr. 30, 1998.

10. Gurr, *Violence in America*, 32–33.

11. Butterfield, *All God's Children;* Horace V. Redfield, *Homicide, North and South: Being a Comparative View of Crime against the Person in Several Parts of the United States* (Philadelphia: J. B. Lippincott, 1880); Los Angeles, from my research sponsored by the National Consortium on Violence Research, "Homicide in Los Angeles: An Age Standardized History" (forthcoming). Note that Lane's data are not comparable because they are trial-based.

12. Dov Cohen, "Culture, Social Organization, and Patterns of Violence," *Journal of Personality and Social Psychology* (forthcoming); for a critique of the data analysis in Richard E. Nisbett and Dov Cohen, *Culture of Honor: The Psychology of Violence in the South* (Boulder, Colo.: Westview Press, 1996), see Rebekah Chu, Craig Rivera, and Colin Loftin, "Herding and Homicide: An Examination of the Nisbett-Reaves Hypothesis" (manuscript, July 24, 1998).

13. Norbert Elias, *The Civilizing Process*, trans. Edmund Jephcott, 2 vols. (New York: Urizen Books, 1978–1982). For a series of articles dealing with state development and the criminal justice system, see Xavier Rousseaux and René Levy, eds., *Le Pénal dans tous ses états: Justice, états et sociétés en Europe (XIIe–XXe siècles)* (Brussels: Publications des Facultés Universitaires Saint-Louis, 1997). See the introduction to Pieter Spierenburg, ed., *Men and Violence: Gender, Honor, and Rituals in Modern Europe and America* (Columbus: Ohio State University Press, 1998), and Wilbur R. Miller, *Revenuers and Moonshiners: Enforcing Federal Liquor Law in the Mountain South, 1865–1900* (Chapel Hill: University of North Carolina Press, 1991).

14. Recent work by Michael A. Bellesiles, "The Origins of Gun Culture in the United States, 1760–1865," *Journal of American History* 83 (1996): 425–455, has made clear that in the pre–Civil War era, American gun ownership was much lower than most have assumed, c. 20 percent of all families.

15. These periods loosely conform with Mary Ryan's sense of the public sphere,

as detailed in *Civic Wars: Democracy and Public Life in the American City during the Nineteenth Century* (Berkeley: University of California Press, 1997).

16. Albert W. Alschuler and A. G. Deiss, "A Brief History of the Criminal Jury in the United States," *University of Chicago Law Review* 61 (1994): 867–928. Lawrence M. Friedman, *Crime and Punishment in American History* (New York: Basic Books, 1993), 242–250.

17. Cited in International City Manager's Association, *Municipal Police Administration*, rev. ed. (Chicago: International City Manager's Association, 1943). A less officially endorsed but probably equally important manual appeared in 1921: Elmer D. Graper, *American Police Administration: A Handbook on Police Organization and Methods of Administration in American Cities*, Bureau of Municipal Research and Training School for Public Service, New York City, Handbooks on Public Administration (New York: Macmillan, 1921).

18. See the forthcoming work of Dov Cohen, "Culture, Social Organization, and Patterns of Violence," who uses the notion of crystallization to account for the irrationally high homicide rates in the American South and West. The notion of "crystallization" captures the sense that a social organization comes into self-sustaining balance.

19. Daniel Czitrom, "Underworlds and Underdogs: Tim Big Sullivan, and Metropolitan Politics in New-York, 1889–1913," *Journal of American History* 78 (1991): 536–558. See James F. Richardson, *The New York Police, Colonial Times to 1901* (New York: Oxford University Press, 1970), 69–72. George Washington Matsell seems likely to have been born as plain George in England, not Ireland; only his youngest brother, James Henry Abdeel Columbia Matsell, was known as the family's "Yankee boy." *Documents of the Board of Aldermen*, vol. 22, doc. 43 (New York, 1855). Recently, historians have begun to reexamine the concept of "whiteness," focusing on its multifaceted implications. See, for example, Werner Sollors, ed., *The Invention of Ethnicity* (New York: Oxford University Press, 1989); David R. Roediger, *The Wages of Whiteness: Race and the Making of the American Working Class* (London: Verso, 1991); Noel Ignatiev, *How the Irish Became White* (New York: Routledge, 1995); and Alexander Saxton, *The Rise and Fall of the White Republic: Class Politics and Mass Culture in Nineteenth-Century America* (London: Verso, 1990).

20. Charles Dickens, *American Notes for General Circulation* (first published 1842; New York: Penguin, 1985), 130.

21. A distinction missed in George Cooper's otherwise fine *Lost Love: A True Story of Passion, Murder, and Justice in Old New York* (New York: Pantheon Books, 1994).

22. The picture is in the Carnegie Museum of Art, Pittsburgh. Here and in one other place, I violate my own rule of using no primary materials other than those for New York City itself. The Blythe painting is so unusual that it is worth breaking the rule. Most contemporary illustrations of courtroom or crime scenes were

done to sell lurid pamphlets or for new media in sensational cases, and in this book I make every effort to deal with the ordinary and the everyday.

23. See, for example, Roediger, *Wages of Whiteness*, and Ignatiev, *How the Irish Became White*.

24. Benedict R. O'G. Anderson, *Imagined Communities: Reflections on the Origin and Spread of Nationalism* (London: Verso, 1983); Eugen J. Weber, *Peasants into Frenchmen: The Modernization of Rural France, 1870–1914* (Stanford, Calif.: Stanford University Press, 1976).

25. Max Weber, *Economy and Society: An Outline of Interpretive Sociology*, ed. Guenther Roth and Claus Wittich; trans. Ephraim Fischoff et al. (Berkeley: University of California Press, 1978), 54.

26. The twentieth-century ratio of homicide rates between the two nations set the United States about five (4.8, r^2 of .37) times that of England (except for World War I). For the more specific and longer-term comparison of Liverpool and NYC, the ratio is a bit closer, 3.2 (r^2 of .43), and the time span nearly two centuries. (For London: a ratio of 7 and an r^2 of .65. Liverpool correlated *less* with London than it did with NYC.)

27. My thanks to Clive Emsley for alerting me to this quotation in David Philips, "'A New Engine of Power and Authority,'" in *Crime and the Law: The Social History of Crime in Western Europe since 1500*, ed. V. A. C. Gatrell, Bruce Lenman, and Geoffrey Parker (London: Europa Publications, 1980), 174. It followed on the hammer murders of two families in the Ratcliffe Highway, East London, in December 1811.

28. Paraphrased in Richardson, *New York Police*, 190.

29. Clive Emsley, "'The Thump of Wood on a Swede Turnip': Police Violence in Nineteenth-Century England," *Criminal Justice History* 6 (1985): 125–149.

30. These figures are probably as complete an accounting as possible, because high constable Jacob Hays compiled a manuscript of all people sentenced to the city prison. The only omission here would be that some offenders may have been pardoned after Hays compiled his list. I have used only the offenders from New York City, although the pardon rate for all murderers is the same. Jacob Hays, *An Account for Prisoners Received into the New York State Prison* (c. 1822), Museum of the City of New York. Using his full list of forty-five murderers to estimate time served for murder, I calculate that 50 percent served less than a year and a half, but a few long-timers raised the mean to about three years.

Comparable trial data for other places in the United States are difficult to find. One can calculate from data in Clare McKanna's study of three late-nineteenth-century Western counties, which is based on coroner's inquests, that between 64 and 71 percent of the cases went to the indictment stage; if all of these cases went to trial, then there was a much more careful follow-up. I have not been able to establish such figures, and the proportion of indicted cases coming to trial is impossible to guess. See Clare McKanna, *Homicide, Race, and Justice in the American West, 1880–1920* (Tucson: University of Arizona Press, 1997), 17, 54, 121.

31. See, for example, the strange story of Quimbo Appo, who seems to have murdered several people, some in self-defense, but who managed to get pardoned. John Kuo Wei Tchen, "Quimbo Appo's Fear of Fenians: Chinese-Anglo Relations in New York City," in *The New York Irish*, ed. Ronald H. Bayor and Timothy J. Meagher (Baltimore: Johns Hopkins University Press, 1996), 125–152. The tables of commutation were conveniently republished by Inspector Thomas Byrnes in his *Professional Criminals of America* (1886; reprinted, New York: Chelsea House, 1969), 394–396.

32. William Francis Kuntz II, *Criminal Sentencing in Three Nineteenth-Century Cities: Social History of Punishment in New York, Boston, and Philadelphia, 1830–1880* (New York: Garland, 1988), 462.

33. *New York Times*, Nov. 23, 1854.

34. Source: for England, V. A. C. Gatrell, *The Hanging Tree: Execution and the English People, 1770–1868* (Oxford: Oxford University Press, 1994), 8–9, 10, 616–619; for the United States, the Espy file.

35. Kuntz, *Criminal Sentencing*, 73.

36. Because most shipwrecks were not within national boundaries, and because the victims would not necessarily have been the same nationality as the ship, creating per capita rates may be impossible. Certainly no one seems to have tried. The only such list seems to be *Principal Marine Disasters, 1831–1932* (Washington, D.C.: U.S. Coast Guard Public Information Division, c. 1946), a typescript publication consisting, with a handful of exceptions, of American and British disasters of the nineteenth century.

37. The $r^2 = .28$; .39 with World War I removed.

38. The $r^2 = .76$ for the twentieth century, .69 for the nineteenth and twentieth. In an important article, Howard Taylor argues that nineteenth-century English crime was deliberately underreported in order to save prosecution costs. "Rationing Crime: The Political Economy of Criminal Statistics since the 1850s," *Economic History Review* 51 (1998): 569–590.

39. Frank Neal, *Sectarian Violence: The Liverpool Experience, 1819–1914; An Aspect of Anglo-Irish History* (Manchester, Eng.: Manchester University Press, 1988), 2.

40. Paul Laxton and Joy Campbell, "Homicide and Manslaughter in Victorian Liverpool: A Research Report" (Liverpool: Department of Geography, 1997), 4.

41. Herman Melville, *Redburn: His First Voyage* (Garden City, N.Y.: Doubleday, 1957), 184.

42. Dickens, *American Notes*, 136; Melville, *Redburn*, 184.

43. Melville, *Redburn*, 218.

44. The $r^2 = .26$.

45. Rosemary Gartner, "Age and Homicide in Different National Contexts," in *The Crime Conundrum: Essays on Criminal Justice,* ed. Lawrence M. Friedman and George Fisher (Boulder, Colo.: Westview Press, 1997), 67. For a synthetic essay that offers at least one explanation for the differences, see Terrie E. Moffitt, "Adolescence-Limited and Life-Course-Persistent Antisocial Behavior: A Developmental Taxonomy," *Psychological Review* 100 (1993): 674–701, who argues that today there are two kinds of young offenders, those who begin early and offend throughout their lives (corresponding to the flat nineteenth-century distribution), and those who do so temporarily (corresponding to the bump in contemporary youth offending). The difference, Moffitt argues, is in the earlier onset of physical maturity today interacting with a much longer time span to adult responsibilities and privileges. Work by Jeff Grogger, "Market Wages and Youth Crime," *Journal of Labor Economics* 16, no. 4 (Oct. 1998): 756–791, confirms Moffitt's insights by showing how the youth employment market affects youth crime.

46. This is an old observation that has had its most recent explication in David T. Courtwright, *Violent Land: Single Men and Social Disorder from the Frontier to the Inner City* (Cambridge, Mass.: Harvard University Press, 1996).

CONCLUSION

1. Franklin E. Zimring and Gordon Hawkins, in *Crime Is Not the Problem: Lethal Violence in America* (New York: Oxford University Press, 1997), point out that the property crime rates of the United States and other Western nations are more similar. This faintly cheering news still leaves our violence record unexplained.

2. On the possible rise in interpersonal violence anticipating the Civil War, see Randolph Roth, "Why Northern New Englanders Seldom Commit Murder: The Role of Honor" (paper presented at the conference of the Organization of American Historians, April 1998, Indianapolis, Indiana).

Index

Text: 10/14 Palatino
Display: Snell Roundhand Script and Bauer Bodoni
Composition: Integrated Composition Systems, Inc.
Printing and binding: Haddon Craftsmen, Inc.